EDUCATION, EDUCATION, EDUCATION

EDUCATION, EDUCATION, EDUCATION

REFORMING ENGLAND'S SCHOOLS

ANDREW ADONIS

Biteback Publishing

First published in Great Britain in 2012 by
Biteback Publishing Ltd
Westminster Tower
3 Albert Embankment
London SE1 7SP
Copyright © Andrew Adonis 2012

Andrew Adonis has asserted his right under the Copyright, Designs and Patents
Act 1988 to be identified as the author of this work.

ISBN 978-1-84954-420-7

10 9 8 7 6 5 4 3 2

A CIP catalogue record for this book is available from the British Library.

Set in Dolly and Steelfish

Front cover photograph (above) © Mirrorpix
Front cover photograph (below) © David Churchill
Author photograph © Rex Features

Extracts from Ben Okri's 'Lines In Potentis' by kind permission of
The Marsh Agency Ltd.

Printed and bound in Great Britain by
CPI Group (UK) Ltd, Croydon CR0 4YY

To the pioneers of academies and everyone working to improve England's schools, building a better society before our eyes.

CONTENTS

The poor have no childhood. It must be bought and paid for.
Charles Dickens

The future does not belong to those who are content with today,
apathetic toward common problems and their fellow man alike, timid
and fearful in the face of new ideas and bold projects. Rather it will
belong to those who can blend passion, reason and courage in a personal
commitment to the ideals and great enterprises of American society.
Robert Kennedy at the University of California

FOREWORD: 'TELL EVERYONE THAT THE FUTURE IS YET UNMADE'

When, shortly before becoming Prime Minister, Tony Blair said that his three priorities were 'education, education, education', John Major quipped that he had the same three priorities but not necessarily in the same order.

I had been yearning for this moment since my own school and university days in the 1970s and early 1980s. That someone in power would do something about the jungle which passed for an education system, from which few emerged with anything resembling an education.

Now at last, I thought, it might be different.

Tony Blair was clearly going to win. He was the inspirational progressive leader I had been hoping for since joining the Social Democratic Party on the day of its launch, a month after my eighteenth birthday in 1981. For a short while I thought Roy Jenkins, the brilliant social moderniser of the 1960s, might be that leader. But the SDP failed, and until Tony Blair came along there was no politician who excited me. Margaret Thatcher I saw as inevitable after the ungovernable, sclerotic 1970s, but the idea that 'there is no such thing as society' was obviously mad and dangerous.

Now, at last, there was a leader. And one who appeared to be concerned about education and all those other things which didn't work in Britain. Not just the schools but the council estates, the hospitals, the police, the prisons, the trains, indeed almost everything which involved the state apart from the army, the Queen and the BBC.

After graduating in 1984, I spent fourteen years as an academic and journalist, writing books about political history and the English class system. For much of this time I was at the *Financial Times*, when I got to know Tony Blair and David Miliband, his policy director. We talked about the dire state of Britain and what New Labour needed to do. One thing led to another and in 1998 I went to work for Tony – as he was to all his staff – first as his education adviser, then as Head of his Policy Unit, and ultimately as Minister for Schools.

As soon as I started in No. 10, I focused on one objective above all: how to reinvent the comprehensive school.

Across much of England comprehensives were palpably and seriously failing. I regarded this not only as an educational crisis, but a social and economic crisis too, since the poor standard of education and socialisation among school leavers was so obviously at the heart of England's problems at large. I saw failing comprehensive schools, many hundreds of them, as a cancer at the heart of English society.

Looking back, this wasn't an exaggeration. The typical sixteen-year-old in the 1990s was leaving a comprehensive with two or three GCSEs, and likely as not these didn't include English and maths. 'We Don't Need No Education' wasn't just Pink Floyd blaring out in my boarding school as I revised for O-levels in 1979. It was the reality of my generation and the one after.

The first half of this book tells the story of my efforts at education reform in the decade after 1998. It is largely about the evolution of academies, the new type of all-ability independent state school, with dynamic independent sponsors taking charge of their management, which the Blair government introduced to replace failing comprehensives, and which are continuing to develop under David Cameron's coalition government.

What started as a small, tentative and controversial project has grown, over the twelve years since its launch in the spring of 2000, into a nationwide movement for educational transformation.

It was a slow and tough ordeal to get academies started. Looking back, developing the policy was the easier part. Implementation was far harder. It took about a year to devise the academy policy before its launch in March 2000. It then took two and a half years to open the first three academies in September 2002, and only fourteen academies opened in the following two years combined (2003 and 2004).

Getting this first group of academies designed, sponsored, located, built and opened was the most gruelling challenge of my twelve years in government.

In retrospect, the tipping point came with Tony Blair's commitment in July 2004 to establish at least 200 academies. This was more than four years after the launch of the programme. It was followed soon after by Tony's third election victory in May 2005, after which I became Minister for Schools. Implementation then accelerated rapidly. Ten academies opened in September 2005, and another fifty were by then in development. By now, these new independent state schools were proving highly popular with parents, and their results were improving fast on those of their predecessor comprehensives.

In telling the tale of academies, I also tell a story about pioneering reform in government. On becoming a minister, I eagerly read Gerald Kaufman's witty book *How to be a Minister*. Yet looking back, 'being a minister' wasn't the difficult bit. The civil service hold your hand, put you in a cocoon, and all but the completely incompetent survive. The real challenge is how to be reformer: how to achieve something worthwhile and substantial which wasn't going to happen anyway. Hence my concluding chapter – 'How to be a reformer' – which gives my reflections on how to drive and lead change.

The second half of the book looks to the future. England today has a part-reformed education system. It is urgent that all underperforming schools, primary as well as secondary, become academies, and I set out the case and a plan for this in Chapter 10. I support free schools, which are simply academies without a predecessor state school, and which have been central to the academy policy from the outset, and I make the case for these too as a means of tackling disadvantage, providing choice and boosting innovation.

Academies and free schools are only part of the further reform needed to build world-class schools nationwide. Education in England is still far too weak an engine of social mobility, skills and citizenship. In order to build a genuine one-nation society without the entrenched class divisions and poverty of the past, the chasm between private and state education – the elite and the mass – must be bridged. I set out a plan for this in Chapter 8. Universities, particularly the top universities, have got to serve the generality of state schools as well as they serve private schools, and I set out a plan for this in Chapter 9. Above all, a new deal is required to make teaching the foremost profession in the country, including a large expansion of Teach First and a big increase in the starting salary for new maths and science teachers. This 'new deal for teachers' is set out in Chapter 11, alongside the imperative to expand under-fives services, particularly Sure Start support for parents and children from the poorest families.

England needs to be up there with the leading nations of Europe and Asia in developing a '90 per cent' education system: schools where at least 90 per cent of sixteen-year-olds reach a basic GCSE standard, wherever they live, whatever their background, in place of the '60 per cent' education system of today. All secondary schools should have sixth forms and make academic and technical education beyond GCSE a core part of their mission. I suggest a new A-level Baccalaureate (A-Bacc), embracing the best of the International Baccalaureate (IB) and assessing a wider range of subjects and skills than existing A-levels for those on track to higher education. I also suggest a new 'Technical Baccalaureate' (Tech Bacc) for those not proposing to go – or go straight – to university, combining essential literacy and numeracy standards with technical qualifications, and assessed work experience, leading directly into work or apprenticeships, or to higher technical education. All this is set out in Chapter 11.

Teenagers need to be prepared much better to become citizens and to value democracy. More should be expected of them and more responsibility should be accorded to them, in their schools and communities. At the age of sixteen, they should be treated as citizens – young and maturing citizens – and be given the vote with a polling station in every secondary school on election day. This too is set out in Chapter 11, together with the proposal that schools systematically become community hubs, including health and library services, and community sports and arts facilities, and not continue just as teaching sites for children and teenagers.

This, in summary, is my 'manifesto for change', brought together as a set of concrete reform proposals in the Appendix. I see no reason why this manifesto could not be embraced by all the political parties, for education is too important to be subject to narrow political tribalism. It is an unashamedly progressive agenda, aiming to strengthen society and social cohesion.

To make this manifesto happen, the state, as the ultimate and leading expression of society, must give a strong lead. I am not aware of any other basis upon which social transformation has taken place in the modern age.

‡

I ought to say a bit more about my own background, to help make sense of why I see education, the state and the whole way we prepare young people for adult life as so important.

My dad, a Greek Cypriot immigrant to Britain in 1959, who got a job first as a waiter and then as a postman, was soon left alone with the care of two young children – me and my younger sister – in a council flat in Camden Town. He was working all hours to make ends meet and could not look after us, so from the age of three I was brought up in a Camden council children's home in Borehamwood, a drab London overspill town whose only exotic feature was Elstree Studios, where we were once taken to watch the filming of the sitcom *On The Buses*.

For the next eighteen years, I grew up in three institutions, and my fate turned on some remarkably selfless and dedicated individuals who worked in them.

The manager of my children's home became a surrogate mother. Together with my father and my excellent social worker, she fixed with Camden council for me to go on to boarding school at the age of eleven. She even chose the school.

Then there were three successive headmasters of Kingham Hill School in Oxfordshire, the third of whom, David Shepherd, sent me to visit his old Oxford college, Keble, whose history tutor, Eric Stone, offered me a place and, over the next three years, spurred me on to become an historian and university lecturer myself.

All this gave me a burning sense that education matters fundamentally. That inspirational teachers, and all who work with children, matter fundamentally. That institutions matter fundamentally. That the state matters fundamentally. And that values, sometimes expressed through religion, matter fundamentally.

Maybe this is heightened perception from unusual experience, but it is my profound conviction that, while the family is the fundamental social unit, institutions beyond the family, particularly schools, shape children almost as much and often more so.

The manager of my children's home, Auntie Gladys as we called her, was a local authority official in charge of a council institution, yet she had spent her previous career in Barnardo's homes and regarded Camden council's bureaucracy and lowest common denominator values with brisk contempt. She was unmarried, and the children's home was her life. She dealt with the red tape, created a strong institution, talked about duty, discipline and responsibility, and took all her charges off to Borehamwood Baptist Church every Sunday morning. I don't recall anyone objecting until they were twelve or thirteen, when it was fine if they wanted to stay behind.

Values and structure were equally strong at Kingham Hill School. Chapel every morning, seven days a week, and a whole set of other daily and weekly routines: 'housework' before breakfast; 'prep' after tea; the Cadet Force, starting with parade and drill, every Monday afternoon; games every Wednesday and Saturday afternoon, including rugby and cross-country running throughout the winter, whatever the weather. I disliked a lot of this regimentation, and a lot of the teaching was indifferent. But Kingham Hill was a school of only 230 boys divided into seven houses, so in each house everyone knew everyone and I soon made friends with similar interests. Of the twenty teachers, a handful were brilliant, and in my case taught me to debate and play the organ, and I took the Oxford entrance exam in a class of one.

Oxford, with its one-on-one tutorials and its galaxy of talent and opportunity, was another brave new world, which gave me a passion for politics and history, and the self-confidence to pursue them without being too intimidated by the gilded and polished products of the 'public' schools who dominate our public life.

Both my school and my Oxford college were independent foundations, established (in both cases by Christian philanthropists) within a few years of each other in the late nineteenth century. They were pioneering 'academies' of the Victorian age. By my day they were more or less secular, yet their values remained strong, their sense of mission and tradition profound, and, by comparison with so much else in English education, they worked.

The crux issue for progressive reformers today is not whether the state matters and needs to command significant resources - of course it does - but how it translates its social and educational duties into institutions which work and which promote a successful common life. Ruthless pragmatism should apply case by case, informed by two centuries of experience in building a liberal, cohesive society, the cardinal lesson being that in the social sphere the state works best when it works with and through strong autonomous institutions in a strong civil society.

Where schools and institutions for children fail, society fails and individuals suffer, often irreparably.

I am still scarred by the turn of events after Auntie Gladys retired as manager of my children's home shortly before I was to go to boarding school. Her replacement had no grip or authority. Within days, the place started down a *Lord of the Flies* spiral, a dozen children beginning to fight, to steal, to bully, in a spirit of dangerous cruelty. This was soon after I had started at one of Borehamwood's comprehensives, which after primary school was a vast adolescent jungle where neither the headteacher nor many of the teachers knew our names, let alone our talents. Within a few months, my childhood began to fall apart.

It was put together again at boarding school. Yet even there, year by year, classmates fell by the wayside, particularly after O-levels, when many of them – including some of the most able – left school virtually unqualified. Only a handful of my friends went on to university. All this was just taken for granted.

I am writing a few days after the bicentenary of the birth of Charles Dickens. Who better evokes the perils, the vulnerability, the desperation of the childhood of the poor? Dickens also grew up in Camden Town, and gave Bob Cratchit his home there. Were Dickens to return, Oliver Twist, Smike, the Artful Dodger and David Copperfield would roam contemporary London, pitched perhaps amid the riots of August 2011. And looking at today's House of Commons, Dickens would be just as contemptuous of the MP Gregsbury in *Nicholas Nickleby* who has 'a tolerable command of sentences with no meaning in them'.

On setting about the creation of academies, I was mindful of Machiavelli's celebrated advice in *The Prince*:

> It must be remembered that there is nothing more difficult to plan, more doubtful of success, nor more dangerous to manage than the creation of a new system. For the initiator has the enmity of all who would profit by the preservation of the old institutions and merely lukewarm defenders in those who should gain by the new ones.

He might have been writing about the reform of English education.

Yet equally compelling to me have been Churchill's words on the occasion of the opening of the new chamber of the House of Commons, replacing the one bombed by Hitler: 'We mould our institutions and they mould us.'

Fatalism and inaction in the face of social crisis are immoral.

We all have a duty to act. There is so much more we can and must do together to build schools fit for our children and for our future as a society.

The poet and novelist Ben Okri puts it brilliantly:

> *Here lives the great music*
> *Of humanity.*
> *The harmonisation of different*
> *Histories, cultures, geniuses*
> *And dreams.*
> *Ought to shine to the world ...*
> *Tell everyone that the future*
> *Is yet unmade ...*
> *Here, now, under the all-seeing*
> *Eye of the sun.*

Andrew Adonis
London, 12 March 2012

HACKNEY DOWNS TO MOSSBOURNE

Deserted, dilapidated and vandalised. Concrete ruins were all that remained of Hackney Downs School, a graveyard of the 'worst school in England' closed five years before.

It was a drizzling autumn morning in 2000, a few months after the launch of the academies policy. This was one of hundreds of outings over the eight years in which I sought to establish academies up and down the country. Just one, yet perhaps the most symbolic.

Hackney Downs had long been a by-word for disaster in inner-city comprehensive education. The very name conjured images of a school out of control, militant teachers, no learning, mass truancy, children leaving with pitiful – if any – qualifications. A school which aspirational parents, working class as much as middle class, did everything possible to avoid.

The image was close to reality. Hackney Downs may once have been a successful grammar school, founded in 1876 by the Grocers' Company, one of the historic livery companies of the nearby City of London, its alumni including Harold Pinter and Michael Caine. But that was long past. As a comprehensive in the 1970s and 1980s, it became a sink school, finally closed by ministerial order in 1995 after damning inspection reports and media vilification. By then, virtually no students were leaving with decent GCSEs. The subject at which the pupils did best – Turkish – wasn't even formally taught at the school. Among the fifteen- and sixteen-year-olds, inspectors found a significant number struggling to divide 168 by 12 and some unable to say how many pence there were in £1.85.

It was an extreme form of the malaise afflicting so many comprehensives in the inner cities: low standards, poor leadership, bleak, even unsafe schools and the flight of aspirational parents.

This is what the inspectors had to say about Hackney Downs before they closed it:

> Often the teacher appeared to expect very little from the pupils except misbehaviour, and the pupils lived up to the expectation. Most classes were subject to constant interruptions by a few disruptive boys whose often coarse and occasionally foul-mouthed comments addressed to one another and to the teacher ensured that little or no education took place. There was continual low level disturbance to which virtually all the boys contributed. Teachers often had great difficulty in getting lessons started. Boys often drifted in at various times during the first ten minutes and it was not uncommon for the first fifteen to twenty minutes to be spent gathering the group and establishing a sense of order.

However foolhardy, I was determined that one of the first of the new academies should be in Hackney precisely because the borough – the second poorest in England – was so symbolic of past failure. If academies could succeed in Hackney, they could succeed anywhere. It was tempting fate to set one up on the actual site of Hackney Downs. But the site was immediately available and the council was prepared to give it to the academy and to support the project.

The ruin of Hackney Downs wasn't a promising scene to show Clive Bourne, the academy's potential managing sponsor. As we wandered round, I did my best to persuade him that the past was the past, and with the government's help he could create a completely different future. We would fund a new flagship building. I would do my best to ensure that the local officials in Hackney, and in the Education Department in Whitehall, were supportive. I even had a suggestion for the founding headteacher: the brilliant no-nonsense head of a high-achieving Catholic state secondary school in nearby Newham, who had hugely impressed me on a recent visit to a failing comprehensive in the borough to which he had been seconded on a rescue mission.

Why Clive Bourne? An East End boy made good, who left school at fifteen and went on to build a successful overnight-parcels business, Clive was passionate about education. He was also a JP in Newham, and saw from the Bench all too many of the consequences of teenagers failing at school. He was put my way by Michael Levy, Tony Blair's fundraiser and envoy and himself a proud and brilliantly successful Hackney Downs Grammar alumnus. Clive's East End roots, his values, his determination and his business acumen all suggested to me a highly suitable sponsor.

Clive didn't hesitate long. If I did what I said about sorting the red tape and the funding, he would put up the required £2 million of charitable sponsorship and drive the project forward personally, 'just like the business I set up all those years ago'. We even agreed the name for the new academy: Mossbourne, after his father, Moss Bourne.

So Michael Wilshaw, the Catholic headteacher from Newham, became the founding principal. Richard Rogers designed a flagship school building. I chased progress at my weekly session with the Education Department. And I worked hand in glove with Sir Mike Tomlinson – the former Chief Inspector of Schools, who became chair of the independent Hackney Learning Trust, to which the council's failing education bureaucracy was contracted out in 2002 – to navigate the difficult local politics.

One issue we didn't initially crack was the sixth form. Clive Bourne and Michael Wilshaw rightly wanted the academy to have a sixth form, but the other Hackney schools and further education colleges objected vociferously at this departure from the local pattern of schools stopping at age sixteen, with students then transferring to college if they stayed on in education at all. The local FE colleges weren't much good, but the Hackney Learning Trust and Education Department officials sided with them, and among the many blockages I sought to unblock week by week – operating from No. 10, and not myself the decision-taker – I couldn't resolve this one. The academy was anyway going to start only with eleven-year-olds and then build up year by year, so I parked this as a problem to be solved at a later date.

Four years later, in September 2004, Mossbourne Community Academy was opened by Tony Blair. It was the fourteenth academy to open, but, given its location, it was from the outset a symbol of the academy policy at large.

Doing a recce before the official opening, I was stunned not so much by the buildings as by the students and the teachers. The spacious multi-coloured £28 million Richard Rogers construction and state-of-the-art facilities were breathtakingly impressive, more like a university than a school, including lecture theatre, sports hall, bright open-plan study and social areas, glass-fronted classrooms and abundant PCs. But more striking was the behaviour of the children, all of them from the surrounding area, proud in their smart grey uniforms with red trimming and ties, lined up quietly in the playground before filing in for assembly, and clearly enjoying their classes. As for the teachers, their professionalism was palpable.

Michael Wilshaw's approach to school leadership was the precise opposite of most inner-city comprehensive heads of the day. Whereas they would talk about 'making allowances' for behaviour, discipline and expectations in the socially and racially mixed inner city, the Wilshaw mantra was that to make a success of an inner-city school, compared to other schools, you needed to be more not less strict, expect more not less of the students, and compromise less not more with the world beyond the school gate. 'Many of the children come from families imposing little structure themselves so we have to provide it for them,' he told me when we first met.

From day one, discipline, respect, hard work and politeness were at the core of Mossbourne Academy. The pupils stood up when a teacher entered the class, and at the start of lessons recited the mantra: 'I aspire to maintain an enquiring mind, a calm disposition and an attentive ear so that in this class and in all classes I can fulfil my true potential.' Parents were given clear instructions on how to support homework and good behaviour. Supporting all this was intensive pastoral support, with staff following up on absentee children and visiting them and their parents or guardians at home to sort out problems as soon as possible.

Equally atypical until the academy era was Michael Wilshaw's conviction – not mere words, but profound belief – that inner-city all-ability schools could and should achieve as highly as the best schools in the country. And that to make excuses or fatalistic allowances for children from deprived or dysfunctional families – 'what do you expect from kids off these estates?' was a comment I heard countless times from heads and education officials on my visits to failing comprehensives – was to betray not only the 'kids' but also the fundamental vocation of the teacher.

Michael assembled an outstanding staff. The core team worked under him at St Bonaventure's School in Newham, where he had been head for eighteen years. They live and breathe the academy's ethos and standards he insists upon. The code of conduct for staff – dress, punctuality, preparation, service – is as high as for the pupils. Rigorous ability setting applies in all key subjects. Each year, Mossbourne's new intake of eleven-year-olds arrive at 7.30 a.m. three days a week for extra reading practice. Older children can attend Saturday school and holiday workshops for catch-up sessions. Every student has individualised targets. There are termly reports to parents. Lesson observation by the academy's leadership team takes place constantly. Staff are always in the playground, around the academy at lunch and in breaks, and at the school gates in the morning and evening. There is a full programme of sports and after-school activities which staff are expected to organise and all pupils to participate in.

'Mossbourne is a grammar school with a comprehensive intake,' says Michael Wilshaw. 'I realised long ago that if you work with disadvantaged children you can't be woolly. It's about meticulous standards, standing up for children, using Sir and Miss, lots of homework, very clear boundaries, no excuses and high expectations. In return, the students get the very best of what we can offer.'

The Wilshaw mission is to give all children the start in life which middle-class children take for granted:

> We do intervene in the way that parents in more prosperous homes will do. It's a philosophy that works for poor children. I don't see ourselves as Tiger mother. We're aspirational but we're not a

hothouse, we don't push children to the edge. People tend to think our children are miserable but they're not, they're extremely happy because they see that they're working in a good school and they see that they're making progress and they achieve way above what they originally thought they would achieve.

Back in 2003, every part of Michael Wilshaw's philosophy was music to my ears. Much of it corresponded to my own education. This was the comprehensive ideal in practice.

More to the point, all this was music to the ears of Hackney parents. From the outset the academy was vastly oversubscribed. Mossbourne immediately became the school of choice in its Hackney Downs and Clapton community, so it had a genuinely comprehensive intake. Most of the children were from poorer families – more than 40 per cent were eligible for free school meals, three times the national average – but there were plenty of aspirational parents including some from gentrifying Hackney's middle class who were giving the academy a try rather than decamping to the suburbs or the private sector. A friend in No. 10 moved close to Mossbourne to get a place for his son, waving the acceptance letter at me one morning as if his son had got a scholarship to Eton.

I regularly took or sent potential sponsors, and anyone else who needed persuading of the merits of academies, to visit Mossbourne. 'Let's not have this argument,' became my standard response to objections from MPs, councillors and defenders of the old comprehensive model. 'Just go and see an academy for yourself, and tell me what you think.' They usually came back saying they wanted one.

Two years after the opening, Michael Wilshaw asked me to award the prizes at an inter-school public speaking competition at the academy one Saturday afternoon. Yes, a Saturday, and he was there himself with several staff. The final was between St Paul's and Westminster, who beat other big-name London public schools in the quarter- and semi-finals. Mossbourne's team – the only one from a state school – had been knocked out early in the day. Being only thirteen- and fourteen-year-olds, then the oldest students in the academy, they never stood much chance. 'No matter,' said Michael when I commiserated. 'I've told them they've got to stay for the final so they can see how to win next year.'

Three years later, 2009, was Mossbourne's first GCSE year. More than 80 per cent of the students gained five or more good GCSE passes including English and maths. Not only was this the highest score in Hackney, but it also made Mossbourne one of only a few dozen all-ability schools nationwide to reach 80 per cent, putting it in the top 1 per cent of schools nationally in terms of the achievement of students of similar background.

It was awesome yet poignant. Clive Bourne had recently died and never saw his academy in its full glory, including the sixth form to which these students progressed. The sixth form was established following a relentless campaign by Michael Wilshaw and Mossbourne's parents and governors. When I became Minister for Schools after the 2005 election, and could take these decisions personally, I simply overruled the objections and official advice to the contrary, allocated the necessary funding and told Michael to get on with it.

However, the best was yet to come. In 2011, Mossbourne's first sixth-formers gained the most stunning university offers of virtually any state school in the country. Nine students won places at Cambridge, two to read medicine. In all, seventy students won places in the highly selective Russell Group of leading universities. 'We expect a majority of our young people in the sixth form to enter Oxbridge and the Russell Group,' said Michael – by now Sir Michael – on the front page of Mossbourne's website. 'Nothing short of this will satisfy us.'

Twelve years after Clive Bourne's grim tour of Hackney Downs, Mossbourne Community Academy is a model for 21st-century education, pioneering opportunity, social mobility and the reinvention of the inner-city comprehensive. It is the flagship of the national academy movement.

Within Hackney itself, Mossbourne is not an island but the vanguard of a revolution in secondary education.

Early sceptics worried that academies would simply cream off students from other schools, sending them into decline and replacing one hierarchy of schools with another to little net gain. Not so. Hackney now has five 'sponsored' academies out of twelve state secondary schools. The other four academies have sponsors as committed as Clive Bourne, bringing hugely valuable contacts and partnerships to their schools and to Hackney. The Petchey Academy is sponsored by the charitable trust of Jack Petchey, one of the East End's foremost businessmen and philanthropists. The Bridge Academy is sponsored by UBS, the international bank. City Academy, Hackney, is sponsored by KPMG, the consultancy and accountancy firm, in partnership with the Corporation of London, which also sponsors academies in Islington and Southwark alongside its three private schools (the City of London Schools for Boys and Girls and the Guildhall School of Music and Drama). Skinners' Academy, Hackney, also has a charitable City sponsor with powerful educational credentials in the Skinners' Company, one of the ancient City livery companies, which sponsors its Hackney academy alongside Tonbridge, the public school in Kent, and two state grammar schools and an academy, also in Kent. And far from declining, the other seven Hackney state secondary schools – several of which are now converting to become academies themselves – are thriving and have seen their results rise substantially too.

Central to Hackney's education revolution is the systematic introduction of sixth forms into secondary schools, following Mossbourne's lead. All the borough's academies, and almost all its comprehensives, now have sixth forms and view A-level and post-GCSE technical education as a core part of their mission, rather than something which happens elsewhere if at all.

In the mid-1990s, average GCSE performance in Hackney schools was barely half the national average. In 2006, it was still nearly ten percentage points below the national average. In 2010, in an astonishing turnaround, Hackney crept above the national average, with Mossbourne leading the pack.

'Hackney parents used to fight to get out of Hackney schools,' says Meg Hillier, a local Labour MP. 'Now they are fighting to get into them.'

Far more parents now keep their children in secondary schools in the borough rather than fleeing to the suburbs. Competition and collaboration between highly successful and improving schools – all of them all-ability by intake, so competing on a level playing field – is boosting them all.

Tellingly, Hackney's employment rate for 16–24-year-olds has also shot up in recent years, despite the recession. Since 2006, it is up from barely 50 per cent, far below the London average, to nearly 70 per cent, above the London average. Jules Pipe, the elected Mayor of Hackney and a strong supporter of the academies, attributes most of this improvement to the transformation in secondary education. 'Parents with means to move are no longer abandoning the borough when their children turn nine or ten,' he says.

The Hackney story is everything I hoped might be possible when Tony Blair launched the academies policy in March 2000. Fittingly, in 2012, Sir Michael Wilshaw became Her Majesty's Chief Inspector of Schools.

What Hackney has achieved in the last decade every deprived part of England needs to achieve, and more. They need to be equally bold in embracing academies and all they stand for.

Meanwhile, Mossbourne and Hackney are not untroubled. Beyond the academy's northern entrance, past the high steel fence with its security guards, lies the huge Pembury council estate. It is home to many academy students. It is also home to the Pembury Boys and other gangs, and to many of the rioters and looters who in August 2011 terrorised the neighbouring streets and shops.

'Youngsters will tell you they fear walking into a postcode where they don't live,' says Michael Wilshaw. 'I kept the gangs out of the academy. But gang activity has got considerably worse in the area. It's material and spiritual poverty.'

Mossbourne is a work in progress. So is every school, even the best.

WHY HALF THE COMPREHENSIVES FAILED

The foundation and re-foundation of schools is a hallmark of every age. It is often the greatest legacy one generation passes to another. King Edward VI, the Tudor boy king, is remembered today as founder of a string of grammar schools which still bear his name.

Since the state started taking responsibility for national education in the nineteenth century, there have been four major phases of school foundation and re-foundation in England. Primary schools were established nationwide in the years after Gladstone's Education Act of 1870. Secondary schools were established, haphazardly, in the decades after the Balfour Education Act of 1902 and then as part of a national system of (mainly) grammar and secondary modern schools in the years after the Butler Education Act of 1944. These primary and secondary schools co-existed with thousands of private fee-paying schools, and with large pre-existing systems of schools run by Church of England and Roman Catholic dioceses. As part of R. A. Butler's wartime settlement, most church schools became state-funded, but retained their autonomy.

The third phase was the replacement of many grammar and secondary modern schools with all-ability community comprehensive schools. This reform – the re-foundation of a large part of the state secondary school system – was implemented across much of the country in the fifteen years after it was mandated in 1965 by Tony Crosland, Education Secretary in Harold Wilson's government (1964–70). Alongside the raising of the minimum school leaving age to sixteen in 1972, the creation of comprehensives necessitated a nationwide wave of school closures, openings, amalgamations and new (mostly shoddy prefab) school building.

Academies constitute the fourth phase of national state school development. There will soon be thousands of academies as the majority of state secondary schools are either founded or re-founded as academies, and academies extend into primary education too.

Academies were born of the failure of comprehensivisation to achieve its goals. For all the idealism of their pioneers, a large proportion of comprehensives were little better than the secondary modern schools they replaced and very few were highly successful. The key objective of academies was to replace failing and 'bog standard' comprehensives (as Alastair Campbell famously described them in 2001) with successful all-ability schools, founded and managed on a different and better basis.

Academies were also intended to help overcome other fundamental weaknesses of the comprehensive era: the rigid and damaging division between state and private schools; the low morale and appeal, and weak leadership, of the state teaching profession; the misconceived role of local education authorities as school managers; and the absence of sixth forms in the half of the country – mostly the more deprived half – where comprehensives stopped education at the age of sixteen.

The roots of all these problems went back decades before Tony Crosland, but comprehensivisation left them all starkly unresolved and in some cases worsened. To understand academies, it is essential to understand why this was so: why, that is, about half the comprehensives failed.

Before becoming Tony Blair's education adviser in 1998, I reflected a good deal on this issue. I also sought to assess, as dispassionately as I could, the attempts by Kenneth Baker and his successor education secretaries in the Thatcher and Major governments to promote improvement.

In government, it is hard to reform successfully unless you have largely worked out your reform plan beforehand. Once in office, even as a special adviser, let alone as a minister, there is precious little time and space to research and think through a subject. I didn't, alas, have a properly worked-out plan on starting at No. 10, but my prior analysis had a crucial bearing on the reform plans I developed thereafter and I recreate it now. It falls into two parts: my view of 'comprehensivisation' from Crosland to mid-Thatcher (1965 to 1986), and my assessment of the reforms to secondary education under Kenneth Baker and his successors in the late Thatcher and Major years (1986 to 1997).

'SECONDARY MODERN COMPREHENSIVES'

A general misunderstanding of the comprehensive revolution of the 1960s and 1970s is to regard it as ending the secondary moderns.

In reality, comprehensives were essentially a continuation of their predecessor secondary modern schools rather than the creation of new schools. They were 'secondary modern comprehensives', as I came to call them, and this is why they so largely failed.

To understand why this was so, and what it meant, we need to go back to the early 1960s.

In 1960, there were across England some 3,700 secondary modern schools, 1,200 grammar schools, 500 church secondary schools, 500 fee-paying independent secondary schools and 200 technical schools. Taking account of the fact that some church schools were also grammar schools, secondary modern schools accounted for about 60 per cent of secondary schools, and they educated about two-thirds of 11–15-year-olds.

However, beyond the age of fifteen, the picture was entirely different. Here the secondary moderns educated only a tiny minority. For few children stayed in secondary moderns beyond the minimum school leaving age of fifteen. Indeed, only a small proportion of secondary modern pupils took public examinations of any kind, and beyond the age of sixteen virtually no secondary moderns had sixth forms. Of pupils staying at school beyond the age of fifteen in 1960, about 230,000 were in grammar schools, and a further 100,000 were in independent and church schools. A mere 50,000 were in secondary moderns. Most secondary moderns did not even offer technical and vocational courses beyond the age of fifteen. These were taken, if at all, at separate vocational colleges (soon to be called 'further education colleges'), which stood entirely above and apart from the school system. As for the technical schools promised in the 1944 Education Act, very few were set up and they never became more than a peripheral part of the supposedly 'tripartite' post-war school system.

So secondary moderns 'educated' the majority – the working-class majority – of children only until the age of fifteen, then sent them virtually unskilled into factory-type jobs or the vagaries of local vocational colleges.

There was another crucial dimension – governance – to the rigidly hierarchical character of the pre-comprehensive secondary school system. Secondary modern schools were the creation of local education authorities. They were set up and managed as, in effect, part of the local council, whereas more prestigious types of secondary school, including the state-funded, enjoyed greater autonomy and much more institutional self-confidence. Private fee-paying schools were entirely independent of the state in their governance. The 'direct grant' grammar schools were similarly independent in their governance, taking pupils on a government contract. Church schools also mostly had a high degree of autonomy in their governance and admissions, as did many grammar schools, partly because their governing bodies tended to be more assertive than those of secondary moderns, and partly because they were often sponsored by historic and socially powerful charitable foundations similar to those behind independent schools. Some of these foundations straddled the independent/church/grammar sectors, like the King Edward VI Foundation in Birmingham, which was responsible for the city's two leading private schools alongside five of its state grammar schools.

Then there was the 11-plus exam, the test sat by all children at the end of primary school to determine whether they went on to a grammar or a secondary modern school. The particular evil of the 11-plus – indeed, a good part of the reason why it was an evil – lay in the fate of those who did not go on to the grammar schools. The grammar schools only took about a fifth of eleven-year-olds, so there was no shortage of talented and able children who went to the secondary moderns. But unlike the German and Dutch technical and high schools, England's secondary moderns were chronically inadequate schools and were never valued in their own right.

This stark reality came home to me from reading a 1967 study of the secondary modern school by David Hargreaves, an incisive and unsentimental Cambridge professor who was later to become head of the national qualifications and curriculum agency. It was the fruit of a year which Hargreaves, then a young researcher, spent at a secondary modern in Salford Docks. He described the school as pretty standard for a working-class community in the mid-1960s. In one notable respect – the school had new buildings – it was better than standard. Yet the description of the school is unremittingly bleak. Most of the boys took no external exams at all and gained no qualifications whatsoever. Only a minority in the top stream of the school were even entered for a local school leaving certificate, for which cheating was widespread among staff and pupils. The new national CSE exam was coming in, a much inferior form of O-level, but there was no encouragement from the headteacher or most of the teachers for even the brightest pupils to stay at school beyond the minimum leaving age of fifteen to take it. As for O-levels, Hargreaves wrote:

> Only one member of staff, who came to the school after teaching in a grammar school, felt strongly that the best boys in the top stream were of sufficient ability to take O-level; most of the other teachers of the higher streams took the view that ... to enter them for O-level after a fifth year at the school would be to mislead the pupils with hopes of academic success beyond their powers. There is also little doubt that some of these teachers were reluctant to teach forms to O-level since they had never done so and were uneasy about their competence to do so.

As for the wider ethos of the school:

> Lessons and exams were treated with contempt by most of the boys ... For many of the teachers and most of the pupils life at

the school was a necessary evil. Life was directed towards a reduction of potential conflict by a minimal imposition of demands one upon the other. If the upper streams passed their [school leaving] exam and the lower streams did not riot, the school was for most teachers succeeding.

This was warehousing, not education.

So, to sum up: secondary moderns were grossly inferior to the grammar schools in their character and self-confidence. They were basic at best in their teaching, and banned from almost all post-compulsory education. And they never developed technical specialisms and curricula, which would and should have led their students reliably to apprenticeships and to higher-level technical and academic courses.

This background is crucial to understanding why comprehensivisation went so badly wrong. A government inquiry into secondary education in 1959 had reported, as if it were a breakthrough of medical science, 'the discovery that a fair number of pupils in [secondary] modern schools are capable of reaching academic standards that in the past have been confined to grammar schools'. But it was one thing to make this discovery; quite another to create all-ability schools with the governance, leadership, standards and ethos necessary to act upon it. Across most of the country this simply did not happen. What happened instead was the straight replacement of most secondary moderns by comprehensives which were little different.

The failure of the 'secondary modern comprehensives' should have been no surprise. What was needed was fundamental reform of the secondary modern school to create fundamentally new and better schools. Instead, there were mostly just new signboards outside the secondary moderns, or amalgamations of secondary moderns to create 'new' comprehensives, whose only novelty was their factory-scale size. ('Big is beautiful' was another assumption of the comprehensive era: small comprehensives were small mostly by reason of unpopularity and failure, not by design.)

The comprehensive reform was supposed to have integrated grammar and secondary modern, but this happened only very partially.

Despite Tony Crosland's self-proclaimed mission 'to destroy
every fucking grammar school in England', and the willingness of
subsequent education secretaries until 1979, including Margaret
Thatcher, to agree to local authority reorganisation schemes,
only three-quarters of the grammar schools were integrated into
comprehensives. These were mostly the smaller, lower-performing
and less prestigious three-quarters. Since there were only about
1,200 grammar schools to start with, against 3,700 secondary
moderns, the latter were the dominant influence – often the sole
influence – on the new comprehensives.

Three things happened. First, about a fifth of all local education authorities – including the entire counties of Kent and
Buckinghamshire – successfully resisted comprehensivisation and
retained most or many of their state grammar schools and secondary moderns. Second, a number of individual grammar schools
with strong foundations and social networks survived within the
state system even where comprehensivisation took place in their
local authority, as with the King Edward VI grammar schools in
Birmingham. And third, where survival in the state system was not
possible, the majority of the most prestigious grammar schools
– including most of the 'direct grant' grammar schools which
had been funded by central government under a long-standing
scheme abolished by Labour in the mid-1970s – decided to go
private rather than go comprehensive. This included schools of the
calibre of Manchester, Leeds and Bradford Grammar Schools, the
Royal Grammar School Guildford, Reigate Grammar and Hampton
School in Richmond.

Furthermore, church schools continued pretty much as before.
Most, but not all, church-sponsored state grammar schools gave
up the 11-plus, but the Church of England and the Roman Catholic
Church retained the autonomous governance and character
(including sixth forms in most cases) for their schools. Crucially,
they also retained their separate admissions, usually based on

church affiliation or attendance. In the absence of grammar schools, this made many church schools highly attractive to aspirational parents, particularly in inner London and other cities, where fulfilling baroque church attendance requirements became an entrance exam for parents far more demanding than the 11-plus ever was for their children.

All this would have mattered less if the new comprehensive schools had radically improved over time. But mostly they didn't. In ethos, curriculum, governance and teaching, all too many of the comprehensives were simply a continuation of the secondary moderns described by David Hargreaves.

There were flickerings of something better, including celebrated comprehensives created entirely anew with sixth forms. Holland Park and Pimlico comprehensives in central London were ILEA showcases, with high-profile and passionately committed chairs of governors in Caroline Benn (wife of Tony Benn) and Jack Straw respectively. Tellingly, however, these and other showcase comprehensives soon became educational battlegrounds in the face of low standards, poor teaching and hard Left politicisation within the National Union of Teachers (NUT). Holland Park became a 'pure comprehensive', in the left-wing lexicon of the day, abolishing setting and academic prizes, frightening away aspirational parents and becoming a virtual sink school by the 1980s. Both schools are now academies.

However, showcase comprehensives like Holland Park and Pimlico at least had sixth forms. In the 1970s most comprehensives had no sixth forms – indeed nearly half still have no sixth forms – and like the secondary moderns before them they offered little if any technical education. This continued to be the case, even after the raising of the minimum school leaving age to sixteen in 1972. In the comprehensive era, schools with large sixth forms were mostly in the independent and church sectors. And so, unsurprisingly, entrance to universities came disproportionately from these schools. Nor was there any attempt to divest the FE colleges of their technical education in respect of 16–18-year-olds and give this role to the new comprehensives, which might have radically improved their curriculum, quality and popularity. On the contrary, as the number of sixteen-year-olds wishing to stay in education rose, the FE colleges expanded their provision, alongside the creation of a new breed of free-standing sixth form colleges for A-level students.

The first sixth form college, in Luton, was established in 1966. Tellingly, it was the former Luton Grammar School, converted. Within fifteen years there were a hundred such sixth form colleges. Their establishment by local authorities, and the expansion of FE colleges also run by the local authorities, was the result of top-down local authority reorganisations of post-16 educational provision. These reorganisations typically involved closing the few comprehensive school sixth forms in existence, whether they liked it or not. These sixth forms were usually in the former grammar schools (such as Hackney Downs), further diluting any remaining grammar school ethos in the very comprehensives which ought, by inheritance, to have been most successful.

Some of these new sixth form colleges became – and remain – academic powerhouses. But excellent sixth form colleges were, and still are, a small minority of FE college provision for 16–18-year-olds, serving only a tiny fraction of the country. Most FE colleges were, and still are, patchy at best in the quality of their A-level and technical courses for 16–18-year-olds and in their provision of the pastoral support required by this age group. Moreover, whether local colleges were good, bad or mediocre, it was a serious policy error to divorce A-level and technical education entirely from more than half of all secondary schools. It not only sent out a message to those attending these schools (mostly from less advantaged families) that 'education stops at sixteen': it also denuded comprehensives of older pupils and role models, and made teaching in them less attractive. On my visits to comprehensives without sixth forms since the 1980s, the main complaint of headteachers, teachers and students has been – and continues to be – the lack of a sixth form. Yet local education authorities and state funding agencies generally refused, and still refuse, to allow comprehensives without sixth forms to set them up, even where the schools are successful and local colleges are vast in size and/or poor in quality.

So each year about 300,000 sixteen-year-olds were – and mostly still are – forced to transfer to another school or a college if they wanted to stay on in full-time education. Among this group, incentives to stay on were (and mostly still are) weak. Unsurprisingly, the high proportion of English teenagers dropping out of education at the age of sixteen came – and continues to come – largely from this 300,000, concentrated in lower-income families.

As for the comprehensive ideal of all-ability schools developing the talents of all children fully, this was not even distantly recognisable in most comprehensives. Leadership, ethos, discipline, the qualifications of teachers, and the quality of teaching and learning were often pitiful. Eric Bolton, Her Majesty's Chief Inspector of Schools in the 1980s, reported year after year on the 'stubborn statistic' of 25–30 per cent of lessons being consistently judged by inspectors to be unsatisfactory. This was an average figure; the situation in the 'secondary modern comprehensives' was far worse. Teaching across the ability range is tough enough, particularly with challenging pupil intakes. But doing so without teachers qualified in key subjects, together with weak leadership and discipline, exacerbated in many comprehensives by a hard Left ideological hostility to ability setting or proper systems of rewards and sanctions, reinforced failure with failure.

Bruce Liddington, later a transformational headteacher and one of my key officials in helping to establish academies, recalls that when in 1972 he started teaching at Northcliffe High School, a secondary modern in Conisbrough near Doncaster in South Yorkshire, he and a colleague recruited at the same time were the only teachers at the school with honours degrees or postgraduate qualifications. 'The head deliberately appointed us in order to set down a marker about the quality of teaching that would be necessary as the school went comprehensive,' he says. But few other such teachers arrived and little changed. The school continued to fail as a comprehensive, and thirty years later it was an early candidate to be replaced by an academy.

Weak management bedevilled comprehensives. Like the secondary moderns before them, comprehensives were set up and managed by local councils. In the language of the era, they were 'maintained schools' and part of what was called the 'maintained sector'. Their headteachers and governing bodies were subservient to local councillors and council bureaucracies.

It was an article of faith in the comprehensive era that local authority control was essential to schools being both comprehensive and publicly accountable. This was, and remains, false. The comprehensive principle concerns intake and provision: all-ability intake and all-ability provision, neither of which depends upon a particular form of school governance. As for the accountability and community mission of schools, there are far more effective mechanisms which now promote this, including strong governing bodies, independent inspection, the publication of performance data and greater school choice for parents.

Fatally, the comprehensive principle became confused with dogmatic attachment to a bureaucratic model of school governance which institutionalised weak and unambitious school leadership. Comprehensives failed on governance. The demarcation between local education authorities and school governing bodies was chronically unclear. Headteachers had two masters and only partial managerial control of their own schools. Buck passing was rife and diversity stifled.

This failure of governance was most pronounced in the cities, where local education authorities were most dysfunctional. Among the worst was the Inner London Education Authority (ILEA), England's largest city education authority, whose sweeping ambitions, vast bureaucracy and intense ideological debates did little to remedy the deep and deplorable failure of most of its comprehensives and many of its primary schools.

Then there was the impact of comprehensivisation on the private sector. Not only did the number of fee-paying schools significantly increase as the 'direct grant' schools and other state grammar schools went private rather than comprehensive, but the impact of these schools on the standards and culture of the private sector was profound. Competition from a suddenly enlarged fee-paying grammar school sector galvanised the old 'public' schools, from Eton downwards, who were obliged to match grammar school quality teaching and results in order to get their students into top universities. By the 1980s, the 'public' schools had largely caught up, while remaining as socially exclusive as before.

The Thatcher government's Assisted Places Scheme, which from 1980 until its abolition by the Blair government in 1998 paid private day school fees for a small number of bright children of poor parents – and better-off parents with good accountants – provided a financial cushion for these new fee-paying grammar schools, while blunting the social edge for them of moving into the private sector. Bringing some of these schools back into the state-funded system, as independently managed all-ability academies, was a key part of my academy strategy from the outset.

‡

So it was that half the comprehensives were failing in the 1990s and the education system remained as segregated as it was before comprehensivisation.

I saw all this at first hand as a governor of two 'secondary modern comprehensives' in the late 1980s and 1990s, as education correspondent of the *Financial Times* in the early 1990s, and then again as Tony Blair's education adviser after 1998, when I visited low-achieving comprehensives systematically and was shocked at how bad so many of them were.

I kept mentally comparing these comprehensives with my own academically non-selective boarding school in the 1970s. At my school, barely half of the pupils even took O-levels, a minority stayed on beyond sixteen, and only a few went to university. It was pretty tough, and looking back, name by name, I am conscious of a wholesale waste of talent. But on every score these 'secondary modern comprehensives' were categories worse: in behaviour, results, teaching, extra-curricular activities, ethos, social responsibility, the lot.

This wasn't just – or even mainly – about inner London. Another piece of entirely false conventional wisdom of the 1990s was that failing schools were largely an inner-London phenomenon, the obsession of Islington dinner parties, and that the London tail shouldn't be wagging the national dog. But in reality, every city in England and virtually every local authority in the country contained many truly dire comprehensives, although at a greater distance from London's chattering classes so attracting less attention than the likes of Hackney Downs, Highbury Grove and Holland Park. And most of their higher-performing comprehensives were mediocre at best.

Indeed, the school visit which sticks most vividly in my mind was to Hylton Red House in Sunderland, one of the first comprehensives established in the north-east. There was a mix-up over the dates of my visit and the headteacher wasn't expecting me. In a semi-panic, he put me in an office while he summoned local authority officials. Only when they arrived and the school day had ended would he show me around, with entourage. The main topic of conversation on the tour was the school's intractable problems. There were the buildings, which were dilapidated and filthy. But worse still, I was told, were the pupils. 'Not many of the kids are here to learn,' one teacher said. That much was self-evident: only a dozen of the previous year's 180 sixteen-year-olds had left with five GCSEs including English and maths. But still more shocking was the comment made by someone else in the party. 'Twenty years ago,' he said, 'when the boys left here, they walked down the hill and turned left to get a job in the shipyard or right to go down the mines. All those jobs have now gone. They might as well walk straight on into the sea.' I didn't know how to respond. It seemed too obvious to say that, if they got a decent education, they might prosper on dry land.

Hylton Red House is now closed. It has been replaced by an academy sponsored jointly by the University of Sunderland and Leighton Group, a new media technology company in the city.

The more such school visits I undertook, and the more I studied the data and the history, the clearer it became to me that what these 'secondary modern comprehensives' required wasn't incremental improvement but fundamental reinvention. They needed to be closed and replaced by schools with a fundamentally new and better ethos, new and better governance, new and better leadership, new and better teaching, new and better curriculum, new and better facilities, new and better extra-curricular activities, new and better parental and community engagement. The schools to replace 'secondary modern comprehensives' needed to be strong, self-confident institutions, not council bureaucracies in school buildings. And these new schools needed a missionary zeal to transform educational standards and aspirations in their localities.

All these points were more forcibly impressed on my mind because, at the *Financial Times*, I pioneered the first annual exam performance tables of independent schools and visited most of England's elite private schools to write the copy. After two years, we extended the performance tables to include the highest-achieving state schools too.

What struck me from visiting these schools was that, whereas the worst comprehensives were shockingly bad and far worse than my school, the best state and independent schools were shockingly good and far better than my school. This was not so much in terms of their facilities, which were highly variable, but rather in their teaching, their results, their sports, their drama, their art, and their other extra-curricular and community activities. What stood out, time and again, was their powerful sense of excellence, tradition and purpose rolled into one. Typically, including in the best state schools, there was an historic trust or foundation, and/or one of the churches, standing behind the school and its governance and ethos. If these schools were state comprehensives, they never put it in their title. Among the state schools, few had a good word to say about their local authority as a school manager.

To give just a few examples, at Sevenoaks School, I first saw the International Baccalaureate in action and wished I had been able to take it in place of A-levels, with its six-subject curriculum plus a course on the 'theory of knowledge' and an extended essay based on original research. At Hockerill Anglo-European College, in Bishop's Stortford, I saw an inspirational state day and boarding comprehensive school with bilingual teaching, international students, deep partnerships with schools worldwide and a brilliant music department. At William Ellis School in Camden, I saw a fairly successful community comprehensive in inner London, which, crucially and unusually, was part of a large sixth form consortium with three other neighbouring comprehensives. At Hills Road Sixth Form College in Cambridge and Peter Symonds College in Winchester, I saw veritable universities for seventeen- and eighteen-year-olds, and wished I had been able to attend them too.

I also came to perceive that the most successful schools, state and private, were themselves a considerable resource which could and should be used to found, manage and inspire schools to replace 'secondary modern comprehensives'. Their leaders, governors and brands were hugely powerful yet largely unexploited assets in the wider education system. They were unexploited partly because of the historic private–state divide, but also, in the case of state schools, because local education authorities regarded themselves as the agents and networks to improve schools, whereas in reality they largely lacked the capacity and passion to do so. There was a clear need and capacity for chains of successful schools to be set up under the leadership of England's best headteachers and school governing bodies and trusts, spanning the state and private sectors.

All this led, ultimately, to academies. But I am jumping ahead. Between the setting up of the comprehensives in the 1960s and 1970s and the Blair government of 1997, there was a creative burst of secondary education reform which was to have a significant bearing on my thinking. This was the Education secretaryship of Kenneth Baker between 1986 and 1989.

KENNETH BAKER AND AFTER

The introduction of the GCSE examination in 1986 was the only reform which notably improved the comprehensive system during the entire first two Thatcher terms. GCSE was the first qualification geared to the whole cohort of sixteen-year-olds, so for the first time the bottom two-thirds of the ability range were taken seriously in terms of curriculum and assessment. GCSE also ended the previous O-level practice of setting a quota on exam success. Sir Keith Joseph, its initiator as Education Secretary, extended this principle to A-level too, rightly deciding that it was unfair and reactionary to continue limiting A grades to less than 10 per cent of A-level entries, as a quota, while requiring exam boards to fail 30 per cent of students as another quota irrespective of the standard they achieved. Although a Thatcherite before Thatcher, Keith Joseph departed, in this respect at least, from the view, then common on the Right, that in education 'more means worse'.

Kenneth Baker, a highly dynamic reformer, succeeded Joseph as Education Secretary amid a long-running dispute over teachers' pay and conditions. He settled this dispute then concentrated on three priorities: the school curriculum, school management and the creation of a new type of technical secondary school. His ground-breaking reforms were the national curriculum, local management of schools, grant-maintained schools and City Technology Colleges.

The national curriculum set out minimum curriculum requirements and entitlements to be delivered in all state schools. Local management of schools devolved budgetary management from local education authorities to schools. Grant-maintained status enabled secondary schools to 'opt out' of local authority control after parental ballots. City Technology Colleges were an entirely new breed of independent state schools, managed by independent charitable sponsors outside local education authorities.

Tory Education Secretaries after Baker introduced some other notable reforms. In 1991, Ken Clarke established an independent national pay review body to determine teachers' pay and conditions in place of the archaic and conflictual negotiating machinery between local authorities and the teacher unions. This started improving teachers' pay and status and ended the endemic industrial conflict of the 1970s and 1980s. He also established an independent schools inspectorate – Ofsted – to undertake regular inspections of all schools and to publish the reports. In 1995, Gillian Shephard introduced national primary school literacy and numeracy tests for every child (SATs), with the results published school by school.

These three positive Clarke/Shephard reforms were retained by the Blair government after 1997. Blair also kept in post Chris Woodhead, the outspoken critic of low standards and the 'comprehensive establishment' appointed head of Ofsted and Her Majesty's Chief Inspector of Schools in 1994. (Managing the government's relationship with the tempestuous Woodhead was to be one of my tasks at No. 10 after 1998. This was my closest lifetime encounter with lion taming. I was fascinated by the lion but determined not to be eaten alive, and just about succeeded.)

However, it was the Baker reforms to the structure of the state school system – slower reforms on a longer fuse – which were to have a fundamental impact on my thinking on how to tackle 'secondary modern comprehensives', both for what they achieved and what they failed to achieve.

At the time, I was supportive of Baker's national curriculum, which imposed detailed requirements on schools to teach a broad, balanced and substantive curriculum subject by subject. Kenneth Baker saw it as conferring an 'entitlement' to a decent education which would transform standards. Except that it didn't. By the mid-1990s, it was clear that the national curriculum was only being properly delivered – indeed was only deliverable – where the quality of teaching and school leadership was up to the job. State regulation was a poor substitute, if any substitute at all, for good teaching, good leadership and good governance school by school. Hackney Downs and Hylton Red House weren't much improved by the national curriculum, while successful schools already had a rich and broad curriculum anyway and objected to its bureaucracy and straitjacket.

Moreover, the fundamental crisis of school standards lay in the teaching of the '3Rs', not in the content of the history or physics syllabi. The results of the first national tests of eleven-year-olds in English and maths, in 1995, showed that more than half of eleven-year-olds, and a far higher proportion in poorer areas, were failing to achieve the standard expected of their age in literacy, with a higher failure rate still in numeracy. Ensuring that children mastered the '3Rs' in primary school, and if not that they did so at the very beginning of secondary school, was the national curriculum priority. And this, again, could only be achieved by good teaching, good leadership and good governance, school by school.

The lesson rightly drawn from this by David Blunkett, Labour's education spokesman from 1995 and highly effective Education Secretary for the entire Blair first term, was to concentrate above all on the teaching of literacy and numeracy in primary schools. And not just by words in a government circular. Primary school teachers needed to be properly trained in teaching English and maths, and equipped to give substantial daily lessons in each.

In the run-up to the 1997 election, David Blunkett's adviser Michael Barber did the groundwork for national literacy and numeracy strategies, which were to become the main school reform agenda of Blair's first term. A brilliantly can-do and insightful London University education professor, Michael had previously been a Hackney Labour councillor and education director of the National Union of Teachers, so he knew every crevice of the political as well as the educational mountain he was climbing. He worked hand-in-glove with Conor Ryan, David's political adviser in opposition and as Education Secretary, who was New Labour – with an Irish lilt – to his core, and a master of facts and detail and how to communicate them jargon free.

Back to Kenneth Baker. His second late-1980s reform, local management of schools (LMS), was an unalloyed and almost immediate success. By delegating budgetary management from local education authorities to schools, LMS turned headteachers and governors into ... proper headteachers and governors. The governors and headteacher now had legal responsibility for their school's budget and the appointment and dismissal of staff. Furthermore, school budgets under LMS were based largely on pupil numbers, so parental choice came to matter as never before because income rose and fell in response to a school's popularity. LMS also meant that schools could recruit staff, and carry out smaller capital projects, without constant referral to the local authority. Whether it is true or apocryphal that before LMS there were heads who had to phone up the council to get a light bulb changed, there were fewer excuses for the lights not working thereafter.

Bruce Liddington, headteacher of Northampton School for Boys by the late 1980s, recalls the transformation brought about by LMS:

> Prior to LMS, schools had tiny delegated budgets. Mine was in the region of £60,000 a year which was intended to cover incidental petty cash, petrol for the minibus, but nothing remotely signifi-cant. The budget for staffing was held centrally and the staffing quota was dictated annually by the local authority. The only flex-ibility was via a bidding method that the head could enter into in order to get additional teachers for particular reasons. This totally lacked transparency and was palpably unfair.
>
> After LMS, I got control of virtually all my budget. The local authority continued to top slice a proportion for their bureaucracy, but the running costs of the school shifted under LMS to the school governing body. It was still ambiguous who was responsible – the school or LEA – for capability proceedings against teachers and the ultimate discipline of employees within the school. However, schools themselves and their governing bodies now decided how many teachers they would have and how many staff they would have, and at what rate they would pay them within national scales. At Northampton School for Boys this meant that instead of £60,000 a year my budget shot up to £5 million a year.

LMS was rapidly accepted by all political parties and became the bedrock of subsequent reforms to enhance school autonomy.

However, LMS exposed other problems. The first was the shortage of funding. Now that schools knew their budgets year by year, cuts couldn't be disguised or simply blamed by central government – which provided most education funding – on local authorities. Bruce Liddington recalls that his budget was cut in real terms in six of the eight years after the start of LMS in 1988. Since LMS, transparency has been a powerful force for increasing education funding, making a straight connection between higher education spending, bigger school budgets, and more and better-paid teachers.

Local management of schools also exposed weaknesses in school leadership and governance. This was particularly the case in comprehensives, large and complex organisations with multi-million-pound budgets and typically upwards of a hundred staff, most of which had no tradition of strong management. Effective management is the essential corollary of school autonomy. Where this was not in place, it needed to be, and after LMS the systematic upgrading of school governance and leadership ought to have been a national priority. But this was not done, which was a huge policy missing link until academies.

The other side of the coin, however, was that, for successful and self-confident school managers, LMS whetted their appetite to take complete charge of assets and staff and to end the managerial role of local education authorities entirely. These go-ahead schools tended to be in more affluent and Tory areas, including such enclaves within the cities and Labour fiefdoms. This generated both the political pressure for Kenneth Baker's third major reform – grant-maintained schools, entirely autonomous of local councils – while also giving it a bitter partisan edge.

The controversy over grant-maintained schools extended beyond the issue of school autonomy. There was a large funding bribe available, and in a further concession to the Tory right wing, grant-maintained schools were allowed to select up to a quarter of their eleven-year-old intake by ability and become quasi-grammar schools, although very few did so.

However, the fundamental argument was about independent governance. Kenneth Baker accentuated its significance by conceding local parental ballots before a school could become grant-maintained. The ballots were fought intensely, with local authorities, the teacher unions, the Labour party and the Lib Dems united against. But the ballots were generally won – strong head-teachers normally have little trouble persuading parents to take their advice – and by 1997 nearly one in five secondary schools and a small number of primary schools had taken grant-maintained status.

Labour came to power in 1997 committed to abolishing grant-maintained schools and bringing all schools back under local authorities. Tony Blair only reluctantly consented to this. He conceded it because his bigger concern was to avoid a debilitating battle in government over the abolition of the remaining 166 state grammar schools against the will of their parents. This he achieved by agreeing with David Blunkett that there would have to be parental ballots before a grammar school could be abolished. (Only one ballot was held – in Ripon in 1999 – and it was lost two-to-one.) That done, he left the future of grant-maintained schools largely to David's discretion, on the assurance that they would be given a reasonable degree of autonomy once forced back under local education authorities.

I was against abolishing grant-maintained status. For the most part, these schools were thriving and delivering a better standard of education than before, and their heads and governors were almost all strongly opposed to losing their autonomy. In my view, there were far too few good schools in the state system without putting even those at risk. Equally, however, it was clear to me that grant-maintained schools were not remotely an answer to the fundamental problem of failing comprehensives. This was for three reasons. First, very few failing comprehensives went grant-maintained, for these were the schools with the weakest leadership and most in the grip of their local councils and militant branches of the NUT. (The

NUT's full-time local officials, many of them paid by local authorities, were vociferous campaigners against grant-maintained schools, and later against many academies too.)

But, secondly and crucially, where failing schools had gone grant-maintained, this was not making them any better. Unsurprisingly so, since vesting complete autonomy in the hands of their existing headteachers and governors was hardly a recipe for success where weak leadership and governance were the problem in the first place. Indeed, some failing schools went grant-maintained as a way of avoiding closure, which should never have been allowed.

A third weakness of the grant-maintained policy is that it placed little premium on the setting up of entirely new schools and offered no new governance models to make it possible for external school promoters to do so. Radical innovation being a key driver of improvement, this was another big policy missing link until addressed by academies.

I therefore regarded grant-maintained schools as largely irrelevant to tackling endemic failure in the comprehensive system.

Kenneth Baker's fourth reform, the City Technology College (CTC), was more promising in this regard. The CTCs were new independent state schools with all-ability comprehensive admissions but an entirely new form of governance. They were set up and managed by independent sponsor-promoters drawn from successful leaders in business and social enterprise, while being not-for-profit and without fees. From the outset the CTCs focused resolutely on progression to higher education and skilled jobs. All the CTCs had sixth forms, purpose-built facilities, a technology-rich curriculum and strong links with employers. By the late 1990s, they were achieving good, even spectacular results.

In all these key respects, the CTCs were fundamentally different and better than all three of the dominant types of state school since the Second World War – grammar schools, secondary moderns and local authority comprehensives.

Only fifteen CTCs were established. Securing the necessary sites, sponsors and investment, and overcoming the intense opposition of local authorities and the teacher unions, proved a colossal challenge even for the indefatigable Kenneth Baker, and his Tory Education Secretary successors from 1989 to 1997 did not set up any more. It was some time before it was even clear that the CTCs were succeeding and they soon vanished from national view. One of Baker's Tory successors in the 1990s told me that the CTCs were seriously misguided: 'maximum aggro and huge expense for minimum reward, and mostly in Labour areas'.

Perhaps this was fortuitous. For as a result of their rarity and low profile, there was little pressure on Labour, before or after the 1997 election, to include the CTCs in the abolition of grant-maintained schools. The CTCs were simply ignored and left alone.

Until, that is, I started paying close attention to them.

ACADEMIES - GENESIS (1998-2000)

The basic of the basics, the '3Rs' in primary schools, was the Blair government's education priority in 1997. For good reason: literacy standards in English primary schools had barely improved since the Second World War, and numeracy standards were lower still. 'A child who cannot read cannot learn' was David Blunkett's compelling mantra.

Immediately after the election, Michael Barber was made head of a new 'standards and effectiveness unit' within the Education Department. Michael's brief was to implement the national literacy and numeracy strategies which he had developed for David Blunkett in opposition. These included teacher training in best-practice methods for teaching literacy and numeracy and a requirement for a daily 'literacy hour' and 'numeracy lesson' in every primary school. The plan was good, the implementation – driven by Michael personally – was highly effective, and primary school standards rapidly improved.

In secondary education, however, the early Blair government did little more than abolish Tory reforms unpopular on the Left. The Assisted Places Scheme, subsidising places in private schools, was abolished, without any credible policy to promote better forms of state–private partnership. Grant-maintained status was also abolished and the 1,200 grant-maintained schools were forced back under local authorities, mostly against their will, albeit with greater managerial discretion than had applied before they became grant-maintained. They became 'foundation schools'. Non-grant-maintained schools – the overwhelming majority of all schools, including virtually all the lower-performing comprehensives – were also given a new legal status ('community schools'), which was an elaborate reinvention of the status quo.

This highly complex reform of the legal status of state schools took more than a year to enact and drained reformist energy from the early Blair government to little positive effect. The School Standards and Framework Act of 1998 was a legislative monster of 145 clauses and thirty schedules, barely any of which did anything to turn bad comprehensives into good ones.

I became Tony Blair's education adviser in May 1998 after these initial changes had been made.

My view of the position in early 1998 was simple. The government had a bold and credible policy for improving primary schools, but no policy worth the name for improving the mass of underperforming comprehensive schools. So we needed one.

I didn't arrive in No. 10 with a worked-up policy, but rather a sense of what made for a good school, from my own school days and from my experience as an education journalist, school governor and university lecturer. I had a profound conviction that the status quo needed fundamental, not incremental, reform. A complete reinvention of the comprehensive school was required.

One statistic shocked me above all. In 1997, fewer than half of all state comprehensives – *fewer than half* – achieved a decent school leaving standard for more than one in three of their sixteen-year-olds, defined by the basic yardstick of five or more GCSE passes at grades A* to C including English and maths.

Most children of middle-class parents were achieving well above this basic GCSE standard, whether they went on to become nurses or doctors, soldiers or physicists, and their parents expected no less. This included the children of my friends and almost everyone I worked with. Almost all private schools, and the best all-ability state schools, regardless of intake, were achieving above this standard for most of their children. Yet more than half of England's comprehensives were failing to achieve it for the great majority of their pupils. In many hundreds of these comprehensives, tiny numbers of pupils were reaching the basic GCSE standard each year.

The socialist writer R. H. Tawney laid down a principle of education policy which I have always taken to heart: 'What a wise parent would wish for their children, so the State must wish for all its children.' Few wise parents would have sent their children anywhere near many of England's comprehensives.

In my experience, avoiding euphemisms to excuse an inexcusable status quo is the first essential in a progressive reformer. Put bluntly, about half of all comprehensives were essentially failing, many of them abjectly. The situation was a social crisis, and it needed to be treated as such. I had said as much in a book written with Stephen Pollard, now editor of the *Jewish Chronicle*, published shortly before the 1997 election and entitled *A Class Act: The Myth of England's Classless Society*. As we wrote:

> Those who can afford to flee the system desert it for the private
> sector; those who have the money to escape to a leafy middle-class
> catchment area leave the inner cities; and those who can't are left to
> pick up whatever is left over for them.

However, diagnosis was the easy bit; treatment altogether tougher. A whole catalogue of issues needed to be addressed. How to improve teacher recruitment and training radically. How to transform standards and expectations in comprehensives. How to empower headteachers and governors to lead strongly and take real responsibility for driving school improvement. How to demolish the Berlin Wall between the state and private sectors. How to end the bureaucratic levelling-down culture within the teacher unions, the local education authorities and the Education Department itself.

More demanding still was how to do all these things together, and how to create a dynamic within the state school system which would drive change in a self-sustaining way, for I had no illusions about the capacity of central government to manage schools any better than local councils.

It wasn't just about getting policies right in all these areas. The politics was highly toxic, which is part of the reason why it had been so hard to forge good policy in the first place. By the mid-1990s, few educationalists or politicians attempted to justify the fact that most children were leaving primary school unable to read, write and do basic maths properly. David Blunkett quickly and skilfully established a consensus behind his primary school literacy and numeracy policies. But when it came to reforming the comprehensives and the local education authorities, it was straight into political trench warfare.

The trenches represented the deep, fearful conservatism of both Left and Right, each side castigating the other while being entirely defensive about its own unwillingness to rethink and change in the face of stark failure.

The conservative Left had spent generations attacking private schools, 'elitism' and underfunding as the causes of England's educational ills. Up to a point, they were correct, of course. But when it came to reform of the comprehensive itself, and the local education bureaucracies which had sustained failing comprehensives for decades, education professors, council chiefs, teacher union leaders, and a fair few Labour and Lib Dem national politicians, took to the airwaves and the columns of *The Guardian* and the *Times Educational Supplement (TES)* to denounce virtually any change besides an increase in education spending. Ritual denunciation usually included an attack on the 'elitist' motives of any reformer who dared to challenge the status quo, and their sad lack of knowledge of the real world of comprehensives and council estates. This was a particular forte of Ted Wragg, then a professor at Exeter University and principal education columnist on the *TES* and *Guardian*, who excelled at personal abuse. I soon became 'ABA' – 'Andrew Bloody Adonis' – and later 'Lord Barmy of Bedlam'. It wasn't even witty.

However, the conservative Right was just as bad. While criticising the 'education establishment' of the Left for its tolerance of low standards and levelling down, it was itself an establishment fiercely resistant to change. It championed private schools without any willingness to overcome the rigid barriers between the private and state sectors. Its strategy for enhancing opportunity was to subsidise a tiny number of places in private schools and establish a few more selective grammar schools, while ignoring the vast majority educated in comprehensives. This was escapology, not a vision or policy for national education. Underpinning it all was an implicit, and often explicit, philosophy of 'more means worse': a reactionary denial of equality of opportunity and any notion that the typical child could achieve as highly as the child of wealthy parents, if educated properly. Even today, some leading private school heads criticise me for suggesting they might set up academies and broaden their educational mission. 'It must be a socialist plot,' one muttered to me.

If levelling down was the curse of the Old Left, social pessimism was the curse of the Old Right. They were equally misguided and outdated.

What was needed was a fundamentally new approach to secondary education unshackled by prejudice and failed policy masquerading as principle. This was not about splitting the difference – 'triangulating', in the jargon of the day – between Left and Right, which was the caricature of Blairism, sometimes alas given credence by a Blairite reluctance to have an argument with anyone outside the extremes of Left and Right. It was about completely rethinking, from first principles, the policies required to achieve progressive goals, which was Blairism at its best.

The challenge was simple. It was to create successful all-ability secondary schools, absolutely no-nonsense about standards and results, achieving the comprehensive ideal in a way that most comprehensives were failing to do, and making it possible to bridge the debilitating divide between state and private education. However, a credible strategy to meet the challenge was altogether more difficult to identify.

Setting about the task, I spent my first few months in No. 10 – the summer and autumn of 1998 – visiting schools and local authorities incessantly. It was soon clear that there were three immediate priorities: to recruit more good teachers; to focus comprehensives on better results; and to end the 'secondary modern comprehensives' by abolishing them outright and starting again with institutions set up and managed on a radically better basis.

The task was to translate these priorities into policy.

TEACH FIRST

Looking back, it is striking how the Blair government's most successful policies – including academies – followed failed or less successful attempts to tackle the same problems. Successful policy is often accretive and reactive. Rarely did we get it right first time, even where we got it right at all. We had to fail to succeed.

Teacher recruitment and appraisal were early cases in point. In 1997, we inherited an acute shortage of state secondary school teachers in key subjects, notably maths and most of the sciences, where there weren't even enough applicants to fill training vacancies, let alone graduates of quality. And quality was in short supply in virtually all secondary subjects. Initially, policy focused on targeted 'golden hellos' – modest cash incentives for recruits in shortage subjects – which had a modest impact. A school-based training programme for mid-career-switchers into teaching set up by the previous government was also proving positive and was scaled up year by year. Real-terms increases in teachers' pay also helped.

To try to use pay to drive up standards more radically, we decided in 1999 to offer a £2,000 pay increase for established teachers, provided they passed a performance threshold within a nationally regulated appraisal regime. The idea was that this would oblige headteachers and schools to take appraisal seriously. But it ended up as a huge bureaucratic form-filling exercise, with virtually all eligible teachers receiving the £2,000. It ought to have been obvious that the creation of a national bureaucracy to administer a less than 10 per cent pay rise was disproportionate. The funding should have been given directly to headteachers and the £2,000 payment made subject to their discretion with no further red tape, which is what we ended up doing a few years later, after wasting colossal amounts of time and money in consultancy fees.

Next came the quest to recruit more top graduates into comprehensive school teaching. It was vital to be no-nonsense about this. Education Department officials, reflecting the sensibilities of the teacher unions, the local authorities and sundry education professors, had an allergic reaction to labels like 'top graduates' or 'top universities', saying they were divisive. They invented long-winded euphemisms – 'higher-achieving graduates including graduates from the more research-intensive universities' etc. – to avoid calling a spade a spade. More worryingly, all too many of them denied that the spade existed, and would bridle at the 'elitism' of saying that Oxbridge and Russell Group graduates were any better than other graduates, when my point was simply that no school can be better than its teachers and without at least some academically high-achieving graduates, who were also good teachers, no secondary school could be excellent. Schools cannot teach to the highest levels at GCSE and A-level, and encourage the most able teenagers to go to top universities, unless they have at least some teachers who were educated at these universities themselves, and who themselves got A grades at A-level.

All this seemed to me stark staring obvious. That it had to be stated, and raised hackles, was itself a symptom of the crisis of the comprehensive school. But doing something about it was hard, for the majority of the most able graduates entirely shunned comprehensive school teaching. This wasn't about an aversion to the public sector or to teaching per se. Despite the gadarene rush to the City in the 1980s and 1990s, the civil service was still recruiting plenty of high-flyers, and a steady stream of top graduates were continuing to go into independent school teaching. Typically, a third or more of teachers in the leading private schools were from Russell Group universities, including a fair number of PhDs (more than twenty at Eton alone in 1997). But only a tiny number of state schools and colleges – mainly the grammar schools, sixth form colleges and highest-prestige (often church) comprehensives – were recruiting top graduates in any numbers.

It was important to understand why. The alien and threatening image of the comprehensive – more crowd control than teaching – was starkly off-putting to most young graduates, particularly those with good degrees who mostly hadn't been to 'bog standard' comprehensives themselves but rather to private or top-end state schools. Only one of my circle of Oxford contemporaries went into comprehensive school teaching. He was the exceptionally altruistic ex-Westminster School head of the Christian Union in my college, who saw it as a prelude to the priesthood. He is now chaplain of a leading south London private school. I am not aware of a single one of my students, from five years as an Oxford tutor in the late 1980s and early 1990s, who is still teaching in a comprehensive. Most of them are in the City. The only one for whom I wrote a PGCE reference is now headmaster of a major private school.

However, there was a deeper problem still. The 'teacher recruitment crisis' was generally portrayed as a recent phenomenon. But in terms of graduates from top universities going into state secondary school teaching, it wasn't. While there had been large numbers of top graduates going into state grammar schools in the post-war decades, there were barely any such teachers in the secondary moderns and their successor 'secondary modern comprehensives'. Oxbridge and other top university graduates shunned the secondary moderns. So the objective wasn't simply to reconnect the top universities with state school teaching – but rather, for most comprehensives, to make the connection for the first time. Given the image of the 'bog standard' comprehensive, this was a phenomenal challenge. It was also a critically important one if the comprehensive school was to be reinvented successfully.

Our initial thinking was that the solution might lie in a new graduate high-flyer recruitment scheme. If this was combined with only a time-limited commitment to teach – akin to the short-service commission, a popular option among graduates wanting to spend a few years but not a whole career in the army – then this might, we thought, attract a stream of top graduates.

This was the thinking behind a new 'fast track' scheme, which I spent a lot of time working on in my early months in No. 10 in 1998. The scheme was launched, but it came to little and it didn't last. This wasn't for lack of money, but because it wasn't attractive to the punters. Insofar as ambitious students and graduates noticed this new 'fast track' at all, it was seen as yet another lacklustre government scheme. The branding was poor. There was no champion. And it was weakened by compromises once the state teacher training agency got hold of the project design and implementation. The short-service element was lost, and graduates recruited through the conventional PGCE route were encouraged to join the scheme lest it be thought 'elitist'.

However, on the rebound from 'fast track' came a breakthrough policy. Just as 'fast track' was foundering, a McKinsey project team came to see me in No. 10 with a plan to launch an English equivalent of Teach For America, a highly successful private-sector-sponsored US scheme which recruited graduates straight from Ivy League and other leading US universities, trained them together over the summer after graduation, and placed them in groups, with proper support, in schools in disadvantaged areas, mainly in the big cities. The commitment to teach was only for two years, which made it highly appealing to young graduates.

A project board led by Rona Kiley, the persuasive American wife of Bob Kiley, Ken Livingstone's Transport Commissioner for London, had already lined up blue chip business sponsors for a proposed English equivalent, to be called Teach First, provided the government would rewrite teacher training regulations to make it possible, pay for the training and salaries of the recruits, and arrange placements in comprehensive schools for teachers selected and supported by Teach First.

After checking out the success of Teach For America, I jumped at the proposal. Education Department officials were fairly negative, lighting on the unit cost, given the commitment to teach for only two years, the short duration of the initial training, and the status of Teach First as an independent charity outside the state teacher training system. But to my mind, the failure of 'fast track' was largely because it wasn't outside the existing system, and wasn't an attractive enough offer to high-flying graduates. Teach For America had been growing for ten years in the US under the leadership of Wendy Kopp, a charismatic social entrepreneur, and there seemed to me no reason why an equivalent scheme couldn't succeed in England. Estelle Morris, David Blunkett's successor as Education Secretary, saw it the same way, and in 2002 we decided to back the scheme.

Teach First has been a huge success. It started small, 184 teachers in the first year, focused on schools in deprived parts of London. It was popular and prestigious from the outset. Driven by strong demand and the outstanding leadership of Brett Wigdorz, the McKinsey project leader who became chief executive, it expanded rapidly. More than half of Teach First teachers have stayed for longer than the initial two years. In 2011, there were 5,323 applicants for 787 places – nearly seven applicants per place – and Teach First now covers most of the country. More than one in ten of all new English teachers in state schools, and 27 per cent of all English teachers in the 40 per cent of schools classified as 'challenging', were from Teach First in 2011. For maths and science teachers, the proportions were, respectively, 17 per cent and 10 per cent. Teach First is reconnecting the top universities with state education, and systematically connecting top universities with schools in the most deprived parts of England for the first time ever. The intention is for Teach First to double in size again by 2014.

There is a close parallel between Teach First and academies. Both are focused on reinventing the comprehensive. Teach First seeks radically to improve their staffing; academies reinvent their governance and leadership. These are two sides of the same coin. Without good teachers, there will be no good schools; but without good governance and leadership, there will be few good teachers. Tellingly, academies were among the first and biggest recruiters of Teach First teachers. It is also striking that many Teach First alumni are now, in turn, pioneering new academies and 'free schools' in deprived areas. This, too, mirrors the US experience, where Teach

For America alumni are behind many of the charter schools and radical education initiatives in deprived communities.

There is an equally close parallel in policy design. Teach First and academies followed a similar 'fail to succeed' process of trial, error and re-trial on a far more radical basis, in seeking a solution to a deep intractable problem. In both cases, the radical reform involved a new public service model of dynamic not-for-profit organisations providing state education. And in both cases, it took the failure of incrementalism to generate political support for radicalism.

But for academies, it was an altogether more difficult, lengthy and painful process of evolution.

FALSE STARTS AND WRONG TURNS

'What is Tony's NHS?' I asked in my diary a few days after starting at No. 10 in May 1998. Nigel Lawson once described the National Health Service as the closest thing in England to a national religion. What was Tony Blair going to do which remotely matched Aneurin Bevan's triumph of social solidarity and national institution building? I wanted it to be an equally profound transformation of England's schools – and so, he said, did he. Education, education, education. 'But it will only be schools if he creates a new structure. None is in sight,' reads my diary.

None was in sight for some time, but I immediately identified a number of strands of reform. Teacher recruitment was one, as just described. Another was to be the 'specialist school'.

John Major's government had encouraged a small number of comprehensives to develop a specialist curriculum in areas such as technology, languages, sport and music, over and above (not in place of) their teaching of the national curriculum. The aim was to give these specialist schools a distinctive ethos, developing centres of curriculum strength. For this they received a modest amount of extra funding, provided they also improved their overall GCSE results year by year. Their intake remained all-ability.

By 1997, barely 200 comprehensive schools had taken up this

specialist option. It was opposed by many local authority and teacher union leaders, and education professors, as a plot to encourage comprehensives to differentiate themselves, which they thought a bad thing. They also feared it would encourage competition between schools, which was worse.

I saw it differently. Differentiation, and a real sense of individual pride, were precisely what comprehensives needed and so often lacked. Moreover, comprehensives already differentiated themselves in all kinds of ways, but generally covertly rather than overtly to avoid offending their local education authorities. This had to change.

As for competition between schools, clear-sighted realism was required. There was already competition. Human nature being what it is, there is no school system in the free world where competition is not evident between schools, particularly at secondary level. This is true even in Finland, the supposed bastion of the community comprehensive, but where, when I visited, I saw thriving choice and competition between schools, particularly in Helsinki at the secondary level. I learned that, in Helsinki, parents of half the children entering secondary school requested a school other than the one originally allocated to them. At the upper secondary level, beyond the age of sixteen, there is wider choice still, with the city's upper secondary schools and vocational colleges competing strongly on the range and quality of their courses. They were increasingly offering specialist teaching in particular subjects, including bilingual education in English and other languages, environmental sciences, music, drama and dance. This innovation and choice was driving higher attainment, according to the Finnish headteachers I met.

In these early days, I spent hours poring over maps and statistics. I soon learned that the notion that England is made up of distinct communities each with its own secondary school, and if only the local populace would do the decent thing and send their children to that school on principle then all would be well, had little purchase on reality.

In a recent critique of academies, Melissa Benn describes herself as 'profoundly distrustful of the concept of parental choice in all its varieties', and urges parents simply to use 'the local community school'. Yet virtually nowhere in England, beyond some rural and small town districts, are there distinct communities served by a single 'local community school'. In cities and large towns, accounting for most of England's population, parents have schools all around them and they are obliged to choose whether they like it or not (and most prefer having a choice to having no choice). Within about two miles of my house in north London, there are ten state secondary schools. It isn't even obvious which is my nearest: there is one at one end of my road, another around the corner in the other direction. As for primary schools, there are six within a ten-minute walk. This is not unusual.

So school competition and choice were there already. The problem was that too often, particularly in the cities, effective parental choice was between poor or mediocre schools which had too little incentive to improve. Although some went up and some went down year by year, in test and exam results and in pupil numbers, even the worst generally kept surviving while failing their children. This was partly because of an acute shortage of places in the few genuinely successful schools. Equally vital to the survival of failing schools were the local education authorities, which generally defended the 'producer' over the 'consumer' and rarely closed failing schools or took effective action to improve them. During my years of visiting failing schools, I often found that chief education officers and local council leaders had not even visited these schools personally, let alone done anything about them.

So I had no problem with 'specialist' comprehensives. Rather, my concern about these specialist schools was that they mostly weren't specialist enough in terms of the curriculum in their specialist area. But they were better than nothing. The evidence was that they were raising standards, and I strongly encouraged their expansion.

I vividly recall visiting a girls' Catholic comprehensive, the

Convent of Jesus and Mary, in a highly deprived part of the London borough of Brent. The brilliant headteacher, Mary Richardson, was every bit the Mother Superior. With steely ambition, great humanity and entrepreneurial flair, she had turned the school from failure to success in less than a decade. Specialist status in modern languages was a key part of this. Mary Richardson had built up a strong modern languages department, rare among inner-city comprehensives, and started a sixth form majoring in languages. She had also taken the school grant-maintained. It was June 1998 and my diary account of the visit is revealing of my thinking two months after I started at No. 10:

> Extremely impressive head – hard as nails; but just the right word for everyone – who has pushed up her five GCSE pass rate from 8 per cent to 58 per cent over ten years. With grant-maintained status and extraordinary success in attracting capital funding, she has practically rebuilt the school, including state-of-the-art IT and music and language facilities. Good old fashioned grit. She hates her local authority and doesn't want to go back under them, leads her staff by example and sends her brightest GCSE students to the Eton summer school to raise their sights for A-levels and universities. Three sixth-formers, all hopefully Oxbridge bound, showed me around, with nametags attached, and incredibly composed. All of this in one of London's most deprived areas. 'I was brought here to close the school: we had the worst results in the borough,' she said, 'but now we have the best results and are far oversubscribed.'
>
> There are crucifixes everywhere, but the Catholicism – rather like the Evangelicalism at KHS [my old school] – was not overpowering or fundamentalist, but gave a sense of order and values to the place. 'It's vital to have an assumed value base in a neighbourhood like this – they've got to shut their estates and often their families out of their mind when they come through the front gate,' she said. She has a wonderful tough black deputy head to deal with the PARENTS when they get abusive and violent. The benchmark of our success is that schools like hers thrive.

I was also impressed by Sir Cyril Taylor, the ceaselessly optimistic and can-do chairman of the Specialist Schools Trust, which acted as the club and promoter of specialist schools. A successful businessman, Cyril Taylor had been Kenneth Baker's right-hand man in establishing the City Technology Colleges. He and his trust became important allies in the reforms ahead.

So we steadily increased the number of specialist schools, until by 2005 almost all comprehensives had specialist status. In taking on the argument that specialist schools were elitist and divisive, we also started to make the case for a deeper reform of the comprehensive. For, however worthwhile, giving modest encouragement to a comprehensive to develop strengths in a particular curriculum area was not going to drive fundamental change. In the autumn of 1998 and throughout 1999, I continued to cast around for the reform which would.

At this point, I went down a number of blind alleys. One was a quest for more sixth form colleges. As described in the last chapter, by the 1990s, there were a hundred sixth form colleges nationwide. Some of them were large and successful A-level powerhouses, among the best institutions in the state sector at promoting access to higher education in general and Russell Group universities in particular. Since A-level provision was poor or non-existent in most comprehensives and FE colleges, I was attracted to setting up lots more sixth form colleges.

In autumn 1998, I worked up a plan to double their number. The idea was to set up a new college in every large town and city district without one. They would offer the full range of A-level provision as well as technical courses. Where there were existing school sixth forms, students would have a choice of where to study. Sixth form colleges would become a national system of flagship 'senior schools' for 16–18-year-olds, ruthlessly promoting access to top universities and apprenticeships, and taking on the independent schools.

It was never going to be easy to implement this plan. It soon got the 'elitist' branding from Education Department officials who, without opposing it outright, began articulating the objections of the FE colleges. The FE colleges were strongly resistant to losing their A-level and vocational courses for 16–18-year-olds, which constituted a large part of their income. The Education Department's further education funding quango quickly countered with promises of higher standards for sixth-formers within the existing all-age FE colleges.

However, the problem wasn't the FE colleges, which were – and still are – ripe for radical reform. If creating new sixth form colleges had simply involved breaking up FE colleges into 'sixth form' and 'adult' colleges, I would have pressed on. The difficulty lay, rather, with the schools. It had never been my intention to close existing school sixth forms. However, smaller sixth forms in comprehensives like the Convent of Jesus and Mary would have been vulnerable, and it would not have been possible to establish many new sixth forms in the half of comprehensives which lacked them if new sixth form colleges were being set up to serve the same teenagers. Indeed, the government's further education funding quango, which had long been gunning for small school sixth forms, latched onto my ideas to suggest that its proposed reform of FE colleges would facilitate the rapid closure of many 'less viable' school sixth forms.

This focused my mind on the essential problem, which lay with the comprehensives. A successful secondary school almost always has a sixth form, or champs hard at the bit if it doesn't have one. And they are right to do so. For today's young generation, education should be full-time until the age of eighteen, through to university or apprenticeship or a job. Sixteen-year-olds might wish to change institution after GCSE to pursue a particular course of study, or to go somewhere 'better', but to forbid schools from engaging in education beyond the age of sixteen as a matter of principle is wrong and a hangover from an age when most teenagers stopped full-time education at fifteen or sixteen, if they had received anything meriting that description in their comprehensive school before that age.

So yet again I came back to the core issue: the 'secondary modern comprehensive'. The essential reason why most comprehensives had no sixth forms, or small and mediocre sixth forms, was because their GCSE results were pitifully bad, and therefore their pool of potential sixth-formers was too small. Placing lots more sixth form colleges above comprehensives would not address this crisis. However tough, the right thing to do was to tackle the essential problem – the 'secondary modern comprehensive' – and not to engage in yet another diversionary strategy. So I dropped the idea.

The second blind alley was a quest to reinvent the local education authority (LEA). Here too, there were powerful arguments for change. Many LEAs were incompetent or positively harmful at the task of school improvement. And they were generally at their worst in precisely the inner-city areas where school improvement was most needed. In my diary in October 1998, I put it thus: 'We need to be promoting the "LEA of the future" which has only a small school improvement staff of its own but is extremely effective at school improvement through a combination of "contract" head-teachers and experts in school turn-around, in place of the current low grade bureaucracies and political wrangling.'

In 1998 and 1999, I pushed hard for reform on these lines, including the contracting out of the school management functions of failing LEAs. David Blunkett was no fan of failing LEAs either, and contracting out the management of failing LEAs became a major preoccupation of the Education Department. The result was an improvement in some of the worst LEAs such as Islington and Lincolnshire.

The question then was whether to go further and seek to replace the entire LEA system with something better. I produced a number of schemes to this end. Some of them looked quite good on paper. But then I drew back. For the more failing schools and LEAs I visited, the clearer it became to me that, while weak LEAs were a problem, the very notion that bureaucracies – however good – were appropriate to the task of managing schools was mistaken. Good schools were rarely good because they had competent LEAs, but because they themselves possessed good governance and leadership. A competent LEA, particularly an effective chief education officer, could help put in place good governance and leadership school by school. But for this, the need wasn't for the wholesale reinvention of the LEA, a reform which would very likely end up with the same people doing similar jobs for higher salaries in a recreated bureaucracy after a massive, lengthy and expensive upheaval, like rail privatisation. The imperative, rather, was for each LEA to have effective leadership and a mindset to support schools to become strong self-governing institutions. Furthermore, where the task was one of fundamental school re-foundation – as it became, once academies started – I was anxious for this to be undertaken by central government in partnership with local councils, because of their local democratic legitimacy.

So the replacement of LEAs was also dropped in the summer of 1999. Instead, I worked with David Blunkett and his team on a set of 'next steps' reforms, called 'Excellence in Cities', to provide greater support in school improvement for LEAs in the major cities. And I continued to ponder how to reinvent the comprehensive.

Abolition of LEAs was not the last false start of my first year in No. 10. A third, more decisive one was happening in parallel. It was called 'fresh start', a policy for relaunching failing comprehensives within the local authority system. For me, this was to be a very personal and bitter learning experience, and it led directly to academies.

'FRESH START'

I live in Islington, near Tony Blair's former home in Richmond Crescent. Tony and Cherie sent their sons to The London Oratory, a Catholic state school in Fulham, rather than to either of their then terrible local comprehensives, Highbury Grove and Islington Green. In their position, I would have done the same. Neither Tony nor, for that matter, I was hypocritical about this. We both supported parental choice within the state system, including church schools, and we were both trying to do something radical to turn around failing comprehensives.

At some Islington primary schools a decade ago, half of the pupils were going on to private schools – including at Canonbury, the school my children attended. Many of the rest went to state schools outside the borough, often an hour or more away. Only a handful of children, mainly from the local council estates, went on to the local comprehensives. It was a burning ambition of mine to see that this disgrace did not continue.

There are now two good state secondary schools in my part of Islington. An entirely new academy opened in 2007, sponsored by the Church of England but with admissions open to the whole local community without faith tests. Also nearby is Highbury Grove, a former grammar school, which as a comprehensive in the 1970s went into a spiral of decline similar to Hackney Downs, but over the last five years has improved significantly, thanks to strong leadership, competition from new academies in Islington and Hackney, and a complete rebuilding. The proportion of Islington's eleven-year-olds going on to secondary schools in the borough has risen sharply, including more of the local middle class.

That is now, in 2012. Back in early 1998, shortly before I joined Tony Blair's staff, I gave Derek Sawyer, the Labour leader of Islington council, a piece of my mind about the state of the borough's comprehensives at a party meeting. Derek didn't disagree, said he knew that 'something' had to be done, and put me on the spot by asking if I would become a governor of a 'fresh start' school which was to replace George Orwell, the borough's worst comprehensive, on Islington's northern border with Haringey. (Like the equally grim Geoffrey Chaucer comprehensive in Southwark, George Orwell was proof that great names don't make great schools. Orwell would have appreciated the irony.)

I accepted the invitation. At the time I was a journalist on *The Observer* and knew little about the 'fresh start' policy. This was fortuitous, for, had it been a few months later when I was at No. 10, I would have known more about the policy but might have felt it inappropriate – or too high risk – to become a governor of a 'fresh start' school, given that this was a government initiative. But as it happened, I was to experience 'fresh start' at first hand.

The 'fresh start' scheme provided extra government funding

to councils which closed failing schools and reopened them, still as local authority comprehensives but with new names, new governors and new leadership. George Orwell was one of ten failing secondary schools to go down this 'fresh start' route in 1998 and 1999.

It was not a happy experience. Many of the key decisions about the 'fresh start' school had been taken by Islington council by the time the school's 'interim governing body' was appointed to oversee the transition to the new school. This included the curriculum and the design of the refurbished buildings. Islington council had already decided on an arts and media specialism and the title 'Islington Arts and Media School', although many of us on the interim governing body thought the new school needed a mainstream academic specialism, maths or science, to tackle pitifully low standards in the core subjects at George Orwell.

More urgent was the chronic mismanagement of the refurbishment of the school's buildings. No one was appointed by the council properly to manage the project. Deadlines were missed and the work deplorable. On the opening day of the 'new' school, there was no timetable, no IT, the bells and fire alarms weren't working, and the school was a dangerous building site. Chaos reigned. A near riot, with racial overtones, took place a few days later. The police descended; arrests were made; and it nearly led to the immediate closure of the school.

Leadership and governance were equally fraught. Within the space of barely six months, there were two different governing bodies: an 'interim governing body' to oversee the transition, and then a newly constituted governing body to manage the school once open. Both of these were twenty strong, constituted on the traditional local authority model with a mix of council appointees and elected parent and staff governors, their membership constantly changing. Each meeting was like a mini Islington council meeting, complete with factions, pre-meetings and long debates. There was little unity of purpose or vision, there being no sponsoring organisation or agreed mission. A left-wing faction won the election for the chair of the 'permanent' governing body, against a 'moderate' faction.

Islington council was largely useless throughout. The appointment of the first headteacher took place within weeks of the constitution of the interim governing body. The appointee, who was unsuited for the job, got it on the strong advice of Islington's chief education officer, who left the borough for Hartlepool almost immediately afterwards. Shortly thereafter, the local authority's entire education service was failed by Ofsted, and its management contracted out. By then the school was again in crisis. The headteacher was forced to resign and the 'fresh start' was itself fresh-started. Having worked behind the scenes with the borough's acting chief education officer, and fellow governors, to bring this about, I left the governing body, thoroughly demoralised.

It was a sorry story, and I still shudder to think about it. Over time, the school overcame its founding problems and is now performing much better. But it was obvious to me that the 'fresh start' policy was seriously flawed. The local authority which had allowed George Orwell to fail so badly over so many years was hardly likely to be successful in managing its relaunch. Tellingly, other 'fresh start' schools experienced similar problems. Two of the initial ten were soon closed outright, and several others have since become academies. 'Fresh start' clearly wasn't the answer to failing comprehensives.

CITY TECHNOLOGY COLLEGES

But if 'fresh start' wasn't the answer, what was? In October 1999, as Islington Arts and Media School was in crisis, I coincidentally visited one of Kenneth Baker's City Technology Colleges (CTCs). Or perhaps it was not a coincidence. For the trip to Thomas Telford School, in the Shropshire new town of Telford, was to discuss the proposed National College for School Leadership with the school's headteacher, Kevin Satchwell.

The National College was one of my first initiatives after starting at No. 10. I wanted it to be a Sandhurst for headteachers.

Its conception followed visits I paid to a number of leadership training centres, including Sandhurst. Nottingham University agreed to host the college on a prestigious new site, and we needed a founding director. Thomas Telford had been described to me as the 'best comprehensive in England' and Kevin Satchwell as one of England's best headteachers. So I drove up to Telford with Chris Woodhead, whose support for the college I was keen to enlist, to see whether Kevin might be the person for the job.

Thomas Telford School was everything I wanted Islington Arts and Media School – and every replacement for a failing comprehensive in the country – to become. There was an ethos of achievement and excellence akin to the best grammar schools, yet for pupils of all abilities and backgrounds with a modern curriculum. There was a huge sixth form sending dozens each year to university. The teachers were highly qualified, ambitious and passionate. Every pupil appeared to be succeeding at something, and they were smart, self-confident and enjoying school. There were dozens of sports teams and after-school activities, on a par with the best private schools. The buildings were purpose built and modern, not lavish, geared especially to the technological curriculum. And all under the leadership of the outstanding Kevin Satchwell, the CTC's founding principal: a Brummie equivalent of Michael Wilshaw, passionately committed to education in the West Midlands where he had spent his life in the state system as a teacher and headteacher, with precisely the same tough no-nonsense style, and the same sky-high ambitions for his pupils and his school. Satchwell and Wilshaw also had this in common: a low, despairing opinion of LEAs and the mess they were making of so many comprehensives.

Kevin lost no time in telling me he wasn't interested in becoming director of the National College. But the reason he gave led to a wholly different conversation. What he really wanted to do, 'if your government will let me', was to establish independent state schools across the West Midlands on the Thomas Telford model. He was sure his sponsors would support him. His principal sponsor was the Mercers, one of the historic City of London livery companies, engaged in education for centuries and sponsor-manager of other schools in the private and state sectors, including two of London's historic public schools, St Paul's Boys and St Paul's Girls. 'I can do more for education by running a Thomas Telford chain across the Black Country than by becoming a pontificating education professor, telling everyone else how to do what I'm not doing,' was his typically blunt remark. I said I thought a Thomas Telford chain was a great idea, 'but I'm not quite sure how to get from here to there'. (Twelve years later, Sir Kevin – as he now is – has set up three academies in the West Midlands, all with the ethos and mission of Thomas Telford.)

I decided I needed to visit more City Technology Colleges and get deep into the detail of what made them tick. Over the following month, I visited almost all fifteen of them. The seminal moment was at Emmanuel College, Gateshead, sponsored by the successful Sunderland-based car dealer Peter Vardy. Tony Blair called on my mobile just as I was leaving an inspirational session with a group of sixth-formers telling me about their life stories, the brilliance of their school and their ambitions to get on. When I told Tony where I was, he said: 'Of course I know the CTC and Peter Vardy. I was at Durham Cathedral School with him. Even out in Sedgefield [Tony's County Durham constituency] they want to go to his school.' My diary takes over:

Pacing around the school car park, I told Tony how far we still had to go to make this kind of school the norm. He listened intently, and by the time I had got to the end of the tale of the hostility of Gateshead council, the refusal of the local Labour MP even to visit the school, and Vardy's wish to set up at least five more such schools in the north-east, he simply said: 'OK let's work out how to go for it.'

CTC after CTC, it was the same story. At Harris CTC in Crystal Palace – the student body half black, half white, all high-achieving – Lord Harris of Peckham, chairman of Carpetright plc and confidant of

successive Tory leaders, told me the school was 'one of the most
important things in my life'. Like Satchwell and Vardy, he said he
would found a chain of schools modelled on his CTC, in his case
across his native south London, if encouraged to do so.

I went on to analyse the data for all fifteen CTCs, all of which
had by 1999 been open for at least eight years. Virtually every CTC
was both very high performing and demonstrated exceptional
student academic progress. In educationalist jargon, they were
'high value-added'; in plain English, they provided a good education. Significantly, almost all the CTCs had large and successful
sixth forms and sent lots of students to Russell Group universities.
They all had an exceptional array of sports, arts and after-school
activities. And these features were as true of the few CTCs which
had replaced failing schools as of the majority which started off
as brand-new schools, although the former, unsurprisingly, took
longer to achieve high standards.

Why were the CTCs so successful? Over the course of my visits,
I came to see it in simple terms. It was governance, independence,
leadership, ethos and standards. The CTCs had all five and they
were mutually reinforcing. The CTCs had highly capable and effective governing sponsor-managers, who ran their schools free of
the shifting sands of local and national education bureaucracies. The
sponsors were not 'here today, gone tomorrow', like all too many
local authority chief education officers. They were making long-
term commitments to their schools. Virtually all their founding
sponsors were still in place a decade after the launch of the CTCs,
passionately committed to their schools. The sponsors set ambitious
goals and ran their governing bodies in a businesslike way to achieve
these goals. Strong headteachers were appointed and supported
by these sponsors, instilling an ethos of success, discipline and high
standards in every aspect of the CTC's work. The best of these headteachers stayed in post and did not job hop every few years.

It was simple, really.

So now, at last, I had some building blocks for a radically new
type of independent state school to replace the 'secondary modern

comprehensive'. The crucial difference with 'fresh start' was the presence of sponsor-managers with the skills, commitment and control needed to drive the new school forward from inception to opening and beyond, with a single vision and with full responsibility and accountability. These sponsor-managers were unambiguously in charge: they and their schools were independent of local authority management and the management of the failing comprehensives they mostly replaced, enabling them to break free from past cultures of failure and to strive for excellence unshackled.

However, the CTC model had to be changed for these new independent state schools to reinvent the comprehensive. They had systematically to replace failing comprehensives and not (like CTCs) be conceived of as a small parallel system, separate from the state school mainstream. They needed a broader base of sponsors, including from existing successful schools, higher education and other successful public institutions. They needed to be established so far as possible in partnership with local councils, which needed to be encouraged to welcome them as local community schools and be generous in granting them land and facilities. There could also be no pretence that private sponsors would fork out anything but a fraction – which we initially set at £2 million – of the capital cost of the academies, unlike the CTCs where the unrealised ambition was for the private sponsors to meet a large part of the capital costs. Independence would come because that was what the state wished and willed, not because the sponsors had 'bought' it.

The funding context was crucial. School capital spending was rising fast which gave a one-off chance to provide facilities for these new independent state schools.

Equally critical was political will. After Kenneth Baker left the Education Department in 1989, there was no will to set up new CTCs. I remember, as the *FT*'s education correspondent in 1993, interviewing John Patten, then Education Secretary. Propped up on his desk, updated weekly, was a card displaying the number of mostly high-performing schools which had gone grant-maintained. On mine, ten years later, was a card with the number of failing comprehensives at various stages of being replaced by academies. Ministers, even the most dynamic, possess a finite supply of time and energy. Where they concentrate it tells you everything about their priorities, whatever they say in their speeches.

The biggest conceptual difference between CTCs and academies lay in their relationship with the comprehensive school system. Kenneth Baker saw CTCs as the harbinger of a new form of technical education, providing a minority alternative to the community comprehensive. Hence their name 'technology colleges', the emphasis on business sponsors, their brief to develop a technology-focused curriculum, and the decision to set wide catchment areas with a proportion of places reserved for students passing an aptitude test in technology.

There was a lot to be said for the original Baker vision. There is an important role for dedicated technical schools within a genuinely comprehensive education system. Kenneth has now returned to the charge with the 'university technical colleges' he is establishing under the academy umbrella, as described in Chapter 9, and I am glad to be assisting as a member of his Baker Dearing Educational Trust. However, when I analysed them in 1998/9, what struck me forcibly about the CTCs was that from the outset they had become mainstream secondary schools, not niche technical schools. This happened from the moment they opened their doors because they offered a very high standard of general education and responded to the desperate yearning of parents in their areas for good secondary schools. If fifteen independent state schools could be so successful in this way, why not, in the right conditions, 150 or 1,500?

In forging the academy programme, I was also influenced by international experience in introducing independently managed state schools. In England, before academies, there was no effective means for anyone besides a local authority, or in a few cases the churches (and the churches only within the local authority system), to establish and manage new state-funded schools, even in areas of serious failure. This lack of 'contestability' stood in stark contrast not only to the 'charter schools' in the United States, which the Clinton administration had embraced and which, while it was early days, were generating much-needed dynamism, optimism and parental support in American cities confronting similar educational failure to England's. It also contrasted with liberal Holland and social democratic Sweden, widely regarded as models of equitable public service provision.

In the Netherlands, a large proportion of schools have historically been independently managed, and school promoters have the right to set up new schools in the state system where they can show sufficient parental demand. In 1992, Sweden introduced a radical reform allowing the establishment of 'independent state schools' outside their local authority system to promote greater diversity, choice and higher standards, within rules to ensure fair all-ability community pupil admissions. I visited the Netherlands and Sweden in autumn 1999. The president of Sweden's independent schools association was a social democrat, who stressed the impact of the new schools in raising standards across the system. The number of independent schools was rising fast, particularly in Stockholm, where discontent with the status quo was greatest. As with charter schools, it was early days, yet a strong case was made that these new schools were raising standards without inequity. There was certainly no disputing their popularity and parental support.

'A REAL BREAKTHROUGH'

All this came together in a plan for independent state schools, to replace failing comprehensives and to provide for entirely new schools, which I put to Tony Blair and David Blunkett in November 1999. With Tony, I was frank about its potential 'to go big', and he seized on it immediately.

I had to be more circumspect in cultivating the idea in the Education Department. David Blunkett and his trusted advisers Michael Barber and Conor Ryan, never afraid to be bold in tackling school failure and overcoming deprivation, welcomed it as a small but potentially worthwhile initiative, which was a fair evaluation at the time. Senior officials were more sceptical. One of them, who had worked for Kenneth Baker on the City Technology Colleges, told me that 'even with all Ken's drive, and all those Tory donors, they only got fifteen set up and local authorities have kept them in quarantine ever since. You'll be lucky to do four or five.' I treasured another comment relayed to me: 'It will keep Adonis tied up for a while, instead of him making mischief over here.'

So a few days after watching the excruciating Millennium Dome celebrations on New Year's Day 2000, I got to work with Conor Ryan on a policy announcement for a small-scale programme of independent state schools. The announcement was included in a speech on 15 March by David Blunkett to the Social Market Foundation on the theme of tackling school failure. It was deliberately low-key and got only inside-page press coverage. David rightly didn't want to over-egg it and I took the view – which I took for years to come – that the less media coverage of these new schools the better. They needed time and space to establish themselves. Moreover, the education media was dominated by teacher union leaders opposed to reform, who had most of the education correspondents in their pockets since the journalists depended on the union general secretaries for their daily stories and shock-horror quotes. (The media is more balanced nowadays; far more voices speak up for reform, thanks in part to the rise of the academy movement.)

There was another reason for wanting these independent state schools to be seen as a small experiment. Only if they were considered a minor irritant, not a major reform, would they stand a chance of being tolerated by the forces of conservatism entrenched in the Education Department, the local authorities, and all three political parties, not least my own. It had to be a case of small change leading to big change. But from the outset I always envisaged the big change. As I wrote in my diary the day after the announcement: 'The long-term implications are profound. In effect, we have accepted the principle of independent schools within the state system. With this wedge in the door, a real transformation of the comprehensive is possible. It is a real breakthrough.'

The immediate reaction was largely predictable. 'A half-baked idea from the US,' said the head of the Local Government Association. 'This is something that is not acceptable. This is the beginning of removing education from local government. We don't need another untested and alien gimmick.' 'This whole business smacks of a touch of panic,' said one teacher union leader. 'They seem to be realising that their initiatives are not working.' He was right about that.

The most positive reaction came, surprisingly, from the *Times Educational Supplement*. I had spent an hour explaining the rationale for academies to the editor, and she gave this fair assessment:

> It would be easy to dismiss them [academies] as recycled city technology colleges and benefiting the few rather than the many. But as the mixed results of Fresh Start show, something very radical is needed to break the cycle of low expectations and underperformance ... Children growing up in the most deprived and challenging circumstances need the very best schools and teachers and not, as too often happens, some of the shabbiest and ill-equipped buildings, or least experienced, temporary or demoralised and exhausted staff.
>
> City Academies may not be the solution for more than a handful of cases of chronic underachievement ... [but] fresh, independent management, combined with complete refurbishment, could release new professional energies and help break down the social polarisation of inner-city schooling.

This taught me an important lesson: you can never spend too much time explaining policy, and rebutting unfounded criticism, and should never presuppose opposition.

WHAT'S IN A NAME?

The name 'academy' was settled at the last minute. It came down to a choice between 'independent state schools' or 'city academies'. The first described what was in the tin; the second invoked the strong Scottish 'academy' brand of community school. Two things settled it. The word 'independent' would wind up the Left. 'Academy'

avoided this. It was also snappier and could be incorporated into
the title of individual schools – 'Mossbourne Academy' etc. – which
would create a brand. The word 'city' was there because, initially,
academies were intended for cities; it was soon dropped as projects
came forward in Walsall, Ramsgate and Northampton.

The brand potential swayed me. How many all-ability English
secondary schools have 'comprehensive' in their title? Virtually
none. The comprehensive brand is weak. I wanted a brand to
compete with 'grammar school' and 'independent school', the
two strongest in the business. A decade later, 'academy' is doing
precisely this. Tellingly, although each academy is entirely free to
settle its title, almost all sponsored academies have taken 'academy'
in their title and are proud of it.

But announcing names and policy statements was the easy bit.
Now we had to get some real academies up and running.

ACADEMIES – LAUNCH (2000-01)

The academies policy was bound to be tough to implement, given the innovation required and the scepticism on all sides. But I hadn't anticipated it would be both tough and personal.

It was personal in two senses. From the outset, inside and outside government, the policy was associated with me personally. This happened not only because it was true, but also because no one else much wanted to 'own' such a controversial and high-risk idea. And it was well known, not least in the media, that I had been pressing hard for radical reform of secondary education including independent state schools.

What I hadn't anticipated, however, was that prime responsibility for implementing the policy would also fall to me personally. Being a special adviser and based in No. 10, I had no formal position to take on this role, and I did not wish for it. I had plenty else to worry about, particularly after June 2001 when I became Head of the No. 10 Policy Unit. And I had never wanted to be a manager. My idea, once the policy was announced on 15 March 2000, was to keep a watching brief while the Whitehall machine took charge.

But it didn't. Days passed and inertia reigned. So I had to take the lead.

Who was going to recruit academy sponsors? Who was going to speak to local authorities, identify failing comprehensives to be replaced by academies, and forge projects? Who was going to drive and chase progress within the Education Department? Who was going to ensure that the necessary resources – financial, educational and administrative – were there? Who was going to tell the story of academies and rebut anti-academy claims and arguments day by day? I quickly realised that, if I didn't get going in all these areas, no one else would.

Having no formal responsibility, I didn't discuss how to do it with anyone. I just did it. I drafted a prospectus for sponsors. I got on the phone and set up meetings with potential sponsors and local authorities. I got the wheels of the official machine moving through endless phone calls and meetings with ministers, advisers and officials. I started keeping lists and project files. Once a proper academies team was set up in the Department, which took several months, I went over to Sanctuary Buildings for weekly meetings with the team, as well as enlisting officials to attend my meetings in No. 10 about individual projects.

It was constant improvisation. I had become de facto chief executive of the academies programme, doing the job part-time with no formal powers and with half a secretary as my only direct support.

I didn't expect this intensive engagement to last long. For a good while I kept hoping that after 'a few more months' I would be able to step back. But the months became years, the handful of initial projects became hundreds in a multi-billion-pound programme, and it was to be nearly a decade before I finally moved on.

FIRST STEPS

The first imperative was to build a team and generate some projects.

Without Tony Blair, there would have been no academies. Tony immediately took to academies as one of his emblematic public service reforms. I whetted his appetite with regular reports from the front, and traded on his account day by day to get academies going.

Prime ministerial authority, even when potent, is largely invisible beyond foreign affairs and the management of mega national crises. It is rarely exercised in person, but by proxy. For the proxy to be effective, he or she needs to understand instinctively how far to push ahead, while being confident that the prime minister will not only be supportive but will also say so unprompted and whenever asked. The moment ministers, officials or third parties sense that the proxy is freelancing, their authority vanishes. Tony was brilliant in this regard. Most of the time we barely needed to speak to be on the same wavelength. He never hesitated or expressed ignorance when confronted about my doings, whether he knew about them or not. At decisive moments – ministerial meetings, speeches, encounters with potential sponsors – he would pitch in, all passion and purpose, with a lawyer's command of the brief after a momentary explanation or glance at a note put in front of him.

However, prime ministers and their advisers are powerless without a machine. To get going, I was dependent on allies. David Blunkett's key advisers Conor Ryan and Michael Barber, with David's imprimatur, got a project unit established within the Education Department and kept nudging the machine. Michael Levy, Tony Blair's fundraiser and Middle East envoy, offered to help secure philanthropic business sponsors, and played an invaluable role in recruiting first-rate business sponsors with deep pockets. Within No. 10 itself, three people were critical. Jeremy Heywood, Tony's brilliant principal private secretary, encouraged the civil service to be positive. Sally Morgan, Tony's political secretary, watched my back within the party, where a number of colleagues were none too supportive even within No. 10 itself. An ex-teacher, Sally was deeply interested in academies and after No. 10 went on to become a trustee of Ark, one of the best academy chains. She is now chair of Ofsted. And David Miliband, Head of the Policy Unit until the 2001 election, was by now a close friend and strongly encouraging.

I talent spotted within the Education Department and soon latched on to Sir Bruce Liddington, one of the most successful state school headteachers of his generation. Bruce, introduced in Chapter 2, became head of Northampton School for Boys, then a failing comprehensive, at the age of thirty-five. By the time he left, shortly after the launch of academies in 2000, it was one of the top-performing comprehensives in the country including a sixth form of 500 and fourteen Oxbridge offers. For this he was one of the first state school headteachers to be knighted. Yet, knighthood apart, his ebullient can-do manner was the antithesis of Whitehall's Sir Humphrey. Recruited as one of the first 'education advisers' for academy projects, I soon turned him into a universal trouble-shooter, relying on him to negotiate project deals and bang heads together where I could not do it personally. Bruce stuck with me throughout the academy years, and is now chief executive of E-ACT, one of the largest academy chains.

After the launch, I knew the phone wouldn't immediately start ringing with enthusiastic potential sponsors, council leaders and parents groups. (People tend not to phone No. 10 – they can't get the number, for starters – so you have to phone them first.) But I too glibly assumed that, once they realised the opportunity was there, sponsors of firm intent would come forward and some council leaders would show themselves positively inclined.

It was more of an uphill struggle than that.

For the first two months, no sponsors or local authorities declared firmly. It was a case of one conversation or suggestion leading to another and then another, many of them leading nowhere at all. A number of good potential sponsors got cold feet either at the scale of the task or the likely controversy, while some of the enthusiastic were unsuitable. 'I had no idea it was this grim,' said one business leader after I showed him around one of Middlesbrough's worst comprehensives. 'It's easier building a factory in China.'

Michael Levy introduced me to a string of self-made entrepreneur-philanthropists. A number became powerful sponsors.

The first was Frank Lowe, a genius sports marketer. Frank had been born and brought up in Harlesden, in the deprived north London borough of Brent, and his mother still lived there. He was keen to found an academy specialising in sport, if it could be located nearby. Once she met Frank, Jacky Griffin, Brent's feisty and unusually can-do chief education officer, supported an academy to replace Willesden High School, one of London's worst failing comprehensives, provided we would entirely rebuild the dilapidated school as part of the deal. Soon afterwards, there was an edgy meeting at the school, including Frank, Jacky, the school's headteacher, local councillors, Education Department officials and Frank's fifteen-year-old son, who said to me as we walked around the bleak, leaking buildings, the boys chewing gum and spitting in the corridors: 'I didn't realise people had to go to schools like this.' After the tour, we all crammed into the headteacher's dingy office and agreed the very first academy project. The date was 15 July 2000, four months after the launch. It was to be the first of hundreds of such meetings over the next eight years.

By a similar process, Clive Bourne was soon partnered with a project – now Mossbourne Academy – on the site of Hackney Downs School in Hackney as described in Chapter 1. David Garrard, a property entrepreneur, took on a project in Bexley; Peter Shalson, another entrepreneur, in Edgware; and Barry Townsley, a City director, in Hillingdon.

The next projects came via David Levin, an old friend who was headmaster of City of London School for Boys, one of London's leading private day schools. A giant of an outgoing South African, David made two vital introductions. The first was to Michael Cassidy, chairman of the policy committee of the City Corporation, the school's governing foundation. The Corporation, historic governing authority of London's 'square mile' financial district, has a long philanthropic tradition in its deprived neighbouring boroughs. Michael Cassidy 'got' the academy concept immediately, seeing it as a means for the Corporation to do more in education than running privileged private schools. He persuaded the Corporation to become a sponsor, and in partnership with Southwark council, which provided a site for an entirely new school, the City of London Academy was born in Bermondsey. It was to be the first of three Corporation academies (the other two are in Hackney and Islington).

David Levin's second introduction was to his wife, Jenny, who ran a strategy consultancy for independent schools. One of her clients was Ewan Harper, the highly dynamic chief executive of the Church Schools Company, a charitable chain of eleven historic Anglican private schools. The chair of the charity's board was

Dame Angela Rumbold, an ex-Tory MP who had been Schools Minister under Kenneth Baker and helped him develop the original City Technology Colleges. Ewan and Angela seized on the academy policy as a way of extending their school chain into deprived communities 'as our founders would have wished'.

I approached the council leader in Lambeth, which like the neighbouring borough of Southwark wanted an entirely new secondary school, and persuaded him that an academy was just what he – like Southwark and Hackney – needed to signal a radical break from past failure. The initial meeting with Ewan Harper was frosty. Lambeth's education officials did not warm to Ewan's brisk account of how he intended to import his superb private school management and standards into the state system. But the next meeting went better and work soon started on this new academy just off Clapham Common. In parallel Ewan also agreed to take on Ducie High School, on the edge of Moss Side in Manchester, one of the worst gang-infected comprehensives in the country. Ewan soon honed a user-friendly yet businesslike patter for local authorities, which together with its impressive track record is why the United Learning Trust, the academy wing of the Church Schools Company, is now one of the largest academy sponsors, with more than twenty academies.

A number of City Technology College sponsors were in the vanguard in these early months. Kevin Satchwell at Thomas Telford agreed to found the first academy in the West Midlands in partnership with his lead sponsor, the Mercers livery company. The major West Midlands city councils – Birmingham, Wolverhampton and Coventry – rejected my overtures out of hand. But after visiting Thomas Telford, Bill Thomas, the Labour leader of Sandwell council – a retired teacher, passionate about education – phoned to say: 'I want one of these as soon as possible: it will be a beacon on the hill for the working-class kids in my area.' He offered a site next door to West Bromwich Albion Football Club.

The Haberdashers, another ancient City livery company responsible for prestigious private schools, and which had also established a City Technology College in the 1990s, was also in this first wave. The Haberdashers' CTC – Haberdashers' Aske's Hatcham College in New Cross – was an oasis of excellence in the south-east London borough of Lewisham. Dr Liz Sidwell, the CTC's principal – like David Levin, a robust liberal South African who escaped apartheid, so was shocked yet undaunted by England's class system – offered to partner the CTC with a failing school elsewhere in Lewisham borough. Lewisham volunteered Malory School on its Bromley border, one of the borough's worst schools, and its replacement academy was federated with Hatcham CTC, with common management, uniforms, ethos and expectations. Liz Sidwell is now (in 2012) the Schools Commissioner in the Education Department, promoting academies to replace failing comprehensives nationwide.

Sir Harry Djanogly, sponsor of Djanogly CTC in Nottingham, agreed to do the same and his CTC doubled in size to incorporate a neighbouring failing school.

Philip Harris – Lord Harris of Peckham, founder and chief executive of Carpetright, whom I mentioned earlier as another of the original CTC sponsors – was another prime mover in this first wave. A formidable social as well as business entrepreneur, he agreed to take one of south London's most notorious gangland schools, Warwick Park, in his native Peckham. Southwark council, by now seizing academy opportunities, welcomed him with relief. Philip and his school transformation team, headed by Dr Dan Moynihan, principal of Harris CTC in Crystal Palace, soon developed a chain of south London Harris academies. There are now fourteen and rising, and they are a byword for quality and excellence. Whenever I see Philip in the House of Lords he reels off the latest stats on his academies' achievements together with the story of a boy or girl he met on his last academy visit and what they want to do with their life.

Peter Vardy, also encountered earlier in my 1998/9 tour of CTCs, was Philip Harris in the north-east. Emmanuel College, his popular and very high-achieving City Technology College in Gateshead, was almost as important to him as his hugely successful car dealership. With his brother David as his education project manager, Peter wanted to create a chain of academies across the north-east, where parental enthusiasm for Vardy academies was exceeded only by the stubborn refusal of most of the region's local authorities to respond to it.

Peter wanted to set up academies in Newcastle and Gateshead. Neither council would agree. Middlesbrough was more receptive, followed farther afield by Doncaster, both of which volunteered chronically failing schools to be replaced by academies. King's Academy in Middlesbrough and Trinity Academy in Doncaster are now among the most successful state schools in the country. Peter's evangelical Christian associations were soon seized on by academy opponents. Yet his academies' admissions are entirely non-religious, their teaching and curriculum rated excellent by Ofsted, and parents are queuing up.

The Church of England became an early academy promoter, and was soon the most numerous sponsor of all. Some C of E academies, like Greig Academy in Haringey, replaced failing inner-city C of E schools. Most others were the work of diocesan bishops keen to develop new Anglican secondary schools in deprived areas to strengthen the church's social mission. With my strong encouragement, C of E academies generally eschewed faith-based admissions for all but a small minority of their intake (if that). Local authorities tended to be keen on the C of E as sponsor. The church was an existing and popular manager of state-funded schools, and there was an imbalance across most of the country between Anglican primary and secondary schools, with too few secondary.

So I soon had a good number of sponsors. My bigger initial problem was to square local authority chief education officers and council leaders and/or chairs of education. Without at least two of these three in support in an authority, nothing happened. Often a highly encouraging conversation with a councillor or education director, who would talk with passion about replacing intractable failing school x or y with an academy, was apologetically countermanded after they took wider soundings. Calls would go unreturned for days; meetings could take weeks, even months, to organise, if they happened at all.

I soon realised that council leaders were divided not into Tory, Labour and Lib Dem so much as 'do nothing', 'do something' and 'dither', with most in the first and third camps. I also found that chief education officers tended to be more ideological – and more ideologically opposed to academies – than the politicians, although when they were supportive, as a number soon were, this was generally decisive.

Tellingly, the local political leaders generally most in favour of academies were MPs, irrespective of party. Seared by encounters with angry and distraught parents in their constituency surgeries, and not generally beholden to their local councils, they would give me chapter and verse on the full horror of school x or y and the negligence of the council in standing idly by. Three exceptionally proactive constituency MPs, Simon Hughes (Southwark), Siobhain McDonagh (Mitcham) and Graham Allen (Nottingham North), came and asked me for academies within weeks of the launch, 'although as you know my party is against the whole thing', the Lib Dem Simon Hughes said cheerfully. His deprived inner south London borough of Southwark now has nine sponsored academies, one of the highest concentrations in the country.

MINISTERS AND MANDARINS

By the summer of 2000, I felt I was working on a 500-piece jigsaw with only a few patches complete and most of the pieces still a jumble.

An exasperated diary entry in late June catches the mood and the moment:

> The problem isn't sponsors but finding enough LEAs and credible projects to make a good start on 5–10 over the summer. I can't get the thing joined up. There is no real enthusiasm for any of this in DfEE [the Education Department] and I am driving the whole thing forward personally, spending hours a day in detailed calls about

sites, LEAs, sponsors etc. And then seeking to galvanise the DfEE officials to take the necessary follow-up action.

I had soon put the first ten or so projects together, as just described. But inadequate leadership, drive and support for academies within the Whitehall machine was to dog the academies programme throughout its life. It continues today, and it is a case study in the weakness of British government in carrying forward big projects.

The Department's name says it all. I use 'Education Department' throughout this book to describe it, but the Department's name and scope have changed five times in the last twenty years. At one point while I was Minister for Schools, even the word 'Education' was dropped. Overnight I found myself in the 'Department for Children, Schools and Families', whose acronym DCSF I could only recall by mentally dubbing it the Department for Curtains and Soft Furnishings.

The name would not have mattered so much if the organisation concerned was professional and stable. Yet neither was the case. Over my decade in No. 10 and as Schools Minister, it was subject to six Secretaries of State, three Permanent Secretaries and four directors-general in charge of the Department's schools directorate. In the five years before I became Minister for Schools in 2005, there were also four successive Ministers for Schools responsible for academies. And there were no fewer than seven Education Department officials in charge of the academies programme during its first eight years, although the figure could be put at ten, for at several points more than one official was in charge within the Department's complex and ever shifting hierarchy.

Within months of the launch, I was not only de facto chief executive but also virtually the only point of continuity in the entire programme, and I became more so with each passing year. One of my main challenges was to keep the team of officials responsible for academies energised and focused as the world around them kept disintegrating and reshaping. It was vital not to slow down, nor allow others to do so, amid the constant flux.

This is not to suggest that ministers were uninvolved. David Blunkett endorsed and launched the academies policy in the spring of 2000. David Miliband as Minister for Schools from 2002 to 2004, and Ed Balls as Secretary of State from 2007 to 2010, became deeply interested in subsequent policy decisions and individual projects. The other Secretaries of State – Estelle Morris, Charles Clarke, Ruth Kelly and Alan Johnson – all engaged to some extent in their shorter tenures. But my main point of engagement with them was simply in seeking to persuade them to support expansion of the programme.

It was a similar story with the civil servants. A few senior officials became animated by academies. David Bell, deeply knowledgeable as a former Chief Inspector of Schools, was supportive as Permanent Secretary after 2006. Neil Flint, Chris Wormald, Ralph Tabberer and Peter Houten created an academies division capable of managing a large programme after 2005. Dunstan Hadley, the very model of the private secretary, ran my office as Minister for Schools efficiently, acting as my eyes, ears and discreet adviser on comings and goings across the Department. Sir Bruce Liddington was a critical support. There was also a small, dedicated group of lower-level advisers and project managers, several of them ex-headteachers recruited for their expertise who dealt assiduously with project after project.

However, the notion that Britain has a 'permanent' and 'expert' civil service is largely a misnomer. Most career civil servants change jobs every year or two, unrelated to the needs of the state. They mostly possess superficial subject-specific knowledge and front-line experience and few skills beyond those acquired at school and university. Barely any senior Education Department officials had taught in a school, let alone managed one. Not many were school governors. Unless they were parents, as likely as not they hadn't even visited a school since they attended one. Project management skills were in especially short supply, not least among those possessing the title.

Just as an official was getting on top of an individual project or policy issue, they would suddenly disappear, often at a few weeks' notice. There were a few notable exceptions, but for the most part staying in the same job for more than two years, at most, was seen as a mark of failure. Often, changing job – or even department – was a prerequisite for promotion. I lost Chris Wormald, the best of the directors of the academies programme, after just a year, when he left for another Whitehall department in order to be promoted one civil service grade. When I took this up with Sir Gus O'Donnell, the Cabinet Secretary, Gus protested he was powerless to act because departments were managed autonomously. 'My dear Andrew, I am only Head of the Home Civil Service,' he said with a smile.

It is no accident that Whitehall is so bad at managing change. It rarely views change programmes – academies are one of the biggest programmes of recent years – as projects requiring continuity of management and real expertise in processes and policy. It is largely hand-to-mouth.

But with enough well-intentioned and capable people around, and large budgets to employ consultants doing jobs that should have been done at a fraction of the cost by civil servants, we muddled through.

A good part of my job was to act as persuader in chief. Much of the leadership of the Education Department, and most local authority directors of education and council leaders, expected or hoped that this latest Blairite fad would soon wither and die, or at least be kept small and to the margins like the City Technology Colleges. I had to persuade them otherwise.

For several years, hardly a day passed without some education official or expert telling me that, however worthy, academies were peripheral to the 'real challenge' in secondary education. There was no consensus as to what was this real challenge. Depending on the interlocutor, it could be the IT and digital revolution, teacher training, the national curriculum, the testing and exam regime, Ofsted, the careers service, the school year, local education authorities, the funding system, children's services, sport, 'creativity', 'sixteen to nineteen pathways', 'transition from primary to secondary', or any of these in combination. 'Joining up' was an especially fashionable

'real challenge' – in order to 'abolish silos' and 'overcome barriers to learning'. The words 'holistic' and 'seamless' were usually
thrown into this mix: 'joined up' and 'holistic' agencies, or services,
or qualifications, would provide 'seamlessly' and 'holistically'
for all concerned by ... abolishing silos and overcoming barriers
to learning.

A favourite 'real challenge' was the imperative to abolish GCSEs,
A-levels, BTECs and other vocational qualifications as soon as
possible, and to replace them all with a new '14–19 diploma', which,
being holistic and seamless, would engage the disaffected, reduce
exams and exam stress, eliminate drop-out at sixteen, broaden the
curriculum, unleash the creativity of teachers, promote life skills,
transform social mobility and overcome the academic/vocational
divide, all in one. A massive reorganisation of quangos, a favourite
ploy of ministers and officials anxious to demonstrate activity, took
place after 2001 to create a 'holistic and seamless' post-16 education system, with a new Learning and Skills Council overseeing
Local Learning and Skills Councils in place of the previous Further
Education Funding Council and other funding bodies.

I supported reform in some of these areas. Others I regarded as
a distraction, untimely or unwise (the 2001 reorganisation was very
expensive and bureaucratic, and largely pointless). But none of
them were reasons for soft-peddling on the imperative to transform
the governance, ethos and leadership of failing comprehensive
schools. On the contrary, as I argued, even the most worthwhile of
these reforms would come to little or nothing if the schools that
children attended day-in day-out were not good schools. And if
they were good schools, then most of these reforms would either
be unnecessary or differently conceived. The impact of the curriculum, testing, exams, facilities, technology – and virtually everything else concerning a child's education – crucially depend upon
the effectiveness of the school where they take place. I had to make
this argument virtually every day in some forum or other.

It was also important to know what to try to stop. In giant political and administrative machines, it is not possible to stop every

policy you believe to be undesirable or even damaging, whatever your authority. As a No. 10 adviser, husbanding finite time and goodwill, there was a price to trying to stop the pet projects of ministers and colleagues, however wrong-headed I conceived them and however much I knew that Tony Blair would agree with me. I learned to bite my tongue and only to agitate against seriously damaging proposals, like the wholesale abolition of GCSEs and A-levels proposed in 2004.

However, I didn't compromise when it came to the academies policy itself. As soon as the first projects took shape, political and official pressure was relentless to make academies as much like local authority comprehensives as possible. Size, curriculum, age range, governance, teachers' pay and conditions, building design, the school day and year, the precise form of all-ability admissions: the pressure to conform to local or national norms and initiatives was constant. I even had to resist an initiative on teaching children to cook quick meals being imposed as a national requirement on academies. But resist I did, and the model remained intact.

LEGAL POWERS AND LEGAL AID

Crucially, as it turned out, the essential legal provisions needed for academies to be set up were tacked unobtrusively to a piece of uncontroversial education legislation proceeding through Parliament in the summer of 2000.

Instead of seeking to recast the legal framework for schools, we relied largely on existing statutory powers in relation to City Technology Colleges and legislated anew only for the critical additional powers required for the academy model, mainly pertaining to the leasing and transfer of land. There were a few rumblings on the Labour backbenches when these new provisions were debated in the Commons, but David Blunkett oozed reassurance. The legislation passed into law at the end of July 2000 virtually unnoticed.

The timing was fortunate. In the summer of 2000, all eyes were on the imminent general election and few Labour MPs wanted to rock the boat. Had legislation for independent state schools come forward at the start of the second term, instead of the tail-end of the first term, it would have been fought intensely within the government and the Labour party, and at every stage of the parliamentary process. Gordon Brown, by then in conflict with Tony Blair on public service reform, would have ensured as much. This is precisely what happened over trust schools – 'academies-lite' – when legislation for them came forward at the start of the third term in 2005. The trust school concept was watered down significantly between conception and enactment, and academies would not have survived at all in similar circumstances.

In the summer of 2000, I did not anticipate the post-election Blair–Brown conflict, but I always expected that academies would become more controversial once opponents realised that they were intended to be numerous and nationwide, and not a small experiment limited to a few London boroughs with disgruntled journalists. This is why I moved to secure the legal powers as quickly and quietly as possible, and why I resisted all subsequent calls – from friends, foes and the Whitehall machine alike – to 'codify' or 'improve' the legal framework on academies. After the legal changes in the summer of 2000, there was virtually no further legislation mentioning academies while I was responsible for the programme. I deliberately kept academies entirely out of the 'flagship' 2005 Education Bill, despite constant pressure to include them.

There was another reason for taking this approach. Ministers love to parade their flagship Bills, yet the public barely notices. It is 'facts on the ground' – real changes and new institutions taking root community by community – which constitute real reform. This is what matters, not the legal mumbo jumbo which makes it possible in the first place. There is too much legislation and regulation, and it is a particular weakness of Whitehall and its ministers, who are mostly long-serving parliamentarians, to believe that legislation constitutes reform, when at best it is part of a process of reform. In my experience, charisma, persuasion and money, not legislation and regulation, are the great drivers of reform. Obviously, the essential legal provisions needed to be put in place. But what got academies going decisively was winning the argument about the imperative to overcome entrenched educational failure, and funding the early academies from a dedicated central budget, not legislation. And it would have been a huge waste of political energy and capital to have provoked an unnecessary battle on the wider legal framework for schools (witness the fate of Andrew Lansley's health reforms, 2010–12).

However, if Parliament was navigated quickly and unobtrusively, the same was not true of the courts. As soon as academy projects became public, opponents seized on judicial review as a means to stop them. Ultimately they failed, but only after years of lengthy, expensive and immensely distracting court actions, mostly funded by legal aid with the real opponents – the National Union of Teachers and anti-academy pressure groups – masquerading as parents too poor to afford to pay legal fees.

The legal campaign against academies was masterminded not only by these opponents, but also by solicitors and barristers who made a specialism of academies cases and encouraged legal challenges. Ironically, human rights barristers at Cherie Blair's Matrix Chambers were prime litigators. I wondered how many of them sent their children to failing comprehensives.

A critical early legal case concerned St Mary Magdalene Academy, around the corner from my home in Islington. Islington council held an unusual local referendum in 2001, asking the borough's residents whether they wanted a new secondary school and, if so, of what type. Virtually all those voting in the referendum favoured a new school, and the most popular option was for a Church of England school, Islington having no C of E secondary schools. The council thereafter drew up plans with the diocese of London for an existing Anglican primary school to be rebuilt as an all-through academy for primary- and secondary-age children. However, popular enthusiasm and local authority agreement did not stop anti-academy campaigners from fighting the proposal through the courts, with the support of residents in nearby multi-million-pound houses, few of whom used Islington state secondary schools or intended to do so, and who simply didn't want a new school of any kind in their back yard. It was a classic unholy alliance.

The St Mary Magdalene case was by far the most significant of the early legal cases because it concerned the fundamental compatibility of academies with education law and parental rights. Had it been lost, the academies programme would have stopped immediately.

It took years for the case to grind through planning and education tribunals, and then on to the High Court. Not until July 2006 did the High Court finally rule. Mr Justice Wilkie found for the academy on all counts, ruling that it was perfectly reasonable to believe that the academy 'would improve the standards, quality, range and diversity of educational provision in the area'. Crucially, he rejected outright the contention 'that the maintained sector constitutes a gold standard and that any falling away from that standard requires justification'. The notion that Islington's comprehensives might represent an educational gold standard was surreal, but stranger notions have been entertained by judges.

GLASS PALACES

Academies were greatly helped on their way by the surge in school capital investment which started with the three-year public spending settlement of July 2000. 'Spending spree to follow prudence' was the BBC headline on the day of its launch. The extra spending was especially generous for school buildings, rising from £700 million in 1997 to reach nearly £8 billion in 2010, when it was cut by the coalition government. (It will fall to £3.3 billion by 2013.)

Year by year, I secured a slug of this rising budget specifically for new academies, starting in 2000/01 with provision for about ten. This was justified in its own terms, since academies replaced dilapidated schools in deprived areas, or were entirely new schools in such areas. It also enabled me to offer a straight deal to local authorities. In return for agreeing to an academy, they got £20 million-plus of local investment, and a popular school to boot.

I had no compunction in being so blunt. Anti-academies campaigners and some local authorities complained of blackmail. I saw it as the state living up to its fundamental responsibility to ensure a decent standard of education nationwide, and deploying its resources accordingly. Simply pouring money into failing schools and giving them shiny new buildings does little, if anything, to raise educational standards. It can even make things worse, giving the appearance of a fresh start and bringing an initial uplift in local popularity before parents realise that fundamentally nothing has changed. Anyway, academies represented only a fraction of the rising tide of investment going into schools – far too small a fraction, in my view. For local authorities refusing to contemplate academies, there was plenty of other funding. Increasingly, as academies proved themselves, council leaders embraced academies by positive choice and not simply or even largely for the money.

It is hard to exaggerate the sheer bleakness and unfriendliness of most of the comprehensives replaced by the early academies. The poor quality of post-war and 1960s local authority school design and construction. The life-expired flat-roofed buildings, baking in summer, freezing in winter. The portakabins, like mobile camp sites. The concrete playgrounds. The flaking signage, with the names of successive headteachers painted on top of each other at the main entrance.

There are many successful schools, state and private, which have life-expired buildings and inadequate facilities. But almost invariably they are well maintained, bright and smart. By contrast, only rarely, unless newly built or rebuilt, is a failing school impressively presented. The tell-tale signs are poor cleanliness and routine maintenance; the state of the toilets; and an absence of good artwork and displays on the walls of classrooms and corridors. A canny Ofsted inspector once told me that he could judge most schools within ten minutes by three things: meeting the headteacher, looking at the walls and checking the boys' toilets. My experience of the first two is the same (I didn't think it a good idea to be asking to see the third). No school made a more powerful first impression on me, despite its clapped-out buildings, than Phoenix High School in Hammersmith, with its brilliant wall displays featuring the students at work and play. The headteacher, Sir William Atkinson, was – and remains – an inspirational school leader, as well as a great role model for London's black community; and his school is among the most improved in the country.

The grim physical state of so many failing comprehensives resulted from neglect as much as under-investment, reflecting wider management failure. Poor upkeep of buildings and poor quality of management and leadership are two sides of the same coin. Grim and inhospitable buildings encourage disrespect among children and staff alike. This was all the more reason why I was determined that academies should combine reform and investment – including new buildings – in one integrated project to create an entirely new institution, educational and physical. Not only would this target investment on deprived communities, where academies are now often the most prestigious public buildings in their localities. It was also a once-in-a-generation opportunity to align the creation of new institutions with the creation of new infrastructure, the one reinforcing the other to reinvent secondary education.

The early academy sponsors were putting £2 million of private charitable funding into their capital projects. As part of the deal, some sponsors wanted celebrity architects and landmark buildings. I did not object. I wanted to imprint academies on the national mind as symbols of educational renaissance, in the way the Victorians imprinted their vision and values in their stations, their town halls, their schools and their universities. I also wanted academies to pioneer a new generation of school design. So in the early days I supported the sponsors who engaged Richard Rogers, Norman Foster, Amanda Levete and Zaha Hadid.

The comment by a girl at the opening of Norman Foster's Bexley Business Academy sticks in my mind: 'I didn't realise that schools like this were for children like us.' A number of academies have won prestigious architectural prizes. 'A Brixton school designed by Zaha Hadid contributes to the debate on education – mainly by being so excellent,' enthused an architecture correspondent at the opening of Evelyn Grace Academy, sponsored by ARK (Absolute Return for Kids), an academy sponsor which grew out of the City of London and is now a leading academy chain. Evelyn Grace won the 2011 Stirling Prize, beating the Olympic Velodrome.

However, these early projects with celebrity architects were a nightmare to handle as sponsors competed for glamour and government largesse. On Evelyn Grace, I recall months of agonising meetings over the feasibility and cost of a building thrusting diagonally, with amazing flying angles and rectangular shapes. 'Can't it be straightened up and squashed a bit? That would save millions,' ventured an official. The first contractor pulled out as the bill escalated. It eventually came in at £36 million, one of the most expensive academies. On another occasion, Norman Foster told me it was my duty to posterity not to shave a million pounds off one of his projects by dropping some elaborate multi-coloured eco-friendly cladding and other features. But by now I was more worried about my duty to the taxpayer than to posterity, and the cladding went. I learned the hard way that schools, like everything else, have to be built to budgets not to wish lists.

So, as academy numbers rose, I closed the window for celebrity architects and encouraged more standard and functional designs. These owed a good deal to the ambitious early projects – celebrity architects don't become so for nothing – but they were less expensive and showy. The architectural world did not enthuse as much. But just as inspiring as Evelyn Grace to my mind is, for example, Wellington Academy, in Wiltshire, designed by Keith Papa of BDP in London, built of natural timbers, with a stately entrance lobby and open-plan area from which a 300-seat theatre, a cafeteria and classrooms fan off on several floors. Situated in the down-at-heel garrison town of Tidworth, it is far and away the most imposing building in its community and a source of immense local pride. As

I approached in a taxi, the driver said to me: 'You can't miss it: it's fantastic, like that picture of St Paul's rising up from the rubble in the Blitz.'

Academies have had a seminal impact on school design, and the whole conception of the secondary school as a place of beauty, space, light and modern community facilities, in the heart of inner-city and deprived communities. Nearly 400 academies now have state-of-the-art buildings, alongside hundreds more schools through the Building Schools for the Future programme which grew out of the early academy experience. They are among the finest physical legacies of the last decade and a testament to the new standing of education. 'I was amazed,' writes a visitor to one of these new schools:

> It was the most striking school building I had ever seen at a time when many schools were either Victorian factory-model buildings with high windows and an intractable sense of oppression or else 1960s boxes with the smell of hopelessness growing as virulently as the moss on the leaking flat roofs of the mobile classrooms.

'A HUGE JOB STILL TO DO'

So, by March 2001, a year after the launch, fifteen academies had been announced or were in the pipeline. More than half were in London, which was top priority in the drive to replace failing comprehensives.

A start had been made. Yet it was only a start. I set out the task ahead in a note for Tony Blair on returning from holiday in August 2000. 'A perception of transformation is gaining ground in primary schools, from the combination of the literacy and numeracy strategies, extra nursery places, smaller class sizes and sharply rising tests results.' But, I continued, in a tone of impatient exasperation:

> This is not so at secondary level. We have spent much of our energy in reversing early errors, notably the abolition of grant-maintained

status, in avoiding further errors (notably the abolition of the remaining grammar schools against their will), in averting potential crises (notably teacher recruitment) and keeping funding on an even keel. We have also established a number of new programmes, most recently City Academies (the principle of state-of-the-art independent schools funded by the government). But in terms of concrete results, progress has been modest and we have a huge job still to do.

I then went to the heart of the problem as I saw it:

The number of disgraceful urban comprehensives – eyesores, lousy results, middle-class free zones – hasn't reduced much. The number of failing schools is now higher than in 1997. Test results for fourteen-year-olds and GCSE results for sixteen-year-olds are improving only slowly, despite the much better results for eleven-year-olds. We are barely holding our own on secondary teacher recruitment.

Academies had the potential to be transformational, but only if scaled up rapidly:

They ought to make a big impact in their localities and act as national beacons. But until we get up to a steady 20+ new academies a year, in all types of neighbourhood, they won't have a transformative effect on the system as a whole.

Then there was the private sector:

We have simply marked time on private schools. We have overcome the deep antipathy of the private sector to Labour, and reduced the antipathy of Labour to the private sector. But we haven't actually done much to overcome the state–private divide. The performance gap between private and state schools continues to increase. I see no prospect of the private–state divide being reduced much without bolder policies, e.g. private schools sponsoring academies and becoming academies themselves.

However, the sunlit uplands were in sight. A second Blair landslide appeared imminent. This time it would not be wasted. Academies would be scaled up immediately, systematically replacing those 'disgraceful urban comprehensives', as part of a bold second-term strategy to modernise public services at large.

If only.

5

ACADEMIES – CONTROVERSY (2001–05)

Labour was re-elected by a landslide on 7 June 2001. The party won 413 seats, down only five on 1997, against 166 for the Conservatives. Once again, it was largely a personal mandate for Tony Blair.

But it was a landslide in the country, not in the government or in the Labour party. What followed, in terms of reform, was scrappy, confused and enervating. One of the greatest election victories of modern times half-evaporated within days of the election.

THE TB-GBS

The ballot boxes had scarcely closed on 7 June 2001 before the Gordon Brown volcano erupted.

We called it the 'TB-GBs' (teeby-geebies). At one level it was a straightforward power struggle for No. 10. But there were some unusual features. The struggle was exceptionally long drawn-out, lasting a full six years until Tony Blair's resignation in June 2007. And as a struggle for the supreme office it was also unusual in that virtually nothing but power was involved. Churchill v. Chamberlain after Munich, and Asquith v. Lloyd George in 1916, turned on life-and-death matters of state. Thatcher v. Heseltine in the late 1980s turned on European policy, the poll tax and the Tories' chances of getting re-elected without a change of leader. By contrast, Blair v. Brown turned on little more than Gordon's belief that he, rather than Tony, should be in charge.

There could be no pretence in 2001, and not much at any stage thereafter, that Gordon was more popular than Tony. Rather, Gordon persuaded himself that he would be a better Prime Minister, and that he was a more genuine social democrat. He claimed to regard Tony as lightweight and unstrategic, with unhealthy right-wing sympathies, while he was heavyweight, strategic and 'real Labour'. While he read Keynes and Adam Smith, Tony barely even read the newspapers. While he talked about a 'progressive consensus' and 'Labour values', Tony kept banging on about reform, Middle England and the 'third way'.

So, in June and July 2001, the cry went up that Blair and his coterie were intent on marketising and privatising health and education. Academies, foundation hospitals and university tuition fees were held up as proof of this – although they were no such thing – and, for practically the whole of the second term, being for or against these reforms became a litmus test of whether you were a 'Blairite' or a 'Brownite'. Even the word 'choice', in respect of schools and the NHS, became a source of bitter name-calling.

Gordon calculated that public service reform was the ideal battleground to fight Tony. In Labour terms it united the Left, the unions and large numbers of the timorous, sacked and disaffected among the ranks of Labour MPs. Gordon was Mr Moneybags; Tony, Mr Tory. Gordon claimed not to be against 'reform', just Tony's reforms, although he rarely offered alternatives. Moreover, academies and foundation hospitals were too embryonic to be widely popular, while tuition fees were never going to be anything other than unpopular among those who had to pay them. When I tried to break the ice at one 2005 election meeting in a university city by joking that the words 'tuition fees' would be on my tombstone, someone piped up from the back: 'Not soon enough.'

Beneath Gordon's implacability lay the mistaken belief that Tony was weak and that a big shove would push him out of No. 10. I never quite understood why Gordon so misjudged Tony in this respect. Gordon's crucial error was to confuse Tony's casualness and distaste for personal confrontation with a lack of staying power and self-belief. In reality, Tony was the quintessential iron fist in the velvet glove. Looking back, I think Tony had resolved at the outset of his leadership that, electorate willing, he would stay in No. 10 for a decade and then retire as gracefully as possible, which is what he did. I am pretty sure it is a decision he reached from observing Margaret Thatcher's demise across the chamber. 'She should have gone after ten years,' he once said to me. 'You can't keep it together for longer; people want to move on.'

For Tony's staff, the TB-GBs were deeply fraught and unpleasant. For me personally, as Head of the No. 10 Policy Unit in the second term, it was immensely energy and morale draining. Every proposed reform became a kind of international treaty to be negotiated clause by clause, with no spirit of goodwill and much aggression. The whole pace of public service reform and modernisation slowed. Far less was achieved than we hoped or expected. After 9/11, barely three months into the second term, the 'war on terror' in Afghanistan and later Iraq made the climate stormier still, as well as preoccupying Tony himself for days, sometimes weeks on end.

Academies ought nonetheless to have been one of the easier reforms to advance. The programme was already established and underway. There was no need for legislation or even, at this stage, additional funding from the Treasury.

But another obstacle presented itself immediately after the 2001 election. This was the appointment of Estelle Morris as Education Secretary in the post-election Cabinet reshuffle.

Estelle had been a popular Minister for Schools under David Blunkett throughout the first Blair term. A protégé of David's, and a former comprehensive school teacher, she was a strong support to him while softening the edges with the teacher unions and within the Department itself. She was popular in No. 10, partly for being so personable and partly because in the Blair first term Education was seen as the most successful Department. Her cause was also promoted by No. 10 colleagues wary of Tony's and my reformist zeal, for whom she was reassuringly cautious. Tony was far more sensitive to party management in terms of personnel than he appeared from the outside. He also underestimated the importance of departmental ministers, never having been one himself.

I liked and respected Estelle. She was a masterclass in empathy and a highly effective politician from a notable political family (both her father and uncle were long-serving Labour MPs in Manchester).

Her passion was for education more than politics, and she is one of the few Education Secretaries to remain seriously engaged in education after leaving office, Kenneth Baker being another.

But in the summer of 2001 we fell out over policy, which made the seventeen months of her Education secretaryship hard pounding at precisely the moment of Tony's maximum political strength.

There were capability issues in the Education Department. David Blunkett's advisers Michael Barber and Conor Ryan left with him at the 2001 election, along with the Department's long-serving and respected Permanent Secretary Sir Michael Bichard. There were also now forgotten, but serious at the time, crises over exam marking and the competence of the government agencies responsible. By the summer of 2002, trouble-shooting became Estelle's main preoccupation.

However, the basic problem was policy. Estelle fought shy of controversy on the Left and favoured incremental reform. Tony and I favoured bold reform. There was much we agreed on, including the imperative to increase education spending and strengthen the teaching profession. But we disagreed on both the need for bold reform and on the reforms themselves, notably the principle of independent state schools and university tuition fees. It didn't help that I was forthright on the Prime Minister's behalf. Whitehall loves to argue about process rather than substance, and officials were soon winding Estelle up to 'resist No. 10'.

Estelle had just about been content to see academies launched as a small experiment in 2000, although she hadn't been keen. Had she and not David Blunkett been Education Secretary at the time, I suspect that the fundamental principle of state schools being managed independently of local authorities might have been a show-stopper.

At any rate, within weeks of the election Estelle was worrying about going 'too far' down the Blairite road. On academies, the issue soon crystallized on whether the first academies were to be regarded as experiments, with no more, or only a few more, to be started until these had been open for a good while and thoroughly evaluated (i.e. years later); or whether they were path-finders whose early success, in terms of educational dynamism and parental popularity, should lead us to set up more.

Estelle's go-slow was encouraged by her senior officials, particularly Peter Housden, a former local authority director of education, latterly for Nottinghamshire, who joined the Education Department as director-general for schools in November 2001. Peter had a natural authority – he went on to become a Permanent Secretary – which only strengthened his articulation of the local authority 'producer' view.

A key issue in these discussions was the evidence base. We all professed to support 'evidence-based policy' but disagreed about the evidence. I argued, and believed, that the profound success of the City Technology Colleges, which had been open for more than a decade, was ample evidence that the academy model worked. The issue, rather, was the practicality of establishing such independent state schools as replacements for failing comprehensives, and this had been demonstrated by the early projects. The Department countered – in my view simply as a delaying tactic, since they never engaged on the CTC evidence – that academies were a new model in a different context, so we were starting from scratch and needed to watch and wait.

Not until February 2007, seven years after the start of the programme and four months before Tony Blair's resignation, did the National Audit Office publish the first definitive independent assessment of academies, which showed them to be successful. Since then, a string of similarly positive studies have appeared. Which all goes to show that, when it comes to contested reform, consensus on 'the evidence' often follows years after the chance to act decisively upon it. And that, while a regard for available evidence is essential in good policy-making, doing nothing while you wait for more evidence, in the face of a crisis, and in the face of that available evidence, is not a commendable course.

The question 'to expand' or 'not to expand', debated over many months, came to a head in spring 2002. I had by now worked up a further batch of projects but could not get Estelle's agreement to proceed. I was proposing to set up at least ten more academies a year. This figure took account of Estelle's caution: with a free hand I would have raised the number to forty or fifty a year immediately. I was working up a supply of good sponsors and projects, and the Department was now awash with extra capital funding for schools. But ever mindful of Roy Jenkins's advice to me that successful advisers 'argue to solutions not to conclusions', I judged ten academies a year as the best that could be achieved.

By this time, I was walking back and forth between No. 10 and the Education Department's offices in Sanctuary Buildings on Great Smith Street, near Westminster Abbey, almost daily, sometimes twice daily, to try to resolve this and other contentious issues, as well as for my regular academy progress-chasing meetings. (Fortunately, the two are only seven minutes apart at a brisk pace.) Finally, in late April 2002, Estelle and Tony agreed to proceed with about ten academies a year but not to announce this publicly. With intense relief I noted in my diary:

> It is a good case of 'what matters is what works': the application figures for the opening of the Bexley Academy [the first academy to open in September 2002] show 240 first choices and rising, up from forty for the predecessor school last year. This has clearly impressed Estelle, who volunteered them herself in her stocktake with TB this week.

After the 'ten a year' agreement between Tony and Estelle, I immediately set about developing the next group of academies, to open from 2004. This was helped by a ministerial reshuffle a few weeks later, which saw David Miliband become Minister for Schools under Estelle.

In the early years of academies, I was reluctant for them to open before their new buildings were complete. Although this was delaying the openings, I saw it as vital to establish the image of academies as completely new schools. Creating this image was a particular challenge – sometimes a virtual suspension of disbelief at the outset – because in most cases pupils and teachers were transferring wholesale from a failing comprehensive on the same site. Obviously the pupils needed to transfer, but under European TUPE regulations, all the staff of a school being replaced by another also had a right to transfer to the new school. In practice, effective headteachers manage underperforming staff out of a school fairly rapidly, and typically a third or more of the staff of an academy replacing a failing comprehensive would change within the first two or three years. But to compound these transitional challenges, I didn't want the first academies to be opening in building sites. So only five academies opened in 2004, including Mossbourne and Lambeth Academies, both entirely new schools which did not replace existing comprehensives. Ten opened in 2005 and eighteen in 2006. Almost all of these were planned in 2002 and 2003.

Scaling up was made easier because some of the best and most ambitious of the initial sponsors were starting to develop chains of academies. Indeed, some of the initial academies themselves marked the start of chains. Of the first twelve academies opened in 2002 and 2003, four had sponsors drawn from the original City Technology Colleges, including Lord Harris of Peckham and Thomas Telford School. A further three of these first twelve were sponsored by organisations already managing schools in the state or private sectors: the Church of England, the Church Schools Company and the Corporation of London. By summer 2002, the United Learning Trust (ULT) – the academy division of the Church Schools Company – had four projects on the go. Its chief executive Sir Ewan Harper, after his initial frosty encounter with Lambeth described earlier, became so adept at coaxing local authorities to consider a ULT academy to replace one of their failing schools that I was soon being phoned by council leaders saying they wanted not just an academy but a 'ULT academy'. The same was true of Lord Harris, who was developing a hugely popular academy chain in south London.

Estelle resigned at the end of October 2002, after weeks of a

torrid media storm surrounding an A-level marking crisis. I heard
the news arriving at Canberra airport on a visit to study Australia's
graduate repayment scheme, which was to become the model
for the tuition fees reform we introduced the following year. The
Deputy High Commissioner handed me a message: 'Estelle Morris
resigned. Call No. 10 urgent. Boss wants speak.' I duly phoned, to be
greeted by the No. 10 switchboard telling me it was 4 a.m. and did I
really want to wake the Prime Minister? Er, no. By the time I spoke
to 'boss', at lunchtime, he had already appointed Charles Clarke in
Estelle's place.

THE SLOW CLIMB FROM 15 TO 200

On the long flight back to London, I seriously toyed with following
Estelle and giving up. Minutes before boarding, Kamal Ahmed, *The
Observer*'s political editor, caught me on my mobile to say he had it
from 'someone very close to Estelle' that 'constant disagreements'
with me played a 'big part' in her decision to go. I disputed this,
but, with voicemails on the same lines from Patrick Wintour of *The
Guardian* and others, a media flurry was afoot, on top of months
of hostile comments about me personally from Tony Blair's
Labour critics.

Once political advisers become the story, it is generally time for
them to move on, and I worried that I was becoming a Rasputin
behind Blair. In terms of public profile, I was still in the minor
league compared to some of my colleagues in No. 10 and No. 11,
but that made it no more congenial. Roy Hattersley started writing whole *Guardian* columns on why I should be sacked. 'Adonis's
original mind has done more to alienate the Labour party from the
prime minister than any other single cause' sticks in my mind.

I also wasn't sure I would get on with Charles Clarke any better
than I had with Estelle. Although an instinctive radical, unafraid of
an argument with conservatives on the Left, Charles was robustly
his own man. When I phoned from Canberra to congratulate him,
he made it clear, in the nicest possible way, that he intended to take
some time to make up his mind on the key reform issues.

The anxiety extended to academies too. Perhaps I really was trying to push water uphill? While I was convinced that academies could reinvent comprehensive education for the twenty-first century, and many of the most successful state school leaders across the country were enthusiastic, no one much else in the government or the Labour party, apart from the Prime Minister, seemed to agree. Within the government, even supporters of the academy programme saw it as a small-scale initiative, and one of several possible ways of tackling failing comprehensives. Few others considered systematic reinvention of the comprehensive – the founding of completely new schools with strong, ambitious, independent governance and leadership to replace failing comprehensives nationwide – to be the way forward. Perhaps my role was to be Kenneth Baker Mark Two: creator of a small group of successful 'new model' schools, which someone would spot as a good idea a decade or two later and try to scale up.

Once back in London, I didn't resign, although, with the Iraq invasion and continuing TB-GBs over public service reform, 2003 was *annus horribilis*. I came close to leaving again that summer, and again in the autumn. Self-respect, and the imperative to help keep the Blair project alive, kept me going, but the government staggered from crisis to crisis and Tony's position was constantly in jeopardy. 'Lord Salisbury was quite right: politics is cursed profession,' is a typical diary entry of that spring, but it was to get worse. Just as the Iraq invasion was receding, the suicide of the weapons inspector David Kelly in July, amid BBC claims that No. 10 had 'sexed up' the dossier on Saddam's weapons of mass destruction, deepened the crisis.

And it wasn't only Iraq. With the Cabinet and Labour party bitterly divided, the landslide majority of 2001 was now precarious in the House of Commons for any public service reform. In May, it took a huge political operation to prevent legislation for foundation hospitals – autonomously managed hospitals, akin to academies within the NHS – being defeated in the Commons. The party conference at Bournemouth in October was a further public exhibition of division. When Parliament reassembled shortly afterwards, the Labour whips were privately telling No. 10 that the forthcoming legislation on tuition fees would be defeated by a majority of fifty, and some of Tony's advisers started urging him to withdraw it entirely. I countered strongly that this was the Blair 'In Place of Strife' moment. 'If Tony caves in, he will lose all purpose, like Harold Wilson when he abandoned Barbara Castle's industrial relations reforms [set out in her *In Place of Strife* white paper of 1969], after a party revolt led by Jim Callaghan,' I wrote in an office note. Tony remained firm; so did Charles Clarke. But the date of the key parliamentary vote on tuition fees kept being put back, until by January 2004 it could be delayed no longer if the legislation was to proceed.

Houdini-like, Tony survived. Two dramatic days at the end of January turned the tide. The tuition fees Bill passed its second reading in the Commons with a majority of five, followed a day later by the publication of the Hutton report, which cleared No. 10 of responsibility for the suicide of David Kelly. Within twenty-four hours, the political sky cleared and the horizon opened up for a third Blair election victory fifteen months later. But the situation remained unstable. Right up until the eve of the 2005 election, talk of coups and Tony standing down was the perpetual political chatter.

Against this grim backdrop, the fate of academies was far from assured. But contrary to the wider political flow, and my own expectations, Estelle's resignation at the end of 2002 turned out to be the low point for the programme, and its prospects steadily improved throughout 2003. I learned another lesson from this: in times of crisis, simply keeping the main show on the road keeps a lot else on the road too.

Partly this was because the first three academies had opened in September 2002. The idea had at last become reality. All three – in Bexley, Haringey and Middlesbrough – took over from chronically failing comprehensives and were to have a tough time. The spectacularly successful early academies, including Mossbourne and the first

Harris, Haberdashers, Thomas Telford and Vardy academies, were still one or two years away from opening. But these first three academies were popular with parents and were a manifest improvement on the predecessor schools. The new buildings also looked impressive, although Norman Foster's £31 million Bexley Business Academy, with its door-less classrooms and malfunctioning designer Italian toilets, began my disillusion with celebrity architects.

Also, despite my initial misgivings, Charles Clarke and I got on extremely well. Charles relished an argument, usually over copious red wine in his office in the early evening or after Commons votes at 10 p.m., and we developed a strong mutual respect based on uninhibited argument. We were soon bound together, in Blitz spirit, on the tuition fee controversy and other alarums and excursions, together with David Miliband, his Minister for Schools, and Robert Hill, his special adviser, both of them ex-No. 10 friends. Robert had been Tony's health adviser in the first term and his political secretary at the start of the second term. Like Conor Ryan vis-a-vis David Blunkett, Robert was an instinctive reformer and astute adviser, highly effective at aligning the Department and outside partners behind a strong minister.

Charles, David and Robert started meeting academy sponsors and were impressed with them and their projects. I had by now got far more projects in preparation than could be fitted within Estelle's cap of ten a year. On 3 March 2003, I had what my diary records as a 'crucial discussion' with Charles in which he agreed to lift the cap. 'This should allow us to start on more than twenty this year, taking the total to more than fifty,' I wrote, adding euphorically but over-optimistically: 'This will take academies over the tipping point and make them a transformative force in English education. Three years of intensive work is coming to fruition.' Charles also made it easier to recruit sponsors by reducing the £2 million sponsor contribution to £1.5 million, the first step on the way to eliminating it entirely.

Charles remained to be convinced that academies would have a system-wide, as opposed to local, impact on secondary education.

But, whatever the longer-term thinking, planning could now start on dozens of new projects. This was to enable eighteen academies to open in 2006 and thirty-six in 2007.

Twenty of these fifty-four new projects were in London, eleven in Southwark, Hackney, Islington and Westminster alone, increasing the leverage of academies on secondary education in the capital. Reform in the capital was to be boosted further by the launch of Teach First in London in 2003, and by the start two months later of the 'London Challenge' programme, which gave intensive support to underperforming comprehensives, including partnering their headteachers with successful heads from elsewhere in London. All comprehensives in the capital were also encouraged to become specialist schools with a curriculum centre of excellence. Stephen Twigg, the junior Schools Minister and Portillo-slaying MP for Enfield Southgate, became a highly effective Minister for London Schools with a brief to drive the London Challenge forward. A truly transformational comprehensive school reform policy was advancing in London, with academies in the vanguard.

Reform was accelerated by Tony Blair's decision in the autumn of 2003 to commission 'five-year plans' from the principal departments. The nomenclature was a touch Soviet, but the intention was to focus ministers on an ambitious policy prospectus to relaunch the government in the run-up to a 2005 election, making the case for a Blair third term. In this it succeeded, gaining strong momentum after Tony's political recovery at the end of January 2004.

I seized on the education five-year plan to advance academies decisively. I had a simple aim: to set a bold target for the number of academies to be set up within the five years. The number needed to be large, round and credible to give a rocket boost to the programme among sponsors, schools and the media. I also saw this as vital to mainstreaming academies within the Education Department and the Labour party. As a firm commitment in a 2005 Labour manifesto, the target would become a third-term priority, and might just possibly give the academies programme enough momentum to survive the (by now) inevitable transition from Tony to Gordon.

What was the target to be?

'We need hundreds of them, hundreds,' Tony said to me as we left the formal opening of Bexley Business Academy in mid-September 2003. Bexley Academy had already been built and open for a year and we had just heard two hours of tear-jerking tales from the children and staff about life before and after the academy on the grim Thamesmead council estate it served.

A sprawling concrete brutalist 1960s monstrosity, complete with comprehensive school in matching style, Thamesmead was famous as the setting for Stanley Kubrick's *A Clockwork Orange*, of which Wikipedia says: 'it features disturbing violent images facilitating its social commentary on psychiatry, youth gangs and other social, political and economic subjects in a dystopian future Britain'. The school was one of England's worst failing comprehensives. It hadn't even been completed when built and couldn't make use of much of its site because it was water-logged on a flood plain. Its replacement by an academy was as symbolic as Mossbourne rising from the ruins of Hackney Downs.

But there were hundreds of equally deprived, if not dystopian, communities nationwide which needed a similar educational rebirth. So I pressed hard for an academies target of 200 by 2010. In retrospect, this seems unambitious: 267 academies were in fact open in September 2010. But back in early 2004 the number '200' terrified the horses in Sanctuary Buildings, who pointed out that only twelve academies were as yet open with five more due in September of that year, so this implied opening academies at the rate of thirty a year thereafter. 'I simply don't think this is possible,' said a senior official in an initial discussion. Even after intense pressure from me, the Department wouldn't budge beyond a target of seventy-five academies to be open or in planning by 2008, a modest increase on the existing internal planning target of sixty-four.

Underlying this obstructionism was a continuing refusal to contemplate academies as a systematic replacement for failing comprehensives like Thamesmead. There was a constant casting around for something – anything – less radical and less controversial instead. In the Department's presentation to Tony on its proposed five-year plan in December 2003, a new initiative suddenly appeared of 'syndicates around leading schools' as the way to deal with failing comprehensives. It wasn't clear what these syndicates would be or do, but the Department nonetheless proclaimed, in classic waffle-jargon mode: 'Syndicates have the potential to become new centres of gravity within the schools system, using devolved resources and responsibility to drive change on the ground and revitalise the middle tier.'

Sitting next to Tony in the Cabinet Room, I simply wrote 'NO – WE NEED A BIG ACADEMIES TARGET!' on his notepad. He duly asked for one, and after further iteration over many weeks the Department's bid was raised to a precise 137 by 2010, being the seventeen open in 2004 and then twenty a year thereafter. I wasn't having this. It had to be a round number. Who was going to recall, let alone campaign for, 137 of anything? And the rounding couldn't be to just 150. It had to be at least 200, which was eminently achievable given the availability of sponsors and funding. 'It's not as if there aren't many times more than 200 failing comprehensives out there' was my line to all comers.

Eventually Charles and Tony agreed on 200, with the caveat that it was 200 'open or in the pipeline by 2010'. Of these, at least sixty were to be in London, maintaining the momentum on transforming secondary education in the capital.

Predictably, the Treasury did not want a target at all. But No. 11 was by now fighting on multiple fronts with all the departmental five-year plans coming to fruition at the same time, each raising a host of new commitments. Within Education, Gordon Brown and John Prescott were far more concerned about Charles Clarke's bold plan – which I strongly supported – to ring-fence all school funding within local authority budgets and guarantee every school a rising per-pupil budget for three years in real terms, a reform intended to ensure that the increased funding for schools actually reached the front line. This was unpopular with Labour council leaders, as a limitation on local authority discretion. Gordon and John championed their cause and there was a huge row. But with Tony's forthright backing Charles got his way on school funding, and the academies target slipped in behind.

The Education Five-Year Plan, published in early July 2004, was the Blair government's first bold national policy for secondary school reform. As well as 200 academies and guaranteed three-year funding increases to schools, all the other elements of the successful London Challenge programme were to be extended nationwide. This included Teach First and the systematic mentoring of headteachers of struggling schools by heads from successful schools working in similar contexts. Every comprehensive was to be eligible to become a specialist school. And to promote school autonomy more widely, all non-failing local authority schools were to be given the right to own their own land and buildings, manage their assets and employ their staff directly by a simple vote of their governing body.

The Five-Year Plan process converted me to the virtues of medium-term state planning more widely. It forces the government machine, and its leaders, to concentrate on big objectives and how to achieve them, rather than immediate problems and how to finesse them. It also forces a wider public debate about national objectives and how to achieve them. Of course, plans often go wrong, but patch-and-mend just as often goes wrong, with far less accountability and often without any focus on getting it right in the first place.

In my experience, the best ministers are political sat-navs: they have a plan for where they – and the country – need to end up, but they are constantly recalibrating the route in the light of wrong turns, traffic jams and road closures.

The Guardian greeted the 2004 Education Five-Year Plan as 'the death knell of the comprehensive system' because it included 'a massive expansion of the controversial academy programme'. This was a classic confusion of ends and means. Our ambition was to save comprehensive education not to bury it. But to do this required breaking the umbilical cord between the comprehensive principle and the failing 1960s model of the local authority comprehensive school. And this operation was just starting.

6

ACADEMIES – CONSENSUS (2005-12)

Just as the academies programme was accelerating, in the months after the July 2004 commitment to create 200, there came another sudden and nearly catastrophic breakdown. On 15 December 2004, David Blunkett resigned as Home Secretary over the fast-tracking of a visa application for his ex-lover's nanny. In the reshuffle that followed, both Charles Clarke and David Miliband left Education, after barely two years in post. The new Education Secretary – the fourth in three and a half years – was Ruth Kelly, new to the Cabinet and to the Department.

Ruth had impressed Tony Blair in a trouble-shooting junior ministerial role in the Cabinet Office. The appointment was made for complex political reasons and clearly wasn't the best thing for education, which would have been for David Miliband to have succeeded Charles. With an election only months away, there would have been a slowing of pace in any event. Now the whole machine practically stopped. Everyone in Sanctuary Buildings, ministers included, sat and waited for the election.

I said as much to Tony, adding that, as I was also going to be leaving at the election, he would need extra firepower at Education. 'I know that,' he said. 'And I know what I want to do. I want you to go there as Minister for Schools after the election, with a seat in the Lords. Then you can drive the whole thing forward.'

This was a complete surprise. By the 2005 election, I would have done an unprecedented seven years in the No. 10 Policy Unit. Not only had I agreed my departure with Tony but my next job was waiting. I had a contract to write the official biography of Roy Jenkins, my political mentor who became a close friend in the years before his death in 2003. As for Tony's suggestion, it had never occurred to me that I would be viable as a minister under him, least of all if I was parachuted into the Lords. It would be Rasputin all over again. It would also be a spectacular challenge, and I might fail spectacularly.

On the other hand, it made a certain sense. I knew Whitehall inside out and education outside in, and I had largely formed the policy I would be taking forward. Special advisers are much derided but those who concentrate on policy often make service-able ministers, perhaps because their job has many characteristics of an apprentice minister. Also, I had spent years telling Tony that he had to put people in key ministerial jobs who believed in what he was doing. And there weren't many around. A perennial weakness of Blairism was the shortage of Blairites, which became more not less acute in his last years.

The public side of becoming a minister was daunting, indeed terrifying when it happened. But until that moment, I thought I could probably handle it. Despite seven years in the shadows, and a decade as an academic and a journalist before that, I wasn't a politi-cal ingénue. I had been a councillor and parliamentary candidate in my twenties and early thirties. This was for the SDP/Lib Dems, which didn't endear me to Roy Hattersley, but glad-handing and media exposure wasn't a shock, and four years on Oxford City Council's planning committee, with developers and conservation-ists battling it out week after week and my university voters among the most articulate in the world, was invaluable training for many a ministerial poisoned chalice.

There was also the odd fact that I knew the House of Lords inti-mately. My doctoral thesis was on the evolution of the House of Lords before the First World War. This was the era of Lord Salisbury, the last Prime Minister in the Lords, followed by the celebrated battles over Lloyd George's People's Budget and the Parliament Act of 1911. While writing my thesis, I spent a lot of time in the gallery of the Lords and walking its corridors to get the feel. The chamber, its procedures and its ambiance remain largely unchanged since Lord Salisbury's day, even after the removal of most of the hereditary peers and the influx of life peers. The idea of joining the ermined ranks, as a democratic reformer, was intriguing.

So Tony's idea grew on me.

MINISTER FOR SCHOOLS

Because of Iraq, the 2005 election took on a bitter edge and the result was a large majority rather than a landslide (Labour 356 seats, Tory 198, Lib Dem 62). But in other respects it followed a pattern similar to 2001 in that another remarkable Blair victory at the ballot box was immediately discounted by Gordon Brown, who suspended his election truce and renewed hostilities once the polls had closed. From this point onwards, the Brown mantra was the need for an 'early and orderly transition'.

To my amazement, I became an immediate bone of contention. On election day, Tony phoned to say he intended to make me Minister of State for Schools when he appointed his junior ministers after the weekend. (He formed the Cabinet on the Friday.) Unfortunately, he told Gordon too, and the front pages of Sunday's *Observer* and Monday's *Guardian* announced that Gordon would personally stop this 'outrageous' appointment and claimed that Ruth Kelly was also opposed.

Tony phoned on Monday morning to check I was still up for it. I was. The media campaign dispelled any doubts that I had to do it. If Tony couldn't even appoint a junior minister to take forward his government's agreed education policy, after winning a general election, what could he do?

As I arrived at No. 10 later on Monday, Ruth was just leaving the 'den', Tony's office next to the Cabinet Room. She was all smiles and encouragement. When I went inside, Tony said that in deference to Ruth he was going to make me the junior Schools Minister, as Under-Secretary of State. Jacqui Smith would be the Minister of State and number two in the pecking order, so I couldn't be portrayed as Ruth's 'deputy'.

The worst, to my surprise, was nearly over. A bank of cameras greeted me at home the following morning ('Daddy, why are all those cameras pointing at me?' asked my seven-year-old son as he drew the curtains), and there were baptisms of fire in the House of Lords and – more daunting – with John Humphrys on the *Today* programme. The *Daily Mail* kindly set an investigative team onto me and my family and friends. But by the end of May the media, and thankfully Gordon too, had lost interest in me. Ruth and I were getting on fine. I had an immensely dedicated private office team, and I was getting on with it.

Academies were only a small part of my ministerial brief. I devoted lots of time to primary schools, particularly the teaching of literacy, as well as to special educational needs, the school curriculum, school leadership and the education of the gifted and talented. Part of my job was to be Minister for London Schools, where I worked closely with Tim Brighouse, an inspirational guru, in his government-appointed role as Commissioner for London Schools. I was also responsible for the specialist schools for highly talented children in music and dance, and I promoted the expansion and rebuilding of the Royal Ballet School and Chetham's School of Music in Manchester. The teaching profession was Jacqui's responsibility, but I remained keenly engaged, particularly in the expansion of Teach First. And I had to conduct all the Department's business in the Lords. In the first year alone, this involved three substantial pieces of legislation, pinning me to the red benches of the Lords night after night admiring the Gothic stained glass, mosaics and frescos.

I loved the creative potential of ministerial office, including the ability to encourage national figures to make a real contribution. I worked with Howard Goodall in his campaign to get primary schools singing, with Bill Bryson to get a free copy of *A Short History of Nearly Everything* into every secondary school, with Jackie Stewart on tackling dyslexia, and with Michael Palin to promote geography and adventure. A highlight of each year was the National Teaching Awards, created by David Puttnam, which celebrated the work of teachers in all kinds of communities and schools nationwide.

However, academies were my central project. At last I had real power, not just self-imposed responsibility. The power was circum-scribed, since decision-taking ultimately lay with the Secretary of State, which especially in respect of resource allocation, crucial to the further expansion of the programme, was a real not a nominal check. But within that constraint I could take decisions personally. It was a liberation, making it possible to achieve so much more than by constantly pressing decisions on others.

Animating the Whitehall machine started first thing every Monday morning. I held a meeting at 8 a.m. in a large conference room overlooking Westminster Abbey with all my academies directors and project managers. For two hours or more, we would run through the entire list of academy projects, live and planned, deciding on specific action points project by project. Meetings on thorny policy issues or more complex projects followed, and I would immediately thereafter get on the phone to talk to sponsors, MPs, council leaders, fellow ministers, or whoever, to sort issues or progress projects where my personal intervention might make a difference. Sometimes, on the basis of a Monday morning discus-sion, I would decide I needed to visit a school or a local authority soonest sometimes, if I could escape the diary, immediately after these Monday morning meetings. I would follow up with a smaller meeting of directors on Thursday to take stock of action points from the Monday meeting and agree further actions or advice required by the following Monday.

I would also spend at least a day a week – usually Friday – on pre-planned school and local authority visits, mostly aimed at broker-ing new academy projects to replace failing comprehensives. Not being an MP, I didn't have constituency duties, which gave me valuable time to visit schools instead. Generally, I would visit the lowest-performing schools in an area, arranging where possible to be joined by the local MP and council leader and officials, so that discussions and decisions on what to do about them could take place in the immediate context of the (often dire) situation we had just witnessed. I got four academies in one go in Sunderland as a result of one such visit, doing the deal with the thoroughly

Old Labour leader of the council over a tense dinner in a hotel with dramatic views over Seaham Harbour, brokered by David Puttnam as Chancellor of Sunderland University. The historian in me couldn't resist mentioning that Seaham had been Ramsay MacDonald's constituency. 'Yes, and I don't intend to go his way,' came the curt response.

These visits were the most tiring but by far the most exhilarating and productive part of each week. Often I combined them with speaking at a school prize-giving or other school event. I accepted almost every invitation to speak at state schools, although, tellingly, for every one such invitation, there were at least two from private schools to speak at their speech days, debating societies and the like. Life being short, I declined the private school invitations unless the school was sponsoring an academy or considering doing so, when I would seize the chance to preach private–state partnership.

Getting out and about energised me, and helped me to energise others. This wasn't only about academies. I was constantly learning on these visits, and was constantly impressed by how much children and young people are capable of, given the right opportunities and environment.

An abiding concern of mine was to minimise loss of speed and impact caused by bureaucratic friction and inertia within Whitehall. This is why I dealt directly with individual academy project managers, enabling me to get immediately to the unvarnished state of play and to give instructions directly instead of mediating through official hierarchies, paper submissions, private offices and red boxes in the traditional – completely antiquated – Whitehall fashion, which not only loses a good deal in translation but slows and waters everything down. It was important to give front-line and often fairly junior officials doing critical business access to me personally, and for me to impress on them week by week the urgency of the work they were doing. The cascade of ministerial paperwork I mostly handled in the interstices of the working week, often between meetings soon after it came into the office, rather than through overnight or weekend red boxes. I forbade my private office from telling the Department that my 'box was closed' after a certain time each day or week, or during parliamentary recesses, which is the classic Whitehall device for cutting ministers off from the machine for large parts of the working week and year, while making the minister feel important. I was always open for business.

In all this I sought to change the whole perception of the minister. Ministers too often seem – because they *are* – semi-detached, semi-briefed and semi-enthusiastic, insulated by bland officials. This greatly diminishes their capacity to mobilise the immense resources of the state to bring about change. I saw my mission as to appear constantly engaged, briefed and enthusiastic, usually because I was, although there was a certain amount of acting the part.

One of my main challenges, day by day, was to keep the machine moving forward as the world around kept disintegrating and reshaping with ever changing Secretaries of State and senior officials. It was vital not to slow down, or allow others to do so, amid the constant flux. This meant feigning much less interest and emotion than I felt over the decline of Blair and the succession and tribulations of Brown, and keeping largely clear of the political machinations which obsess Westminster and the top echelons of Whitehall.

SCALING UP

On becoming Minister in May 2005, my immediate priority was to move academies from the periphery to the centre of the Education Department.

I was greatly helped by Chris Wormald, who had just become director of the academies programme and who sought, with my strong encouragement, to integrate academies' capital funding with the multi-billion a year 'Building Schools for the Future' (BSF) programme, which had commandeered most of the Department's new capital resources for school buildings. Chris, a brilliant operator and now the Department's Permanent Secretary, combines engaging wide-boy charm with bureaucratic mastery. He soon managed to assume responsibility for BSF as well as academies, integrating the two programmes.

This bureaucratic fence-removal was crucial. Money drives reform, and ever since the start of academies I had been bedevilled by an annual internal competition for capital funding between academies and other school-building programmes. By uniting the David of academies with the Goliath of Building Schools for the Future, academies were no longer competing for resources with 'mainstream' secondary school capital projects. Instead, for capital funding purposes, academies became simply one way of delivering a building project, and attracted in principle the same resources as a non-academy project for the same school. This instituted better cost control, which was much needed after some of the initial projects had escalated beyond not just the £30 million mark but even £40 million. It also made it easier to expand the number of academies without an internal argument each time about funding and where it was going to come from, since there was now no difference except governance (which for a failing school was all the difference) between one funding route and the other. This was decisive in scaling up academies after 2005.

Eighteen academies opened in 2006 and thirty-six in 2007. My aim in my first months as Minister after May 2005 was to get enough good projects underway to hit fifty openings in 2008 (it came out at forty-nine). By early 2006, around sixty projects were in hand for opening in both 2009 and 2010. Putting all this together, we were on track to hit the 200 target in 2010. By now, not only were there numerous academy chains in development, but also I was striking multiple academy deals with local authorities as part of their BSF plans for renovating their entire secondary school estate. Both supply and demand were increasing rapidly.

The BSF programme was prioritising the most deprived local authority areas. These were also the authorities with the highest proportion of failing schools. Their BSF plans had to be approved by the Department, so I used this leverage to extract commitments to academies as part of BSF plans. A breakthrough was Manchester in late 2006, when I reached agreement with the city's remarkable dynamic duo – Sir Richard Leese, the city council leader, and Sir Howard Bernstein, his chief executive – for six academies in the city, each replacing a failing school or schools and each with a strong employment focus and sponsor or sponsors drawn from city businesses or public institutions related to the vocational specialism of the academy (BT, Manchester Airport, Manchester Children's Hospital, Manchester Co-Op, Manchester College of Arts and Technology, and two major construction and engineering companies). I reached similar agreements with Sheffield, Birmingham and several London boroughs. With deals like this, it was soon evident that we could easily advance beyond the existing target of 200 academies.

NOISES OFF

As academies scaled up, so did the controversy surrounding them.

Continuing legal action was one source of steady bombardment. The critical St Mary Magdalene case, described earlier, dragged on until the summer of 2006. No sooner had this case been won than another potentially lethal legal action started. Ostensibly about the proposed University College London Academy in the north London borough of Camden, it went to the heart of the academies policy from a new angle. The issue was whether academy sponsorship was governed by EU procurement law. This sounds arcane, and it was indeed an ingenious legal argument, exploiting my recent decision to allow the Swedish private school company Kunskapsskolan ('The Knowledge School') to sponsor two academies in Richmond in south-west London, on a not-for-profit basis. But had the challenge succeeded, it would have stopped the academies programme stone dead. Few sponsors would have been prepared to go through lengthy and expensive tendering procedures for the privilege of setting up charities of no commercial benefit.

The Department's lawyers warned that there was a strong

likelihood of the UCL challenge succeeding, and they further advised that it might be wise to suspend all new academy projects until the courts had ruled. I rejected this helpful advice out of hand and instructed them to contest the case with the utmost vigour. The prospect of Brussels banning England from improving its schools through charitable endeavour was almost enough to get me signed up to the UK Independence Party. It was even more surreal than the other legal issue bedevilling academies throughout 2006 and early 2007, which concerned their liability to pay VAT on the whole capital cost of their buildings, as independent (although state-funded) schools, if more than a token proportion of their income came from letting out their facilities, which was precisely in line with their mission as community institutions. The Treasury was deeply unhelpful on resolving this issue with HMRC, until Gordon Brown became Prime Minister when it suddenly vanished.

Fortunately, Michael Beloff, one of England's best public law barristers and President of Trinity College, Oxford, took on the European case for the government. Ultimately he won it both in the High Court and the Court of Appeal. But it was another case which dragged on and on. The decisive ruling did not come until November 2009, by when legal action had threatened to halt the academies programme at any moment for the best part of a decade.

However, by mid-2006, I had a greater anxiety on my mind than the courts. For in April the police suddenly appeared on the scene, implicating academies in the 'cash for honours' investigation which overshadowed Tony Blair's final year in office.

'Cash for honours' concerned multi-million-pound loans made to the Labour party by individuals subsequently nominated for knighthoods and peerages. However, just as the media were lighting on this party funding issue, a *Sunday Times* undercover journalist taped an 'academies adviser' boasting over a liquid dinner about honours which he said were available to academy sponsors. When, shortly thereafter, Chief Inspector Yates of Scotland Yard decided to investigate 'cash for honours', the only person who had so far made any recorded connection between the two was the said academies adviser, who was arrested at dawn on 13 April with media fanfare, taken to Stoke Newington police station for questioning about a possible criminal offence under the Honours (Prevention of Abuses) Act 1925, then bailed pending further enquiries.

I was on an Easter break in the chestnut hills above Lucca at the time. When later that morning I turned on my mobile for a once-a-day checking of messages, it exploded with journalists, ministers, advisers, and most of my friends and relatives – but not Inspector Yates – in hot pursuit. I returned to London pdq to steady the ship, which was essential given the initial civil service urge to shut up shop on academies until the police had concluded their enquiries. Yates of the Yard took more than a year to conclude his investigation, by which time Tony Blair had left office, so, as well as implying that there was something wrong, this would have been as fatal to the programme as suspending it while the Court of Appeal ruled on the compatibility of Swedish sponsors with EU law.

I had never met Des Smith, the 'academies adviser' in question, a successful East London headteacher who did some academies consultancy for an education agency. Nor was there a shred of truth in the suggestion that honours were touted in exchange for sponsorship. However, a few academy sponsors and headteachers had been honoured for their work. Within No. 10, and as Minister, I had long urged the case for honouring transformational headteachers and educational philanthropists. My argument was simple and moral. If banking supremos and permanent secretaries get knighthoods with their generous rations, why not the exceptional headteacher and philanthropist transforming schools in Hackney or Hull? What should the state honour that is more worthwhile than transforming children's lives in deprived communities? Ironically, this notion met stiff resistance from the honours bureaucracy, who regarded headteachers, in particular, as not quite cutting the mustard. 'They will have to live with these titles at work and in the pub. How will they cope?' mused one Permanent Secretary. 'In much the same way as you do' was my response.

I kept rehearsing in my mind how I would say all this,

unapologetically, to Inspector Yates if he came to interview me. But the call never came. His officers interviewed senior Education Department officials, then unsurprisingly lost interest in academies and moved on to party donors. But all the while, the investigation hung over academies (and me), and made it harder to recruit sponsors, who feared being tainted. I lost a number of excellent projects as a result.

Throughout these alarums and excursions, I did my best to project relentless optimism and confidence. This wasn't difficult, because 'cash for honours', and virtually all the anti-academies litigation and agitation, were patently ridiculous and wrong-headed. Furthermore, from the summer of 2005 a string of positive verdicts started to come through on the first academies, which by now had been open for up to three years.

A critical moment was the first overall verdict on academies by Ofsted, the schools inspectorate. This came in August 2005 when David Bell, the Chief Inspector of Schools (and later Permanent Secretary at the Education Department), reported that inspection findings on the first academies were 'broadly positive'. 'It is early days, but I welcome a programme that may help consign generations of inner-city failure finally and properly to our educational past,' he added. I repeated these words ad nauseum to supporters and critics alike, along with the 2005 academy GCSE results which showed an average increase in the proportion of pupils getting five or more GCSE passes of nearly three times the national average. There was a similar rate of improvement in 2006.

Looking back, David Bell says: 'I believed very strongly that, here at last, we had a genuine breakthrough in English education and I needed to say this loudly and unambiguously.' The support of the inspectorate for academies helped counter claims that expansion was risky or unevaluated.

However, ministerial instability continued all about. In May 2006, after a mere sixteen months in post, Ruth Kelly was replaced by Alan Johnson, in Tony Blair's last reshuffle. At the same time, Jacqui Smith was replaced by Jim Knight as my fellow Schools

Minister. So, within just a year of arriving in the Department, I was already the sole point of ministerial continuity in schools policy.

It was a relief that the fifth Education Secretary in five years was Alan Johnson, a long-standing friend and mentor. Before entering Parliament, Alan had been General Secretary of the Communication Workers Union. My dad, a postman in Hampstead for thirty years, was one of his branch secretaries and a great admirer. His junior ministerial breakthrough was as Higher Education Minister under Charles Clarke during the tuition fees crisis, when he sold the policy with aplomb as the working-class boy made good who hadn't had the chance to go to university. So he knew the Department well, and we had already gone through the mill together.

To me as a junior minister, Alan was the model Secretary of State: firm, shrewd, encouraging, collaborative. He was an exceptional media performer and, unusually for a Cabinet minister, invariably punctual, not assuming that everyone's else's time was less important than his. I hugely enjoyed working with him. Alan was strongly pro-academies, not least from his experience as an MP for Hull, where there were plenty of low-performing comprehensives. He left me to get on with academies uninhibited.

BLAIR TO BROWN

By the summer of 2006, the 200 academies announced in the 2004 Five-Year Plan were all in the pipeline, with 188 projected to be open by 2010 and more than thirty more in planning. So I started pressing for a new target of 500.

The figure of 500, one in seven secondary schools in England, was bold, round, achievable, and eminently justified given the availability of sponsors and the profusion of failing comprehensives beyond those already being replaced by academies. As I kept repeating, there were still, in 2006, more than 800 comprehensives where fewer than three in ten sixteen-year-olds were leaving with five or more good GCSEs including English and maths. These comprehensives were all basically failing. Unless they had a credible improvement strategy, my view was that they should all be replaced by academies as soon as possible. It was that simple.

The backdrop was Tony Blair's approaching resignation. In early September 2006, well-publicised round-robin letters from disaffected MPs and ministers called on Tony to stand down. These Brown-inspired missives were in response to a return-from-holiday interview in which Tony refused to set a date for his departure. Tony says in *A Journey* that this refusal was strongly influenced by a summer memo from me urging him to delay announcing his departure date in order to avoid becoming a lame duck. The mantra of the summer was that he should announce the date to ensure an 'orderly transition' and 'dignified exit'. I stressed to him that for prime ministers there are just transitions and exits, all more or less undignified and disorderly, and he should give as little notice as possible.

Unfortunately, my advice was entirely counter-productive. For in the face of this revolt and growing Cabinet pressure, Tony announced that he would resign within a year, and lame duckery rapidly set in.

Agreeing a target of 500 academies therefore became critically urgent. As I put it in a memo to Alan Johnson in mid-October:

> The burning political question of the moment is: does New Labour, including serious education reform, end with Tony Blair? No single policy announcement would answer that question more decisively than raising the academies target from 200 to 500. Tellingly David Cameron opened an academy last week. I'm told he was bowled over and promptly announced that the Tories would do more academies and faster.

The rationale for 500 was not simply the number of failing comprehensives. In my memo to Alan, I noted that I had recently agreed twenty-four academies across Manchester, Birmingham and Sheffield. These cities had a population of two million between them, which implied 450 to 500 academies across urban England.

And even this was far lower than the academy density in much of inner London, where by now there were twenty academies open or soon to open in just five boroughs (Hackney, Lambeth, Islington, Southwark and Haringey) with 1.1 million population between them. As for sponsors, there were by now twelve academy chains with three or more academies each, and between them they accounted for more than a third of academies open or in the pipeline. So there was no shortage either of demand or capacity.

Even with Alan sympathetic, it wasn't easy getting the Education Department behind the 500 target. But then to my dismay the issue escalated to become a full-blown TB-GB confrontation, the last one on public service reform. Thankfully, this was managed not by me but by the excellent Conor Ryan, reincarnated as Tony's education adviser in No. 10 for the third term. In the process, the target came down to 400, and Gordon never even agreed this figure. Tony simply announced it, in a speech at the end of November 2006 to mark the tenth anniversary of his 'education, education, education' pledge. Academies, he argued, were now an 'integral part' of the education system, bringing 'more choice and higher standards', and there needed to be far more of them.

One of Gordon's advisers muttered to me the day after the speech: 'There will be consequences, serious consequences.' One consequence, I assumed, would be the termination of my ministerial career. But then I had never expected to stay in office beyond Tony's resignation in any event. For me, the purpose of being a minister is to pioneer reform and social change from passionate conviction, so I didn't see myself serving under Gordon any more than he might wish to serve over me.

The new target of 400 gave me the energy and focus for a last sustained spurt of academy-making in the first six months of 2007. By the time Tony stood down on 27 June, there were still only forty-six academies open, but eighty were due to open within the following fifteen months and 150 more were in the pipeline. Moreover, in February 2007, there was a strongly positive report on academies by the National Audit Office, the public spending watchdog, and their popularity and results were continuing to flourish. Academies were still work in progress, but I was relieved that I would be leaving government with a large and fairly successful academies sector in place.

Except that I didn't leave.

A few days after Tony announced the definite date of his departure, in early May 2007, I was on a train returning from a school visit when two curious things happened. A text appeared on my mobile from Nick Robinson, the BBC's political editor. 'You're staying. GB just told me,' it read. Just as I was contemplating this intelligence, the phone buzzed. It was Dunstan, my private secretary. 'You won't believe this, but the Chancellor's office have just been on the line wondering whether you might be available to see him tomorrow afternoon.'

It was to be my first conversation of any length with Gordon for nine years, since I went to work for Tony in 1998. Before then, we had had a regular and friendly dialogue, but it stopped overnight.

The remarkable thing about the conversation in the Treasury that May afternoon, with Gordon scribbling on a yellow legal pad with a thick black felt-tip pen throughout, is that it was as if the previous nine years hadn't happened. Without any preamble on either side, we talked amicably as if there had been no interval, let alone interruption. He disarmed me by saying I had been doing 'excellent work' at Education and he wanted it to continue. After two hours discussing everything from academies and apprenticeships to universities and umpteen other things, including the latest books we had both been reading, we agreed to visit an academy together and I said I was looking forward to working for him. I left in a bit of a daze, and walked around St James's Park admiring the pelicans and contemplating the peculiarity of politics.

The academy visit took place a few days later. It was a success. Courtesy of Michael Snyder, chairman of the policy committee of the City Corporation, Gordon and I spent two hours at the City of London Academy in Southwark. The academy was completely new, without a predecessor school, drawing largely from council estates in Bermondsey. But the smartness of the students and their enthusiasm for their work and for all the facilities of the pristine academy was a world apart from the estates. After a tour, the headteacher hosted a discussion with twenty or so parents. Gordon was visibly moved as they spoke about the academy and what it meant to them and their children. I couldn't have scripted the final exchange, when a Caribbean parent said to him: 'What you need is lots more schools like this, that's what you need, Mr Brown.' 'That's what we are doing and this guy is responsible,' Gordon replied, gesturing at me.

I could not have scripted the next three years either. It is literally true that in Gordon's entire time as Prime Minister he and I did not have a single disagreeable conversation. Our dealings were invariably amicable and constructive, with strong mutual respect. He appointed me to the Cabinet for the last year of the government, as Transport Secretary, even though it is highly unusual for a peer to head a department. He backed virtually everything I was doing and seeking to do, including my last great controversial project, the proposed high-speed rail line from London to Scotland. In the last five days of his premiership, in May 2010, I was at his right hand throughout as we tried unsuccessfully to negotiate a coalition with the Lib Dems after the inconclusive general election. I helped draft his resignation statement and didn't leave No. 10 until after he had departed for the Palace to resign. I came to admire him, particularly for the way he handled the international financial meltdown after the Lehman Brothers collapse in September 2008.

Looking back, that Southwark Academy visit was the moment, eight years after their launch, when academies sealed a national consensus. Academies had survived the transition from Blair to Brown. Days later, the Conservatives joined in too.

The Tories had been broadly pro-academy from the start. Kenneth Baker was supportive and academy sponsors included a number of leading Conservatives, notably Lord (Philip) Harris and Stanley Fink, a leading light in the ARK academy chain, who was to become the party's Treasurer.

David Cameron spoke increasingly warmly of academies after becoming Tory leader in 2005 and visiting several of them. Then in a seminal speech to the CBI in late May 2007 – deliberately pitched in the middle of the Blair–Brown transition – David Willetts, the party's education spokesman, raised this endorsement several notches by stating explicitly that the Tories now saw academies, not grammar schools, as the engines of modern social mobility. This drew on a line I had been peddling for years, and believe profoundly, that academies are the 'new grammar schools', taking the best of the grammar school ethos and emphasis on rigour, qualifications and effort, including A-levels and sixth forms, but making it available to all children without selection rather than to a small minority through the brutal 11-plus.

But Willetts did not stop there. He included in his speech an attack on the remaining grammar schools for being middle-class preserves holding back social mobility. This wasn't a career-enhancing line in the Conservative party, and a few months later he was replaced. His successor, Michael Gove, dropped the anti-grammar school riff, but he became still more committed to academies. He lost no opportunity to praise Blair and Blairites to the skies, claiming I was wonderful but was being sidelined by the statist Brownites and in particular by Ed Balls, the new Education Secretary. He proclaimed himself determined to remove the 'shackles' on academies and committed the Tories to a new breed of 'free school' academies to be established by local parents, while enabling all successful schools to take on academy status. When I left Education in 2008, he seized on this as vindication for all he had been saying. I had finally, he claimed, been 'hounded out'.

Leaving aside the tactical party politics, all this steadily consolidated the new academy consensus. It was a fundamental, and fundamentally progressive, change in Tory policy carried out under a brilliant blaze of rhetorical fireworks on Michael Gove's part, which he continued into government after May 2010. No new grammar schools have been set up by the Cameron government. Instead the drive has been for more academies and all-ability 'free schools', the latter being simply academies which do not replace existing state schools.

It wasn't, however, true to say that I didn't get on with Ed Balls, the sixth Secretary of State with whom I worked on academies in almost as many years, or that I had been muzzled.

Ed and I go back a long way – right back to Keble College, Oxford, where we were both students and overlapped. I then followed him to the *Financial Times* in the early 1990s, and followed him again into special adviserdom a few years later. The Blair–Brown adviser period was tense, but in retrospect this was not because of policy differences so much as the straight fact that he worked for Gordon, and wanted his principal to succeed, and I worked for Tony, and wanted my principal to succeed. The fundamental problem was that the two principals had difficulty co-existing, which set the advisers at each other, rather than vice versa. Ed has the great pugilistic and intellectual qualities of Denis Healey.

There is no critique of academies which makes them 'right-wing' unless Alice is in a Wonderland where educational failure becomes left-wing and investment and reform to combat it are somehow right-wing. The difference between supporters and opponents of academies within the Labour party was – and remains – essentially the difference between conservatives and radicals. The conservatives are reluctant to challenge the institutional status quo and the vested interests defending it, and tend therefore to be passive and excusing in the face of educational inequality, while radicals are intolerant of inequality and prepared to do what it takes in terms of school reform to combat low standards and realise the comprehensive ideal of equality of opportunity.

In my discussion with Gordon in the Treasury on that May afternoon, he got this argument entirely. And so did Ed, who is a radical not a conservative.

There was no issue of substance which separated Ed and me on academics. Between us we agreed two changes to the model. The first was to remove the requirement for sponsors to contribute £1.5 million per academy. The time was ripe to do this. The sponsor contribution – originally £2 million – was part of the original policy to demonstrate the long-term commitment of sponsors. But few opponents thought academies more palatable because they came with £1.5 million; on the contrary, this simply led to claims that sponsors were 'buying' schools. It also made it more difficult to recruit enough first-rate sponsors, particularly existing successful schools, state and private, and public institutions such as universities, which were prepared to commit management time but not cash on top. By 2007, I was already waiving the £1.5 million requirement in respect of new projects taken on by academy chains.

The second change, allowing formal local authority co-sponsorship of academies, was equally pragmatic. This was to encourage more authority-wide academy strategies like those being pursued successfully in Hackney, Manchester and Southwark with the strong support of their council leaders. It was a mood music change, making it easier for councils to embrace and sell academies locally, not a change of substance, for local authorities were not permitted to become the principal sponsor of an academy and the principal sponsor continued to appoint a majority of the governors and so retained control.

From the outset of the academy programme, I had in any case treated local authorities as 'co-commissioners' of academies, and rarely imposed an academy or a sponsor against the wish of a local authority. Increasingly, as in Manchester, local authorities were not only suggesting sponsors but also persuading significant local enterprises, public and private, to become sponsors. The fact that local authorities now wanted to call themselves co-sponsors, while respecting the academy model, was further evidence of the growing consensus behind the policy.

So academies survived Tony Blair. During the Blair–Brown transition, both Gordon Brown and David Cameron had pledged their support, sealing a political consensus which even a few months before I would have thought improbable.

This accomplished, by 2008, I felt it was time for me to move on. April 2008 marked the tenth anniversary of my becoming

Tony Blair's education adviser. I changed role several times over the decade, and the work was sufficiently broad and varied that the continuing thread of academies never became narrow or unduly obsessive. But it was academies which kept me engaged in education reform for so long. The academy movement was now self-sustaining, and I wanted to embark on another reform project in whatever time Labour had left in power. Transport, and the dreadful state of the privatised rail system in particular, was a long-standing concern of mine, so in the summer of 2008 I startled Gordon by asking if I could move to Transport in the coming reshuffle. 'No one has ever asked me for Transport,' he said. 'It sort of shows' was my response.

When I left the Education Department on 5 October 2008, 133 academies were open and another 300 were in the pipeline.

It hadn't been easy keeping at it for a decade. I often got despondent. What kept me going week after week, crisis after crisis, was constantly visiting schools, talking to teachers, children and parents, being both amazed at the good things happening while also often appalled at the tolerance of failure and the writing-off of talented young lives. Every time this happened I was overawed with the sense that we the government, we the politicians, and I personally as someone with responsibility and a measure of power to make things different, could not let this continue with a clear conscience. And since I had a credible plan to make things better, and there was nothing better on the table, it was my duty to get on with it.

Reading my diaries to relive the story of academies, I come across this entry for Sunday 14 December 2003. It was at the end of my worst year in government – the year of Iraq and the incessant and debilitating Blair–Brown conflict – and it sums up why I stuck at it:

Lots of work on academies, including a Friday visit to Frank Lowe's breathtaking construction, just open in Willesden [Capital City Academy, another Norman Foster building]. 'It looks like a bloody university,' said the driver as the stately, columned building reared up round the corner. Unbelievable, and almost had me in tears as we met the kids, bright, animated, uniformed and proud of their school, mentally comparing it all to the dump of Willesden High School [which the academy replaced], which I took Frank to three years ago to persuade him to take this on.

It was Frank Lowe who used to quote G. K. Chesterton to me: 'I've searched all the parks in all the cities and found no statues of committees.'

If I had my time again, I'm sure more could have been achieved. But at least we weren't leaving it all to a committee.

WHY ACADEMIES SUCCEED

If you set up a school and it becomes a good school, the great danger is that's the place they want to go to.

Fortunately, John Prescott was right. The great majority of academies are good or rapidly improving schools and children want to go to them. That is the best evidence of their success, and facts, figures and independent studies all now show this to be the case. They also show that, far from success being a zero-sum game where academies thrive only for neighbouring schools to decline, the effect of academies is to improve other local schools too, by example and through collaboration and competition.

Less well appreciated is the reason for the success of academies. It is a statement of the obvious that their success depends upon what makes them fundamentally distinctive. But this distinctiveness is widely misunderstood.

GOVERNANCE IS THE KEY

Academies are independent state schools but it is often stated, wrongly, that the magic academy ingredient of their success is independence alone. Rather, it is strong, independent governance and leadership. To be effective, the governors – and the headteachers and management teams they appoint and sustain – need to be unambiguously in control of their schools without managerial interference from local and national bureaucracies. Independence therefore matters. But it is good governance plus independence, not independence alone, which is the distinctive feature of academies.

For academies replacing failing comprehensives, strong and effective governance starts with independent sponsor-managers.

It is crucial to understand that 'independence' and 'sponsorship' go together and cannot be separated. In respect of failing schools, few if any of the benefits of independent sponsorship would flow either from 'independence' (simply giving failing schools freedom to get on with it) or 'sponsorship' (expecting external governors to lead an institution while still subject also to local authority administration) on their own.

When an academy is set up to replace a failing comprehensive, the comprehensive is closed outright. It is the successor academy which is managed independently of local and central government, after a complete re-foundation which vests this independence in the hands of a managing sponsor with control of the school, subject to a contract with the Education Department setting out basic requirements and giving ministers the power to revoke the contract in case of failure.

For successful schools, extending autonomy to their existing governing bodies – and, again, by extension to their headteachers and management teams – can be a spur to greater success. This is the rationale, which I support, behind the decision in 2010 to allow schools judged good or outstanding by Ofsted to become academies without sponsors. (I don't support the Coalition's decision to pay them to do so.) However, successful schools are usually schools with strong and effective governance, unlike failing schools which almost invariably have weak and ineffective governance. This distinction is crucial to the reinvention of school governance which lies at the heart of sponsored academies.

Two independent studies of pre-2010 academies – by Stephen Machin and James Vernoit of the London School of Economics (LSE), and by the National Audit Office (NAO), the national public spending watchdog – highlight four measures of their success: improved exam results; popularity among parents; a positive impact on neighbouring schools; and a strong impact in combating disadvantage.

In terms of results, academies are improving their GCSE scores – including English and Maths – far faster than both the national average and schools with similar pupil intakes. Graph B, from the NAO report, shows a dramatic difference in both respects, with academies converging fast on the national average. Graph A, grouping academies by year of opening, shows the rate of improvement to be especially dramatic among those academies which have been open longest, as ought to be expected. Academies which opened in 2002 have more than trebled their scores since opening, and those opening in the following three years have mostly doubled their scores, while the national average increased by barely a quarter. Graph C shows most academies to be well within the top quarter of all schools nationwide in terms of the rate of improvement relative to the scores of pupils when they started at secondary school and what they would on average have been expected to achieve at GCSE (a measure called 'contextual value-added').

Graph A

Academies: average improvement – 5A*–C GCSE inc Eng & Maths, by opening date

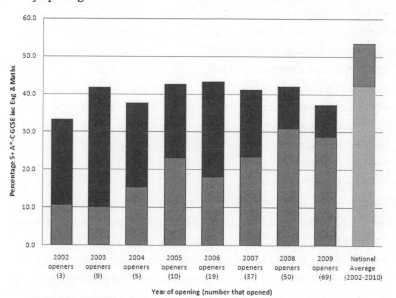

Graph B

Percentage of pupils achieving five or more A*–C grade GCSEs or equivalent in academies, comparator schools and all maintained schools, 2003–4 to 2008–9

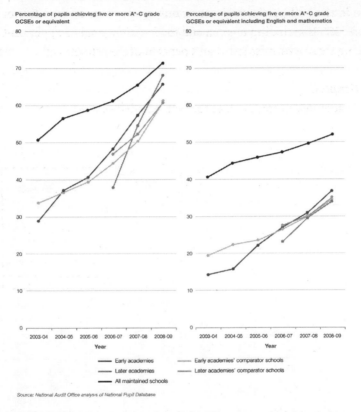

Percentage of pupils achieving five or more A*-C grade GCSEs or equivalent

Percentage of pupils achieving five or more A*-C grade GCSEs or equivalent including English and mathematics

Year

Year

——— Early academies
——— Later academies
——— All maintained schools

Early academies' comparator schools
Later academies' comparator schools

Source: National Audit Office analysis of National Pupil Database

Pupil truancy rates have also fallen faster in academies than in comparable schools, which is another leading indicator of success. In 2003, pupils in academies were absent without permission for nearly 11 per cent of school half days. The proportion steadily declined to nearly 8 per cent in 2010. The scale of truancy and non-attendance in failing schools, and its effects, are insufficiently appreciated in the national debate on education. It is not just good teaching that matters to a school: the pupils have got to be there in the first place. In 2010, 450,000 pupils (7.2 per cent) missed the equivalent of a month or more of school each year, and more than a million pupils (16.4 per cent) missed half a day or more of school a week. These are staggering numbers. Most of these children are in underperforming comprehensives. The impact on their education is stark: of persistent truants, only 35 per cent achieve five or more GCSEs including English and maths, compared to 73 per cent among those who miss less than 5 per cent of the school year.

Graph C

Academies' average contextual value added scores

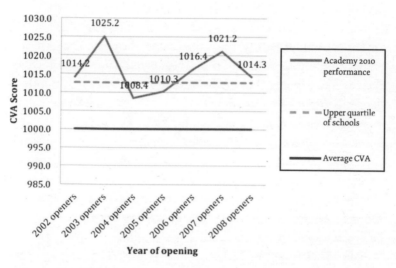

Over and above these improvement statistics, there is one simple test of a successful school: do parents want to send their children to it or not? Academies pass this test decisively. Academies attract two applicants for every place, on average, whereas the comprehensives they replaced were mostly undersubscribed. They also offer far more places. So parents are voting with their feet.

The LSE study finds that the proportion of children from very poor families is lower in academies than in their predecessor failing comprehensives. This has given rise to criticism that academies are being 'colonised by the middle class'. In fact, it simply demonstrates that academies are better community schools – better, that is, at serving their whole communities – than failing comprehensives, which are largely shunned by parents able to secure places elsewhere. Academies are attracting aspirational parents, including middle-class parents, and a good thing too. They are becoming genuine comprehensive schools and overcoming the social segregation of the past. This point is brought out in the NAO study, which finds that 'academies are not generally drawing their pupils from further away than other nearby (non-academy) schools, and indeed academy pupils on average travel a shorter distance to school than pupils at neighbouring schools'.

Not that academies are remotely turning their back on the poor. On the contrary, the NAO finds that, while the *proportion* of pupils eligible for free school meals (FSM) is generally lower in academies than in the schools they replaced, the *number* of such pupils is generally higher. It also finds that the proportion of FSM pupils in academies is significantly higher than the national average. Something thoroughly desirable is happening. Because academies are popular and successful, their pupil intake increases, often dramatically. This is not only for the good for their communities. It is especially good for the least advantaged, far more of whom receive a decent education than was the case before academies.

The social reformer Richard Titmuss observed long ago that 'services for the poor will always be poor services'. This is as true of schools as it is of hospitals, doctors' surgeries, libraries, shops, public transport and other public services which, in a good society, bind the community together.

In this regard, education statistics are often misrepresented. Eligibility for free school meals is too readily equated with children who come from 'poor' or even 'working-class' families. Yet to be eligible for free school meals, parents must either be receiving out-of-work benefits or have a family income below £16,200 a year. Most parents above this level are far from 'middle class', and many are comparatively poor. Simply to specify the criteria for receiving free school meals highlights the benefits to a school, and to the poorest pupils themselves, of having a balanced intake.

In my observation, schools with very high proportions of pupils from very poor families only flourish where they also recruit from among the aspirant in their local communities whatever their class or income. Where this happens, they can still succeed spectacularly, as with the ARK academies in Southwark, which serve large and very deprived inner-London council estates. For these academies, large concentrations of the very poor are a fact of community life, but their intake nonetheless includes a good cross-section of ability and a good number of ambitious families.

The independent studies of academies find that, as well as improving their own results fast, academies also tend to raise pupil performance in neighbouring schools. The LSE study attributes this, rather inelegantly, to 'the increased choice/competition mechanism that has scope to deliver significant positive external effects'. In plain English, by raising standards and providing greater choice, academies encourage other local schools to raise their game too. But because they are required to be all-ability schools, they can't do this by recruiting only academically high-ability students, like a grammar school. So other schools have it fully within their power to flourish too. John Prescott's genuine concern – that academies might undermine neighbouring schools – is therefore unfounded. We saw this in respect of Hackney in Chapter 1, where five successful new academies are co-existing with seven pre-existing comprehensives, all of whose results have increased such that the borough's GCSE results have been around the national average for the last three years, whereas fifteen years ago they were barely half the national average. And far more children now stay in the borough for secondary education. Academies are generally win-win for all concerned, including for neighbouring schools.

Earlier I noted that in most of densely populated England there is no such thing as the 'local school' which serves a distinct neighbourhood simply by virtue of its location. Most urban communities are served by several secondary schools, and by still more primary schools. I said that there are ten state secondary schools within about two miles of my house in north London. School choice and diversity are facts of life. School reformers and leaders need to work with the grain and not assume that all would be well if we could somehow restrict choice and reinvent the 'automatic local comprehensive' – a school which virtually all children in a neighbourhood attend simply by virtue of proximity – which in most communities never was and never will be.

Moreover, it is utterly vital to the success of academies to have in mind that the most motivated exercise the most choice. As well as doing their very best by the least able children, academies need to compete hard and overtly on what they can do for the most able and motivated children. This means competing hard on academic achievement, on success in gaining university places, and on the range and excellence of their extra-curricular activities. It is part of the reason why a constant refrain of this book is the importance of sixth forms and post-16 education, which shape the university and employment aspirations and destinations of teenagers and thereby so much that happens in a school before the age of sixteen too. Mossbourne Academy's website, proclaiming on the front page the number of Oxbridge and Russell Group university offers of its sixth-formers, needs to become the website front page of every academy in the country.

Those who bridle at school choice and competition often remark that there is 'no such thing as school choice', only the right of parents to express preferences, and that where schools are oversubscribed 'schools choose children rather than children choosing schools'. This is a good soundbite but largely nonsense. In the English system, schools can only 'choose' from the ranks of those who apply or are allocated to them in the first place. Parental choices are all-important: obviously for the parent, who can't get their child into a good school unless they choose to apply to it, but equally for the school, which unless it attracts lots of positive choices will quickly become a sink school, full of pupils whose parents did not choose it but were allocated to it because they could not secure places elsewhere. This is the situation of many failing schools, from which it is hard to recover.

A popular school cannot of course determine precisely how many parents will apply, and the more popular it is the more over-subscribed it is liable to become. Only the bureaucratic mind thinks supply and demand can be matched perfectly; the same mentality which tends to think that citizens should take what they are given and not complain. However, in an academy system of competition between all-ability schools, the process of selection is not arbitrary: it is subject to criteria giving a broadly equal chance to all applicants within its community to gain a place. Schools are not 'choosing' pupils: indeed they have no choice about their intake, once they have determined fair all-ability oversubscription criteria.

Because of catchment areas and co-existing selection systems, including the remaining grammar schools and faith schools with religious attendance tests, this process is far from pure. But the larger the number of successful academies and other schools there are, recruiting hard on the basis of genuine all-ability admissions, the more parents will secure a school of choice for their children, as is proving to be the case in places like Hackney, Southwark and Bristol where the academy system is most advanced. The overriding aim of policy ought therefore to be – as it is with academies – to boost the number of good schools where there are insufficient of them.

In pioneering academies a constant concern of mine was to ensure that academies had sixth forms where their sponsors wanted them, as they almost invariably did. So sixth forms are the norm in academies, whereas they were the exception in the failing comprehensives they replaced. All but twenty-nine of the 203 sponsored academies open in 2009 had a sixth form, with staying-on beyond GCSE rising sharply, year by year, in most of these academies.

A social and educational transformation is taking place here. The bane of the 'secondary modern comprehensives' I described earlier was that they mostly stopped education at the age of fifteen or sixteen and were largely unconcerned about what happened to their still young teenagers thereafter. Academies are doing what the best secondary schools have always done: making education a true pathway from youth to adulthood, taking teenagers right through to employment or higher education and not abandoning them midway.

Ofsted inspection data on academies is also positive. Of the early academies, which have had longest to improve, two-thirds are rated by Ofsted as good or outstanding in their overall effectiveness, a significantly higher proportion than for comparator state schools, while more than half of all academies, including those opened more recently, have already reached this standard, which is also higher than for comparator schools.

The views of parents, pupils and teachers about academies are equally positive. Questionnaires in the early academies, carried out shortly after their opening, found nine in ten pupils agreeing that 'most pupils want to do well in tests and exams', eight in ten saying they have 'high expectations', and seven in ten saying: 'Since coming to this academy my school work has improved.' Nine in ten academy parents agreed that 'the academy gives high priority to raising pupils standards of achievement', and 'the academy encourages and supports pupils to define and achieve their aspirations'. And seven in ten parents agreed that 'most pupils like going to this academy', with only one in ten disagreeing.

The surveys also found very high levels of confidence in the leadership of academies. Nine in ten agreed with the statement: 'The principal believes that this academy can make a difference to pupils' learning whatever their family background', and eight in ten agreed that 'the principal makes sure pupils behave well'.

It is particularly telling that Ofsted and parents rate academy leadership highly, for strong leadership is at their core and drives all else. And this, in turn, derives from their independent sponsors.

WHY SPONSORS MATTER

So independent sponsorship is the hallmark of academies and the secret of their success. It generally explains cases of failure too. 'It's really down to the sponsor', is the one-line summary of the most intensively researched study of academies to date.

There is a vital distinction here between governance and

day-to-day management. It is a truism that good schools have good headteachers. But good headteachers do not get appointed and sustained spontaneously. They need to be recruited; they need to be supported; they need to be challenged and held to account; they need an institutional ethos of success and high expectations which exists beyond them personally; and when they stand down – for whatever reason – they need to be replaced by a successor who is strong and effective. This is the job of governance.

Sponsors need three qualities: management capacity, dynamism and positive values. Whether they are individuals or institutions, they need to be passionate about educational opportunity and standards. They need to instil effective governance and management. They need to do what it takes to succeed.

Sponsors and their governing bodies are there to supply academies with ambitious goals, a positive ethos, effective leadership teams and effective performance management.

This is primarily about institutional leadership and high educational standards. But it is also about managing facilities and services, which are other areas of historic local authority weakness. The design and procurement of academy buildings is a case in point. An assessment of new academy buildings by the Commission for Architecture and the Built Environment, comparing new academy buildings with other new secondary school buildings, concluded that 'nearly all the academies scored better than the average for all new secondary schools that had been evaluated', partly because 'their architects have benefited from having adequate time to develop their design in close consultation with sponsors and users'. Academy sponsors and project managers regard building design and facilities management as integral to their educational and community vision, not as a separately managed activities.

Sponsor selection is therefore critical to the success of academies. Sponsors are chosen either because of their educational track record or because of their evident capacity to manage successful social enterprises giving confidence in their ability to do the same

for an academy. Among individual sponsors, as opposed to institutions or trusts, their motivation is often to put something back
into their own communities. David Ross, former deputy chairman
of Carphone Warehouse and sponsor of Havelock Academy in
Grimsby, one of the earliest academies, says:

> I was born and brought up in Grimsby. I really want to make a
> difference for the next generation of children here and put some-
> thing back. I was fortunate enough to go to an excellent school
> [Uppingham, the public school in Rutland], and I want today's
> youngsters to have similar opportunities to make a success of their
> education and get on in life.

David Ross is now a multi-academy sponsor in Humberside and
Yorkshire.

This is Lord Harris's motivation:

> I have been fortunate enough to be successful in business and wanted
> to share that success by investing in the future of education, to give
> young people the best possible chances in life. Education touches
> the lives of so many people in a community and I and my family find
> it a tremendously rewarding experience to see the Harris Academies
> grow and flourish as students come to realise their potential.

Paul Marshall, the chair of ARK schools, describes thus the reasons
why he and his City colleagues formed the ARK academy chain:

> Many of us have had the personal fulfilment and joy of chairing
> our school's governing body and seeing the transformation in the
> lives of individual children. Collectively, as a chain, we have sought
> to implement a model of schooling which truly transforms the life
> chances of disadvantaged children. We have sought to do so by
> implementing a distinctive model (no excuses for poor behaviour,
> high aspirations, depth before breadth, high emphasis on data
> assessment and pupil tracking, schools within schools) which has

worked elsewhere and is now demonstrably working in the UK. We have sought to add capacity to UK teachers by developing new training programmes. For me and most of my colleagues, ARK Schools programme is one of our proudest personal achievements.

A standard critique of academies is that they privatise education and improperly hand over schools to sponsors, putting them beyond the pale of accountability and democracy. One critic, argues that without local authority tutelage of schools 'you are left with, on the one hand, a kind of widespread anarchy, where anyone with special determination, good contacts and influence or a particular plan can push ahead, and on the other, a series of mini fiefdoms, controlled by powerful interests, who are permitted to run schools as they see fit.'

This is not the case. Academies are not-for-profit. They are commissioned by democratically elected government, local or national or both, taking account of parental demand and the existing pattern of local schools. Describing as 'anarchy' a diversity of all-ability community academies with complementary management, curriculum and teaching strengths simply exposes a conservative 'one size fits all' mentality, and a hostility to innovation, which bedevilled the comprehensive era and produced so many failing schools and such low standards. And all in contrast to successful school systems abroad, from Alberta to Hong Kong, Finland to Singapore, Ireland to the Netherlands and Germany.

How could it possibly be better for the city of Manchester to continue with six failing local authority comprehensives rather than replacing them with academies sponsored by local employers and enterprises of the calibre of Manchester Children's Hospital, the Co-Op, the Manchester College of Arts and Technology and BT? Or for Hackney to continue with a mass outflow of teenagers because its comprehensive schools were among the worst in the country, rather than setting up five successful community academies with local corporate and philanthropic sponsors? Or for Camden not to support University College London, one of the world's leading universities, in sponsoring an academy in the borough with curriculum specialisms in science and modern languages, when there is a compelling need for a new school? UCL, the Co-Op and Lord Harris are indeed 'powerful interests', and the more powerful the better for state education.

Nor is the management freedom of sponsors permission 'to run schools as they see fit'. Every academy is funded by the state on a contract stipulating key requirements in terms of admissions, curriculum, performance and financial probity. Academies are inspected by Ofsted, and their performance data is published in the same way as for other state-funded schools.

Before academies, the chain concept barely existed in English education and its growth mirrors similar developments within the independent state school sectors in Sweden and the United States. Chains such as Kunskapsskolan in Sweden and 'Knowledge is Power Program' (KIPP) in the US are at the forefront of school improvement. The same is true in England with highly successful academy chains like the Harris Federation, ARK and the United Learning Trust. The differential performance of chains itself reflects differential qualities of governance, leadership and management between the chains, and this needs to become a focus of public analysis and commentary to encourage best practice and healthy competition between academy chains.

The most successful chains are becoming steadily larger. However, to describe them as 'mini fiefdoms' is to lose a sense of proportion. There are currently (in 2012) more than 150 sponsors of academies, so power is highly diffused across the academy movement. Of these 150, fifty sponsor more than one academy but only seven are sizeable chains sponsoring more than ten academies apiece. Even the largest chains currently manage fewer than twenty-five academies, and all the chains put together represent a tiny fraction of England's 3,330 state secondary schools. They represent nothing like the concentrations of power of the largest local education authorities. Kent and Lancashire County Councils, and Birmingham City Council, each still have 400 or more schools under their tutelage. However, the common factor among these local authority 'fiefdoms' has been low average standards, poor records of school improvement and a lack of respect for parental voice and choice. Academy chains are better in all respects.

The importance of the sponsor can also be seen in the comparison between successful sponsors and those, in a small minority, who have not succeeded. This is especially stark where such academies are in close proximity. In Merton, in south London, Harris Academy Merton, one of Lord Harris's chain, is barely a mile away from St Mark's Church of England Academy, sponsored by the diocese of Southwark. In 2006, the two sponsors launched academies to replace two neighbouring failing comprehensives. The two comprehensives had similarly poor results; they also had similarly impressive new buildings, thanks to a borough-wide PFI reconstruction from which they had both benefited, but which had done nothing to raise standards. Harris Academy Merton's GCSE results have rocketed to near the top in the borough and it is heavily oversubscribed. By contrast, St Mark's Academy has not benefited from the same strength of governance, ethos or leadership. Its GCSE results remain near bottom in the borough. It struggled from the outset – as, tellingly, has another Church of England academy, in the neighbouring borough of Southwark, sponsored by the same diocese, which had recently to engage other sponsors to support a relaunch.

Sponsors, therefore, are fundamental to the success of academies. Where they succeed, they generate an educational 'multiplier effect': governance, leadership, innovation, independence, continuity and capital investment, all mutually reinforcing within a single project to create a new institution.

Continuity is a vital ingredient. The same sponsor and team who plan the academy are fully responsible and accountable for its ongoing operation. This ongoing responsibility is not merely of a few years duration, or even for the tenure of a long-serving successful headteacher. It is a commitment *in perpetuity* by the sponsor, whether they be a trust or an individual who establishes and leads a trust which will continue after them. Commitment in perpetuity concentrates the minds of sponsors on long-term success and sustainability from the very inception of the academy. Unlike the typical local education authority director or individual headteacher or chair of governors, academy sponsors know that they will reap the consequences of poor planning and management into the indefinite future.

Academy headteachers highlight the importance of sponsors. Here is Lynn Gadd, headteacher of Harefield Academy in Hillingdon, sponsored by business philanthropist David Meller, who is developing a chain of academies in Hillingdon and neighbouring Hertfordshire. Lynn has been a headteacher or deputy in state schools for twenty-five years:

> The major differences between headship of a local authority maintained secondary school and being a head of an academy spring from an expectation that positive change will be based on independence, innovation and enterprise. As these expectations form the basis of all planning and development, academy systems and structures develop more dynamically, creatively and rapidly. Sponsors bring a refreshing and positive influence on the development of academies. The sponsors combine the best approaches from the world of business with a true commitment to provide the best for our students.

Dr Dan Moynihan, chief executive of the Harris Federation, and previously headteacher of the outstandingly successful Harris CTC in Crystal Palace, gives his perspective:

> Lord Harris through his success in industry brings an expectation of success and an ability to see problems not as insurmountable but as opportunities. This brings a can-do approach to the academies where everything seems possible and failure is never seen as an option. His personal interest and profile in and around the academies motivates staff and students and gives a feeling that they are part of a special project because of his interest in them. He brings an unrivalled understanding of managing people and very strong interpersonal skills. He allows the professionals to get on with the

job without interfering but also acts as a critical friend and ensures that staff focus on improvement in everything they do.

What of sponsors with a religious motivation? These sponsors, too, are agreed by local and/or national government, having regard to their bona fides and the views of parents.

As Minister, I didn't see it as my job to say which of Richard Dawkins or Rowan Williams I thought was correct, but rather to support the right of communities to have schools which parents want, provided they achieve high standards, promote social cohesion and accept appropriate state regulation including inspection. However, I was anxious to make academies sponsored by faith groups as inclusive as possible in their admissions, preferably with no faith tests at all. And I sought to meet parental demand for greater diversity of schooling within different faith traditions, for example, by providing funding for JCoSS, a new liberal Jewish school in Barnet, north London.

What happens if a sponsor dies, disappears or fails? The government has reserve powers of intervention, including an ultimate power to close an academy and withdraw funding. No such extreme step has been taken in respect of any academy, nor in respect of any of the CTCs, which have been open for twenty years, but the powers are there. As for sponsor sustainability, it is notable that, nearly twenty years after their foundation, all of the CTCs retain their original sponsor, either in the form of the individual sponsor or sponsoring organisation or, typically in cases where the founder has died, in the form of an independent self-sustaining trust. In this they follow the example of most leading private schools, which have long been governed by self-perpetuating independent trusts set up by their original founders. The same is happening with academies, as for example at Mossbourne after the death of Sir Clive Bourne.

GOVERNING BODIES

A critical role of academy sponsors is to endow their academies with strong and effective governing bodies whose job is to set each academy's strategy and budget, promote its ethos, agree its principal policies, undertake performance management, and appoint the headteacher and other key executives.

Within some academy chains, such as ULT, governance takes the form of a central board which manages the chain as a whole, and takes key decisions including the appointment of headteachers, working in tandem with a 'local governing body' with delegated powers. However, for most academies, including those sponsored by chains, there is a single governing body for each school, a majority of whose members are appointed by the sponsor or sponsor organisation. Typically, there will also be a staff representative, a parent governor (although sponsor nominees often include parents), and a representative from the local authority.

Academy governing bodies are generally smaller than their comprehensive school counterparts, which typically have about twenty members. The average size of a FTSE-100 company board in England is eleven. It is hard to see what a state school gains by nearly doubling that size. In my experience, once there are more than eight people around a table, meetings cease to be businesslike and become discussion and debating forums. That is certainly the case with the Cabinet, which had nearly thirty attendees in my day and was essentially a weekly opportunity for networking, gossip and discussion on the doings of the government. There is an important role for discussion and debate, but it is not the same task as the management of a school or indeed the country.

The smallest academy governing body is at Pimlico Academy, sponsored highly effectively by the businessman John Nash and his wife Caroline, which has seven members and is chaired by John personally. John believes that no academy governing body should have more than eight members, a view with which I sympathise provided it is the right eight. More typical are the chains ARK, E-ACT and Harris, most of whose governing bodies have between ten and thirteen members. This is still a third or more smaller than the typical comprehensive school governing body. In the case of Harris, as the chain expands, its governing bodies are taking responsibility for two academies each, in order to promote more effective 'yardstick' comparisons of performance.

A governing body's competence matters as much as its size. Comprehensive school governing bodies are designed to be broadly and numerously representative of 'stakeholders' – parents, teaching staff, support staff, the local authority – with the number and balance between these groups, and even the electoral systems to choose them, elaborately prescribed in government regulations. Sometimes this produces competent governing bodies; too often, it doesn't. By contrast, the principle of composition for an academy governing body is professional competence, in the context of support for the academy's ethos. This is why the sponsor appoints the majority of the governors, in the expectation that the sponsor, being highly competent, and the originator of the academy's mission and passionate about its success, will appoint governors with the necessary skills, values and commitment.

Nothing matters more to a school governing body – or any other governing board – than who chairs it. In virtually all types of state school besides sponsored academies, the chair is elected from among the members of the governing body, emerging from labyrinthine stakeholder elections and appointments. This makes the appointment of a strong and effective chair hit-and-miss. By contrast, in sponsored academies the chair is usually appointed by the sponsor specifically to that post, and is accordingly far more likely to have the requisite skills and commitment. Where the sponsor is an individual, he or she often chairs the governors personally. I strongly encouraged sponsors, however grand or busy, to chair the governing bodies of their academies personally, and many did so. The Bishop of Liverpool – James Jones, a former teacher – for some years chaired the governors of the St Francis of Assisi Academy in the deprived Kensington district of his diocese, while Sir Howard Newby, when vice-chancellor of the University of the West of England, chaired the university's academy in Bristol, in both cases to great effect.

From the experience of sponsored academies, I would introduce three simple, but potentially transformational, reforms to the governing bodies of non-sponsored state schools and academies. First, separate the appointment of members of the governing body from the appointment of the chair. Second, the chair should be appointed by the governing body through open competition, for a fixed but renewable term, with members of the governing body allowed to apply but with the appointment not restricted to them. Third, I would make it possible to pay chairs.

None of this is to downplay the importance of community engagement and accountability. Academies take this seriously. Accountability also comes through independent inspection, the publication of Ofsted reports, the publication of exam and other performance data, and through student and parental choice. However, community engagement and accountability are not the same as governance. A major weakness of non-academy school governing bodies is the conflation of these tasks. When to this is added, as is typically the case with local authority school governing bodies in more challenging areas, a shortage of professionally competent governors, plus their talking-shop size and an uncertain demarcation of responsibilities between the governing body and the local authority, it is no surprise that such schools are too often at the random mercy of recruiting a 'super-head'.

Governance can seem tedious and irrelevant to the work of schools. Educationalists often think so and it almost never features in their discourse. But without strong and effective governance an institution rarely performs well, whether a school, a company, a charity or a government. This is a central insight of the academy model: that governance matters, fundamentally.

'I COULD BE HERE UNTIL I'M THIRTY'

Good governance and strong, ambitious leadership are only the beginning of what it takes to create a great school. An incisive study of sixteen early academies by Philip O'Hear, who helped create several academies as the entrepreneurial chief education officer of Hillingdon in west London and later became a successful academy headteacher himself, and Eric Blaire highlights eight other common factors: (1) vision and values; (2) an ethos of learning, success, good behaviour and mutual respect; (3) excellent teaching and staff development; (4) a culture of continuous school improvement; (5) secure systems, high-quality data and rigorous evaluation; (6) fit-for-purpose buildings and resources; (7) ambitious plans for the future; and (8) sixth forms, with post-16 education integral to the academy.

It is these factors in combination – not just a few of them unrelated – which account for the success of academies.

The sixteen academies in the O'Hear/Blaire study are a good cross-section of the academy movement at large. Half are in London; the other eight spread nationwide in Luton, Bristol, Tilbury, Manchester, Liverpool, Banbury, Middlesbrough and Peterborough. Some have philanthropic individuals as sponsors, including Sir Frank Lowe at Capital City Academy in Brent and Sir Alec Reed at the West London Academy in Ealing, while others have local institutional sponsors, including Barnfield West Academy, sponsored by a successful FE college in Luton, and Bristol Brunel Academy sponsored by Cabot Learning Federation, a trust which has grown out of one of the original City Technology Colleges and now sponsors five academies in Bristol and the surrounding area, this one in partnership with Rolls-Royce and the University of the West of England.

The sixteen academies include six sponsored by the largest academy chains, including the United Learning Trust in respect of Paddington, Manchester and North Oxfordshire academies; Lord Harris in respect of Harris Academy South Norwood; and ARK in respect of Walworth Academy in Southwark and Burlington Danes Academy in Hammersmith, the latter a former failing Church of England comprehensive in which the church is still a partner. All the academies are all-ability community schools without selective admissions tests, apart from one Roman Catholic academy, which succeeded two failing Catholic comprehensives in south London and which gives preference to Catholic families.

In the hands of this diverse range of sponsors, the common factors identified by O'Hear and Blaire have not produced identikit academies. Their curriculums and activities are highly diverse, their specialisms ranging from mathematics and health to sport, enterprise, media and the performing arts. St Matthew Academy, the Catholic academy in Lewisham, has enterprise and business as its specialism, declaring in its mission statement: 'Following St Matthew, who was a tax collector, students can get to know that successful businesses can operate well on Christian, moral and ethical principles and that entrepreneurship, business acumen and success go hand in hand with philanthropy and community involvement.' St Matthew Academy is also an all-through academy taking children from the age of three right through until eighteen.

All the academies have sixth forms. One teaches the International Baccalaureate rather than A-levels. All the academies have smart, distinct uniforms, usually with suits worn in the sixth form. As well as conventional year groups, most of the academies have house systems as settings for pastoral support and also for team games and other activities. In Burlington Danes, the houses are named after the epistles and each one also has an associated role model, including Barack Obama and Aung San Suu Kyi. One of the academies has gone further and is broken down into four 'schools within schools', each with its own headteacher. All the academies have between 900 and 1,500 pupils, apart from Thomas Deacon Academy in Peterborough, which replaced three schools and has 2,130 pupils, making it one of the largest schools in the country. On a large campus-style site, it is divided into six 'colleges', each with significant autonomy.

Most of the academies have between 40 and 50 per cent of pupils eligible for free school meals, which is around three times the national average. None is below the national average.

Looking at their results, it is striking that most of the academies, compared to the failing comprehensives they replaced, have both doubled or trebled their GCSE performance while more than halving the pupil absence rate. These two trends are clearly related. Harris South Norwood has almost quadrupled its GCSE success rate within four years: the proportion of pupils achieving five or more good GCSEs including English and maths has risen from 19 per cent under the predecessor comprehensive in 2007 to 75 per cent in 2011, while the absence rate has been cut by more than three-quarters from 20 per cent to nearly 4 per cent.

In all cases, staffing has been transformed since the academy took over. Almost all the academies are big recruiters of Teach First teachers. Their headteachers are almost equally men and women, most on their second or third headship.

Teaching practice varies. Most have conventional forty-minute lessons, but one has broken the school day down into three ninety-minute lessons plus an hour-long tutorial. Another has 'focus Fridays' for 'deep learning in one subject'. All emphasise discipline and good behaviour. Of Burlington Danes Academy the authors write: 'The Principal is extremely visible, has an open door policy and is rarely in her office. She believes in non-aggressive strict discipline: for example students in Years 7 to 10 line up at the beginning of the school day, at break and after lunch, and stand up as teachers enter the classroom.' Just like Mossbourne.

The academies all have new or entirely refurbished buildings, all immensely striking but varied. Sport looms large, even in those on constrained inner-city sites. As for their wider activities, one has a Combined Cadet Force and a military band; another has members of its first football team, rather than conventional prefects, helping in the breaks. In another, every pupil and member of staff ran four miles to raise funds for a school visit to Uganda.

Reading the sixteen case studies, I am struck by how utterly unrecognisable these academies are from the failing comprehensives they replaced, most of which I visited before the decision was taken to close them.

Nowhere is the transformation greater than at Paddington Academy, a short distance from Paddington Station in inner north-west London. By intake this is the most deprived academy of the sixteen, drawing predominantly from two huge multi-racial council estates. Fully 53 per of the academy's pupils are eligible for free school meals, making it the sixteenth most deprived secondary school by intake nationally.

Paddington's predecessor comprehensive, North Westminster

Community School, was an ILEA showcase when it opened in 1980. One of the largest comprehensives in England, with more than 2,000 pupils spread over three sites, its headteacher for its first twenty years was Michael Marland, a bow-tied guru of the comprehensive movement. Alas, that did not make for a successful school. When I visited in 2004, North Westminster was a deplorable sink school in every sense: buildings dilapidated, bullying and truancy rife, results pitiful, teachers disaffected and supply teachers everywhere. The school's GCSE performance was less than half the national average. The school was pretty well neglected by its local education authority, Westminster.

As we walked around, the school felt unsafe and dangerous. I was with the local Labour MP, Karen Buck, whose son was about to start at the school because he couldn't get in elsewhere. Karen was deeply and rightly agitated, for personal as well as constituency reasons – it makes a profound difference if politicians actually use the state schools they expect the public to use – and she was on the phone to me almost daily thereafter to get the academy project moving.

The first key decision was not simply to close North Westminster, but to replace it with two academies rather than one, so that each could be a 1,000-pupil operation on a single site. ULT became sponsor of one of the academies ('Paddington'), with an individual sponsor taking responsibility for the other ('Westminster'). According to Michael Marland's obituary, 'when walking (his preferred mode of transport) between the school's three sites, he would talk endlessly into his trusty Dictaphone, producing masses of material for his secretaries to type.' He might have done better walking the school's corridors without a Dictaphone.

The transition from North Westminster to the new academies was a nightmare of building sites, pupils being 'decanted' from one temporary building to another, and serious difficulties with the staff and leadership. Yet, since completion, the transformation has been total.

Oli Tomlinson, Paddington's headteacher, sums up her philosophy thus: 'Our saying "the street stops at the gate" ensures there is a defined line of change in uniform, behaviour, language and attitude; the focus is on learning and the academy is safe for all.' Despite the highly deprived intake, in 2011, the fifth year of the academy, nearly 70 per cent of the sixteen-year-olds got five or more good GCSEs including English and maths, against 18 per cent in the last year of North Westminster. In 2011, the academy was rated 'outstanding' by Ofsted. It also got its first student into Cambridge: the son of Iraqi refugees who only arrived in England in 2007, speaking very little English, and who gained three A*s and an A at A-level and is now reading medicine.

In their case study, O'Hear and Blaire attribute much of the success to 'relentless attention to detail, such as daily checking of staff duties (essential in a crowded building) and daily learning walks that sample every lesson with brief feedback'. And despite the success, 'the headteacher judges the academy to be only half way towards implementing its vision which will only be achieved when all children gain at least grade C in English and maths GCSE.'

Teach First has supplied more than twenty teachers, who have helped bring about this profound change.

And therein lies a story.

In autumn 2011, I met the chairman of Marks and Spencer, Robert Swannell, at a round-table business lunch. To my surprise, he wanted to talk about schools. His son, he said, was a Teach First teacher at Paddington Academy, where he went after Cambridge University and Westminster School. We spent the next hour, with the other chief executives, talking about academies, state and private education, and how to create good schools nation-wide. Robert Swannell turned out also to be chair of governors at Rugby School, of Dr Arnold fame, and he wanted to open its boarding facilities to far more children from poor families with boarding need, partly from his son's experience at Paddington. It was a crystallising moment for me on the impact of academies in bridging England's 'two nations' of rich and poor.

But the last word goes to the Paddington Academy student who said this: 'I love it; I don't want to leave; I could be here until I'm thirty – they give us so many opportunities in and out of school.'

OVERCOMING THE PRIVATE-STATE DIVIDE

Two of the greatest challenges in English education today are, first, not simply to reduce the number of underperforming comprehensives but to eradicate them entirely; and second, to forge a new settlement between state and private education.

I put these two challenges together because they go together. It is my view, after twenty years of engagement with schools of all types, that England will never have a world-class education system or a 'one nation' society, until state and private schools are part of a common national endeavour to develop the talents of all young people to the full.

The two also go together in that academies are at the heart of the solution to both challenges. It is academies that are systematically eradicating failing comprehensives. And academies – as independent state schools – are the vehicle by which private schools can become systematically engaged in establishing and running state-funded schools.

So just as the challenge is simple – how to unite state and private schools in a common endeavour – I believe the solution is also simple. Every successful private school, and private school foundation, should sponsor an academy or academies. They should do this alongside their existing fee-paying school or schools, turning themselves into federations of private- and state-funded independent schools, following the lead of a growing number of private schools and their foundations which have done precisely this and would not think of going back, including Dulwich, Wellington, the Haberdashers, the Mercers, the Girls' Day School Trust, the City of London Corporation and the King Edward VI Foundation in Birmingham.

Simple does not mean easy, nor does it mean little. By sponsoring academies I don't just mean advice and assistance, the loan of playing fields and the odd teacher or joint activity, which is generally what passes for 'private–state partnership', however glorified for the Charity Commission. I mean the private school or foundation taking complete responsibility for the governance and leadership of an academy or academies, and staking their reputation on their success as they currently do on the success of their fee-paying schools.

For the private sector, I set this totally apart from the opening up of more places in existing private schools to those who can't pay the fees. This is a good thing for private schools to do to make themselves less socially exclusive, but it does nothing to create more good schools, let alone to breach the Berlin Wall between private and state education.

To leaders in the state sector, I put this forward as a complementary – not an alternative – policy to the brilliant job that so many successful state school leaders and organisations are doing in establishing academies. We need many more good academy sponsors from all successful parts of the education system – whether state schools, private schools, universities and educational foundations – and we need them to learn from each other and collaborate.

The forces against progress are deeply entrenched in both the state and the private sectors of education, mirroring prejudices on the Left and Right of politics which go back decades.

Over the entire second half of the twentieth century, these prejudices made it exceptionally hard to do more than fiddle around at the margins of state–private partnership. This, in turn, bred a deep fatalism which is with us still. Everyone knows that the status quo is terrible – rigid separation between most of the nation's most privileged and powerful schools and the rest. Yet, until academies, no one had a credible plan or will to do much about it except say how bad it was, why it was someone else's fault, and why it would never change because, well, this is England, it's deep and cultural, and it all began with Henry VIII. It's the same fatalism which greeted gridlock in central London before the congestion charge, NHS waiting lists before patients' rights, and rain stopping play at Wimbledon before the roof.

The call now is for activists not fatalists. The future doesn't have to be like the past. There is no reason whatever why the educational Berlin Wall cannot be brought down fairly quickly if every private school and private school foundation sponsors an academy or academies, running independent schools in the state-funded as well as the fee-paying sectors, immersed in promoting excellent education for the least well-off as well as the best-off in society, and progressively combining the best of both.

Before developing this argument, a key distinction needs to be made between the two different 'private' sectors of English education: the private profit-making sector and the private charitable sector. The two are often confused, but they are different and separate. It is the private charitable sector, not the private profit-making sector, which has the potential to drive radical change for the better in England's state schools in the immediate future.

GO FOR THE WHALE NOT THE MINNOW

There is a growing debate as to whether England should follow Sweden and parts of the United States, among others, and allow private profit-making companies to run state-funded schools. I am opposed to this. When Minister, I told private profit-making companies wanting to set up in England that they should sponsor academies philanthropically, and if they could demonstrate great success, then they might be able to make a case. None has yet done so.

In Sweden, commercial operators have been a driving force behind independent state schools. But Sweden's experience has been problematic with a number of recent scandals around profit-taking from state-funded schools. The Swedish education minister recently announced an inquiry into how free schools which fail to meet accepted standards can be prevented from taking out profits.

Furthermore, the position in England is fundamentally different. When Sweden embarked on free schools, it had a weak private charitable school sector. England, by contrast, has one of the largest, and possibly the very strongest, private charitable school sector in the world. The great majority of our private schools – and all of the historic private school foundations which dominate the private school elite – are historic charities. So too are almost all of England's universities, including the most illustrious. The private sector which can make an immediate, substantial and positive difference to English state education isn't the private commercial sector but the private charitable sector. We need to focus on the whale not the minnow.

Consider the statistics. Dwell not on the 7 per cent of school-age pupils who go to private schools, which is the most misleading of the stats. More revealing is the 18 per cent of full-time students over the age of sixteen who are at private schools. And the one in three of A grades in A-level physics, chemistry and history awarded to private school students, earning them a similar proportion of places in most Russell Group universities and half of all places at Oxford and Cambridge.

Consider further. Half of all Oxbridge places means 8,000 ex-private school students at Oxbridge, compared to a mere 130 students at Oxbridge who, at school, were eligible for free school meals. So 130 Oxbridge students are drawn from the poorest 13 per cent of secondary school pupils, while 8,000 – sixty times as many – are drawn from the most privileged 7 per cent. No surprise then that successive reports by Sir Peter Lampl's Sutton Trust, an independent trust which promotes social mobility, reveal that three in four judges, two in three top barristers, and half of leading company chief executives, solicitors, journalists and politicians were educated at private schools. Sport, drama, TV, and both pop and classical music are also largely dominated by the private schools. During a sample week in October 2010, 60 per cent of all chart acts had been educated at private schools.

The teaching profession is an important and under-appreciated aspect of this divide. In the 1970s, the number of pupils per teacher in private schools was similar to that in state schools. Now, on the back of fees which have doubled in real terms in twenty years, private school teacher numbers have doubled relative to state schools. A seventh of England's teachers are now in private schools, and a far higher proportion of teachers with better and higher degrees. And where do these teachers come from? By far the single largest source of new teachers in private schools is experienced teachers in state schools, whereas traffic the other way is minimal. There is net annual recruitment – allowing for transfers the other way – of 1,400 experienced teachers from state schools into private schools, which is more than the entire annual recruitment of Teach First into the state system, and some Teach Firsters also end up in private schools.

So, England in 2012 is governed by a Prime Minister educated at Eton, a Deputy Prime Minister from Westminster, a Chancellor of the Exchequer from St Paul's. Charterhouse, Rugby, Radley, Wellington and Cheltenham Ladies College alumni are all in the Cabinet too, almost all of them children of very wealthy parents. We do indeed have a coalition government: a coalition of Eton and Westminster.

It is only a slightly broader coalition which entertains the country and represents it at sport – football apart (football v. rugby being another continuing divide between state and private schools). This year (2012) opened with Benedict Cumberbatch (Harrow) topping the TV ratings as Sherlock, Michael McIntyre (Merchant Taylors') packing the comedy halls, Dominic West (Eton) on both film and screen, Andrew Strauss (Radley) captaining the English cricket team, and Toby Flood (King's School Tynemouth) and Ben Foden (Bromsgrove School) stalwarts of the national rugby team.

Michael McIntyre is suitably comic on his transition from private to state school after his father, a video entrepreneur, fell on hard times. After starting out at prep school in St John's Wood in 'a bright red blazer with dark trim ... like a ladybird costume', he progressed naturally at thirteen to Merchant Taylors', one of north London's most expensive public schools, whose teachers were 'all dressed like Professor Snape from Harry Potter'. But for sixth form he had to transfer to a local sixth form college. Woodhouse College in Barnet is an A-level factory at the very top end of the state system, but for the sixteen-year-old McIntyre it was terra incognita. 'People were confused by me, as if I was an alien from Planet Posh. That didn't really change much as people got to know me.'

With 'Planet Posh' ruling so much of the social, economic and political life of the country, it is vitally important, for England to become one nation, that the people who run the private schools, and who teach in and attend these schools, become engaged in state education too. I see no other credible way of bridging the private–state divide, which has its roots in the deep isolationism of England's private school sector.

OUT OF ISOLATION

How did it all come to be like this? Like the secondary modern antecedents of the comprehensives, the Victorian antecedents of today's private schools remain highly relevant. Historians of education talk a lot about Gladstone's 1870 Education Act, which essentially started state education. But equally significant were Gladstone's 1869 and 1873 Endowed Schools Acts, which essentially turned the great public schools – and many of the newer grammar schools – previously run in a rackety way by Crown, church or local appointees, into a Victorian equivalent of academies, with new independent governing foundations to control their assets, management and leadership. This Victorian academy status greatly strengthened the private schools as institutions. But their fees, and the conservative use of their charitable assets by their new governing bodies, kept most of them largely closed to all but the upper and upper middle classes. And so they remained as the state secondary system developed in parallel – and separately – in the decades after the 1902 Balfour Education Act.

There was a moment, at the end of the Second World War, when history might have taken a different turn. An official report, published in 1944 on the day Eisenhower reviewed his bridgehead in Normandy, said the social division between private and state schools 'made far more difficult the task of those who looked towards a breaking down of those hard-drawn class distinctions within society'. Churchill himself, visiting his alma mater of Harrow, talked to the boys of 'broadening the intake and the public schools becoming more and more based on aspiring youth in every class of the nation'.

But it didn't happen. Two generations later, the only significant changes to the private school system are that it is larger and richer, and its average educational attainment has risen to among the highest in the world.

The reason for the utter failure of post-war policy to overcome the private–state divide can be explained simply. Both sides of politics, and both sides of education, positively wanted the divide to continue, and – for differing reasons – they adopted a simple one-word policy in respect of private schools: isolation.

On the Labour side, ideological antipathy to fee-paying education, and later also to selective education, bred often intense hostility. But the social and legal position of the private schools, plus – ironically – the personal educational preferences of Labour leaders from Attlee to Wilson and Callaghan, kept at bay any attack beyond the rhetorical, except for the withdrawal of state-funding schemes for small numbers of pupils to attend private schools, which the 1974 Labour government did in respect of the 'direct grant' scheme introduced by Butler in 1944, and the 1997 Labour government did in respect of the Assisted Places Scheme introduced by Margaret Thatcher in 1980.

I treasure Roy Jenkins's exchange with Harold Wilson when turning down Wilson's offer to become Education Secretary in 1965. In his memoirs Roy doesn't say why he turned the job down: he told me it was because he regarded Education as a second-order department and he had no idea of a constructive education policy to pursue, itself a telling commentary on the state and status of education at the time. But here is his exchange with Wilson, as recorded in his memoirs:

'Looking for an excuse [to decline the job], I said that all three of our children were at fee-paying schools and that this surely was an obstacle to being Minister of Education in a Labour government. Wilson brushed this aside as being of no importance. "So were mine," he said.'

(One of them was maths fellow at Keble College, Oxford, when I was an undergraduate there in the early 1980s.)

Tony Blair was the first Prime Minister in history to send his children to state secondary schools. Yet politically and personally – ex-Durham Cathedral School, Fettes, St John's College, Oxford – he was not minded to put himself seriously at odds with the private schools. Instead, there was friendly waffle about mutual respect, and some committees and minor partnership projects, which did not a lot. That is, until the academies policy.

On the Tory side, there was an equal and opposite isolationism. Most Tory ministers and MPs went to private schools and sent their children to them. They still do. So long as Labour kept the dogs off, they had no desire to court controversy by proposing any role in the state system for private schools and their foundations. Better to let sleeping dogs lie. On the Tory patrician left, epitomised by the Etonian Sir Edward Boyle, Education Minister under Macmillan and Douglas-Home, two more Etonians, there was also a dose of patrician guilt and support for comprehensivisation, but only so long as it did not affect the private schools.

However, for the Tory mainstream, the gnawing fear was of dilution. The dominant view was 'more means worse': the view that there were only a small, and pretty fixed, number of 'good' schools, mostly existing private schools and the remaining grammar schools, and they needed to be preserved in aspic. This secured, the only safe and politically viable Tory reform of private schools was to open up a tiny number of places in private day schools to children with poorer parents. Hence the Thatcher government's Assisted Places Scheme which with much fanfare paid private school fees for 30,000 children out of a private school sector of 500,000 children and a state school sector of more than eight million. This, as I noted earlier, was not so much an education policy as escapology.

So much for the politicians. The leaders of state and private schools were – and many of them remain – similarly isolationist. It was an article of faith among the leaders of the comprehensive movement that private schools were not only socially divisive but also, in their educational practice, largely irrelevant. This remains a pronounced view, even among some academy headteachers. They say, to paraphrase: 'what can that lot who just spoon feed the children of the rich ever know about education in Hackney and Knowsley?' As for the heads of the private schools, many of them have been only too eager to agree, especially when the suggestion is made that they might manage academies. Pressed further, they often say it's not about ordinary children versus privileged children but about non-selective schools versus selective schools, an argument made by Sir Eric Anderson when Provost of Eton, which I found richly ironic, given that until recently Eton was basically an all-ability comprehensive for the rich and titled.

This mutual isolationism didn't matter much until now, because there was no opportunity for systematic and deep engagement between the two sectors. Now it matters a lot, because before us, if we seize it, is a simple, radical and workable agenda to end the isolationism of the past. It is for every successful private school and private school foundation to sponsor an academy or academies, and transform themselves into state–private school federations.

WHY PRIVATE SCHOOLS SHOULD SPONSOR ACADEMIES

The arguments for successful private schools systematically to sponsor academies are manifold and manifest. We will never build a one-nation society unless we eradicate failing schools and systematically leverage the nation's most powerful social leaders and best educational institutions in the service of the wider community. That means many more good schools, replacing underperforming comprehensives community by community. Academies – independent state schools – are now proven as the successful institutional means of harnessing England's most powerful social leaders and successful educational foundations in the management of new schools. So we need many more such academies, with private schools prominent among their sponsors.

Everything about academies is in the DNA of the successful private school: independence, excellence, innovation, social mission. The benefit is not only to the wider community, it is also to the private schools themselves, whose mission is enlarged, whose relative isolation is ended, and whose social engagement, beyond the families of the better-off, is transformed.

To those on the Left, and in the state and academy sectors, who see private schools as an irrelevance, I hope I have said enough about their huge footprint in almost every national elite to show why the isolationism of the past cannot continue if excellence and opportunity in education are to be for the many not the few.

To those in the private schools, and their governing bodies, who are reluctant to embrace academies, I appeal both to your professionalism and to your moral and charitable missions. It was excusable to stand apart from state-funded education when the state and its leaders did not want you engaged in the first place. But that is the isolationist politics of the past. The politics of the present and the future is that the nation seeks your engagement in setting up new independent state-funded academies in a way which does not compromise your independence, and which renews for the twenty-first century your essential moral and charitable purposes.

Depressingly, the politics of private–state school reform is still too often seen in terms of cash transactions. On the Left, the conventional wisdom is that charitable status gives an unfair subsidy to private schools which ought to be ended, while some private school leaders and governors, whenever it is suggested that they might sponsor academies or otherwise support state education in a non-tokenistic way, retort that their parents are already paying twice for education, through their taxes and their school fees, so why should they pay a third time over? Some say they would rather 'give up' charitable status than be expected to do this.

Both these approaches are fundamentally misconceived, for they fundamentally misunderstand the position of private schools as charities. 'Charitable status' is not a badge which can be awarded or taken away from the assets of private schools by the Charity Commission for good or bad behaviour. Nor could the government or even Parliament do this, unless charitable assets nationwide are to be held liable to random nationalisation. Rather, it is fundamental to their very being, like blood in a mammal. However, the assets of Eton, Westminster, Winchester and the rest are only vested in their trustees and current managers on the basis that they are deployed for charitable purposes. Private school charities can no more 'give up' charitable status than they can have it stripped from them. If they do not wish to continue as charities, or if they are unwilling to perform genuine charitable endeavour, then their highly valuable charitable assets should be passed into hands willing to do so. If the governors of Westminster School, for example, then want to set up a separate non-charitable trust solely or very largely concerned with the education of the very rich, that is up to them.

The charitable purposes of these schools could not be clearer. William of Wykeham established Winchester for the education mainly of poor scholars, and only a minority of 'noble commoners'. Henry VI set up Eton for poor scholars. Charterhouse was established by Sir Thomas Sutton, the wealthiest commoner in England, for – yes, more poor scholars. Elizabeth I endowed Westminster School for the same purpose; to this day it is an integral part of Westminster Abbey, its governing body chaired by the Dean of Westminster appointed by the Queen. John Lyon set up Harrow in 1572 as a free grammar school for the education of boys of the parish of Harrow, and the parish objected strongly in the 1870s when the Endowed Schools Act removed this obligation.

I could go on through the statutes, charters and founding deeds of hundreds of private schools. This includes my own alma mater, Kingham Hill School, occupying ninety-six rolling acres near

Chipping Norton in the Cotswolds. Founded in 1886 by a Christian philanthropist, Charles Edward Baring Young, for the free boarding education of orphans and destitute boys out of London's East End, it wasn't even called a school in his day but a 'home'. On his death in 1928, Baring Young left his fortune in charitable trust for the 'home'. Nearly a century later, Kingham Hill is a conventional fee-paying private school, with bursaries financed by income from the trust supporting only a few dozen children from poorer families.

Kingham Hill does a reasonable job as a private school but I suspect that Baring Young, if alive today, would refocus its mission on the inner cities and struggling families. I suspect he would have been an academy sponsor, and might think his academy better located in Stoke Newington than Chipping Norton, where a vast capital asset could be realised. Or perhaps, like Durand Academy in Lambeth,[†] it could partner with entrepreneurial inner-city primary schools to offer all-through education for inner-city children from the age of three to eighteen, with the later secondary years spent at a weekly boarding school. The school could then educate thousands, not dozens, of children from poorer families.

It shouldn't take the Charity Commission to challenge private school foundations in these ways about their charitable missions. Their trustees and governors should look to them constantly as a matter of conscience and duty. And they should do so urgently, for with each passing decade many of these schools have become more not less exclusive, and for generations now, few of them have done anything radical to reconnect with their charitable purposes. Most of them are seeking to provide a few more bursaries. But this is hardly enough, when they could also be running academies whose central purpose is the very mission – educating the less privileged – for which their assets were intended in the first place. Schools that simply sell privilege can't continue to call themselves charities.

As for the idea that these great schools and foundations are not

---

†   See page 186.

capable of making a success of academies with more challenging pupil intakes, this is a comic proposition. The governing body of Eton is chaired by the former minister William Waldegrave. Its members include three professors, three knights, five PhDs and the former private secretary to the Prince of Wales. Westminster School's governing body is chaired by the Dean of Westminster – John Hall, the former chief education officer of the Church of England, who was the driving force behind the church's decision to set up more than thirty academies. His fellow governors include the Dean of Christ Church, Oxford, the Master of Trinity College, Cambridge, two professors, two canons, two knights, one baron and one dame.

Almost every private school governing body in the country is a catalogue of the very great and the very good, locally or nationally, including business, religious and educational leaders. The notion that these organisations, if they have the will to do so, cannot command the resources and the expertise needed to run a successful school or schools in less advantaged areas – if that were true, then England would indeed be Greece, about to default on its whole society not just its state borrowing.

However, there is no need to argue by assertion. The leaders are there. Dulwich is sponsoring an academy in Sheppey. Wellington is sponsoring an academy in Wiltshire. The King Edward VI Foundation is sponsoring an academy in Birmingham. All these academies replace failing comprehensives. The Girls' Day School Trust has converted two of its outstanding private schools, in Liverpool and Birkenhead, into state academies. And five substantial academy chains – built up by the Mercers Company, the Haberdashers' Company, the Woodard Corporation, the United Church Schools Trust and the City of London Corporation – have grown out of the management of historic chains of private schools, leveraging this educational expertise and experience to service academies alongside.

For all these schools and chains, academy sponsorship is a matter of moral and charitable passion. Anthony Seldon, headmaster of Wellington College, describes how he and his governors came to found the Wellington Academy in Wiltshire:

> Wellington College was founded in the 1850s as the memorial for the Duke of Wellington, to provide free education for military orphans in the wake of the Crimean War. The school is proud of its traditions and to this day offers fee support for children who have lost parents in the service of their country. But they are now only a small proportion of the intake.
>
> The governors of the college decided to sponsor an academy to strengthen this original social mission. They deliberately took over a failing school in Tidworth, close to the Tidworth military garrison on Salisbury Plain, to reflect the college's traditions and expertise. The academy takes up to half its pupils from military families. High levels of mobility are an obvious fact of life for children in military families, so the boarding option is particularly important.

The Wellington Academy, like Wellington College, has a boarding house, a Combined Cadet Force, an emphasis on service, academic excellence and holistic development.

Graham Able, Dulwich College's former headteacher who pioneered Dulwich's academy on the Isle of Sheppey, says:

> Dulwich College had been interested for some time in engaging with the academies programme because it seemed to offer such a good fit with the original aims of the founder, Edward Alleyn, in 1619. Over the years the college has been able through bursaries to extend the range of its own intake to parents who could not afford full fees. But there was a limit to how many children could be reached by this approach.

In conversations with Lord Eddie George, the former Governor of the Bank of England, and Lord Andrew Turnbull, the former Cabinet Secretary, who were then chairman and deputy chairman respectively of Dulwich's governing body, I was struck by the strength of their social purpose. 'The academy in Sheppey brings Dulwich back closer to its original mission of developing the talents of all children regardless of their background,' says Lord Turnbull.

With vision and leadership, there could be hundreds more academies sponsored by private school foundations, changing the face of English education for the better.

NEW 'DIRECT GRANT' SCHOOLS

It was one of my key objectives for the academies programme that it should be a vehicle for a modern version of the 'direct grant' scheme, which until its abolition in the 1970s made it possible for leading independent grammar schools to be state-funded without fees. I had in mind a simple model. The private school would become an academy, fully retaining its independent management and character but without fees for any pupils. It would exchange academically selective admissions for all-ability admissions, but with a large catchment area and 'banded' admissions to ensure a fully comprehensive ability range. There would also be a large sixth form, underpinning continued very strong academic performance.

A 'direct grant' sector on these lines is gathering scale. I encouraged and oversaw the transition of five historic fee-paying secondary schools into academy status (William Hulme's Grammar School in Manchester, Belvedere School in Liverpool, Birkenhead High School, and Colston Girls and Bristol Cathedral Schools in Bristol). These schools remain strong academic performers as academies, while expanding their intake and greatly broadening their social range. Their independent foundations and governors continue to manage them and promote their ethos as before. The Cameron government has continued this policy. Batley Grammar School in West Yorkshire, founded in 1612, became an academy on the same basis in 2011, followed by Liverpool College in 2012. Several more successful independent schools are likely soon to follow suit.

For these independent schools, economic security and social mission are going hand-in-hand as they become academies. Some of them are located in northern England where the pool of fee-paying parents is small and becoming smaller. Continuing as fee-paying schools would be at the price of greater social exclusivity, and their governors are keen to make their education more widely available. For parents and the public, the conversion of successful fee-paying urban day schools into academies is wholly beneficial. Each of these conversions provides an outstanding new state academy, raising standards and providing greater educational choice and opportunity.

With government encouragement, there could soon be fifty or a hundred more 'direct grant' academies, serving as beacons of academic excellence within the state system and substantially eroding the division between the state and private sectors of education. Over time these 'direct grant' academies could sponsor new academies, replicating their ethos and success within the academy system.

'THIS HOUSE WOULD ABOLISH THE PRIVATE SCHOOLS'

In summer 2011, I visited the Petchey Academy, one of the five academies in Hackney, sponsored by Jack Petchey, a great East End philanthropist. His academy isn't just about exam results, it is about education for character, for community and for citizenship. They do it brilliantly in one of London's most deprived communities.

They were particularly keen I should see debating teams from Years 10 and 11 debate before the whole of their two year groups. The debaters were articulate and well prepared, just like in all those private school debating societies.

The motion they were debating was: 'This House would abolish the private schools'. It was carried two to one. All the old arguments were there. Unfairness. Privilege. Elitism. Afterwards I asked the girl who had led the charge whether she had ever visited a private school. 'Of course not,' she said. 'Why would they want to have anything to do with anyone from around here?'

Why indeed. It is time to bury the past and build a better future.

UNIVERSITIES, ACADEMIES AND TEACH FIRST

There are two chasms dividing English education and thereby society at large. One is between private schools and state schools, which is debated constantly while, until academies, nothing much was done to overcome it. The other is between Oxford, Cambridge and the next thirty or so most selective universities, on the one side, and the majority of comprehensive schools, on the other. This second divide isn't talked about enough, partly because its seriousness is under-appreciated, and partly because the vice-chancellors of these universities do a plausible job of claiming to be tackling it, while year after year little changes.

The two chasms follow similar contours and are intimately connected. A recent study revealed that just five institutions – Eton, three other public schools and one state sixth form college – send more students to Oxford and Cambridge each year than nearly 2,000 comprehensive schools and FE colleges, i.e. more than half of all the comprehensive schools in the country.

Don't rush past this statistic, for it goes to the heart of England's segregated education system. Eton, Westminster, St Paul's Boys and St Paul's Girls, plus one sixth form college, won 946 places at Oxford and Cambridge between 2007 and 2009, while nearly 2,000 comprehensives and FE colleges with an average of less than one Oxbridge entrant a year won 927 Oxbridge places between them.

We encountered these four private schools repeatedly in the last chapter. Yet again the Eton/Westminster – Cameron/Clegg – coalition reigns supreme. However, the state sixth form college in question is equally significant. Its location? Cambridge. It is Hills Road Sixth Form College, an A-level college which attracts the cream of sixth-formers from the whole Cambridge region, including many sons and daughters of university lecturers.

Hills Road College only exists because most state secondary schools in Cambridgeshire do not have sixth forms, following the comprehensive reorganisation of the 1970s. It is highly selective and only admits students with a string of top GCSE grades. Subdivide Hills Road's intake by its dozens of feeder schools, and they are all a world apart from Eton/Westminster in university admissions. Furthermore, a good number of its students are private school educated until GCSE at the age of sixteen, when they transfer by choice and then count as 'state-educated' for the purpose of university admission statistics.

So Hills Road is a brilliant but highly exceptional state college. It has little in common with the great majority of state further education colleges. These, even where they draw sixth-formers from comprehensives without sixth forms, generally have poor progression rates to top universities.

THE TWO STATE SECTORS

If Hills Road College is exceptional, there are another few hundred state schools and colleges which do fairly well in winning 'top' university places. These include other sixth form colleges in affluent areas without state school sixth forms, as well as the remaining state grammar schools, the City Technology Colleges, leading church schools, and a few dozen of the best academies and comprehensives.

This small minority of state schools and colleges supply the great majority of state-educated students gaining places at Oxbridge and other selective universities. By contrast, the bottom half of comprehensives secure few places in any of the top thirty most selective universities. It is not simply Oxbridge which is a virtual no-go zone for many comprehensives, but also universities like Birmingham and Leeds, Leicester and Nottingham, Reading and Sheffield, the LSE and UCL, Surrey and York.†

These thirty universities account for about a quarter of all degree places; their graduates largely run the country and bag the nation's best-paid jobs. Yet there are more than 500 comprehensives which secure an average of only three places a year in any of them. Only one in fifteen sixth-formers goes on to one of these universities from the lowest-performing 20 per cent of schools, whereas more than half of sixth-formers do so from the highest-achieving 20 per cent. And that one in fifteen is of those teenagers who make it into the sixth form: these schools have a far higher drop-out rate after GCSE than the highest-performing schools, virtually all of whose students stay into the sixth form as a matter of course.

Take the borough of Newham in East London. Newham has a huge sixth form college with 2,600 students, plus an FE college with 1,200 students and two Catholic comprehensives with 800 sixth-formers between them. Yet in 2010 these state schools and colleges together got only seventy students into the thirty most selective universities. Mossbourne Academy in neighbouring Hackney exceeded that on its own in 2011, its first year of A-level results, while Hills Road College got seventy students into Oxford and Cambridge alone.

An important category distinction therefore needs to be made between the top few hundred state schools and colleges, which do a good or passable job at sending their brightest sixth-formers to selective universities, and the entire bottom half of the comprehensive and FE college system which performs abysmally in this respect.

This category distinction between the elite of state schools and colleges and the rest of the state sector is vital to understanding

---

† The Sutton Trust defines the thirty most selective universities as: Bath, Birmingham, Bristol, Cambridge, Cardiff, Durham, Edinburgh, Exeter, Glasgow, Imperial College, King's College London, Lancaster, Leeds, Leicester, Liverpool, LSE, Manchester, Newcastle, Nottingham, Oxford, Reading, Royal Holloway London, Sheffield, Southampton, St Andrews, Strathclyde, Surrey, UCL, Warwick, York.

the reform challenge ahead. For the situation is not as generally described, including by the vice-chancellors of the selective universities, who often talk airily about 'improving' their recruitment from 'the state sector'. In reality, the selective universities barely recruit at all from most of the state sector. They – and we, as a country – basically need to start from scratch at this task. Here again, as with the governance and leadership of the bottom half of comprehensives, what is needed is not incremental improvement but fundamental reinvention.

Understanding this reality leads me to break with another piece of conventional wisdom on university admissions. It is no longer good enough for universities, particularly the most selective universities, to say 'it's all the fault of the schools' and to keep repeating mantras like 'we don't do social engineering' – by the way, what else does anyone do in education? – 'we do our best to help', and 'if only the state schools were better, we could admit more of their students on merit'.

Yes, the bottom half of comprehensives need fundamental reform. They need to be replaced by academies systematically. But for this reform to succeed in breaking down the university–comprehensive divide, the universities themselves cannot stand back and leave it all to others. Every university, including every Oxford and Cambridge college and all the selective universities, needs to take a lead and assume substantial responsibility for improving the bottom half of the comprehensive system.

By this I mean not just more of their existing 'outreach' activities, much of which is skin deep. Nor are more bursaries for students from poorer families going to help much, since bursaries generally go to students who would have gone to the university in question anyway, and most of them also go to students educated at private schools or the few hundred top-end state schools and colleges who get the A-level grades, and have the aspiration, to apply to top universities in the first place. Rather, universities need to take responsibility for helping to transform the bottom half of comprehensive schools in two key respects: in governance and –

among the more selective universities – in encouraging far more of their graduates to teach in these schools, which is the surest route to transforming their A-level standards and aspirations among their students to go on to selective universities.

To keep it simple and systematic, which is the only way movements for change ever get going, I recommend two initiatives. First, every university and Oxbridge college should sponsor at least one academy, taking complete responsibility for its governance. Second, all the selective universities, and every Oxbridge college, should become an active proponent – not simply a supporter – of Teach First.

I can already hear some vice-chancellors complaining about distraction from their 'core mission'. But this is where a fundamental change of mindset is required. Promoting wide social access should no longer be a peripheral mission of universities, including the top universities. It needs to become part of their core mission. Unless universities intend to abandon Britain or become research-only institutions without undergraduate students – neither of which is being proposed even by Oxford, Cambridge, Imperial, UCL and the LSE, the five top universities – then all alike have a fundamental duty to recruit Britain's brightest and best students irrespective of background. This is manifestly not happening at present. It will only be achieved by universities becoming intensively engaged in the reinvention of the bottom half of the comprehensives through academies and Teach First, and regarding this enhanced engagement in state education as a central, not secondary, part of their missions.

In short, universities need to become school-intensive as well as research-intensive and teaching-intensive institutions.

More than thirty universities – as varied as UCL, Nottingham, Liverpool and the University of the West of England – are already sponsoring academies, as a matter of strategic intent on the part of their vice-chancellors and councils. As with private school sponsorship of academies, a tipping point will come when the sector at large follows the lead of the pioneers.

So too with Teach First, which is scaling up fast but with the vice-chancellors still mostly on the stands not on the pitch. If they take to the pitch, and mobilise their students, lecturers and careers services behind Teach First, then the doubling of its intake to 1,500 which is planned by 2014 could lead to further significant expansion. Teach First could easily become a popular and socially transformational 21st-century form of national service for many thousands of high-achieving graduates, enhancing their skills and enabling them to put something back into the education system from which they have gained so much; and to do so in their early and mid-twenties before deciding and embarking upon their long-term careers.

All this needs to happen in the next few years, not the next few decades, for England's top universities to become engines of social mobility rather than continuing – like the private schools – as agents of social privilege and exclusivity, carping about the failure of state schools but doing little systematically to put it right.

UNIVERSITIES AND ACADEMIES

I recall precisely the moment in spring 2005 when the University of Nottingham decided to sponsor an academy.

For some months, I had been in general discussion about the idea with Sir Colin Campbell, Nottingham's long-serving and dynamic vice-chancellor. Then David Samworth, a businessman on Nottingham's court of governors, offered to partner the university in an academy and to put up the bulk of the £2 million financial sponsorship then required. David, third-generation chairman of the family firm Samworth Brothers – whose best-known brand, Ginsters, was the first national sandwich brand – had been passionate about academies since their launch. He was already sponsoring two academies in the East Midlands, in Leicester and Mansfield. He offered to sponsor a third if the University of Nottingham would partner with him.

A failing comprehensive in Nottingham – William Sharp School in Bilborough, a deprived community in north-west Nottingham – had become a possible academy project, following discussions with the local Labour MP Graham Allen and the city council. In

2002, fewer than fifteen of William Sharp's 130 sixteen-year-old leavers had got five GCSEs including English and maths, and the school was in a deplorable state all round.

So I took Colin Campbell and David Samworth to visit the school. It was a typically depressing pre-academy tour. As we walked from class to class, a teacher mentioned a startling fact. So far as she was aware – although she couldn't be sure because the school had no sixth form – no student from William Sharp had ever gone on to the University of Nottingham, although the university was less than two miles away. Whereupon Colin Campbell turned to me and said: 'OK, we'll do this. If we can build a campus in the middle of China [Nottingham University opened a replica of itself near Shanghai in 2005] then we can run a successful school in our own backyard.'

One of Colin's pro-vice-chancellors – Professor Di Birch – led the project with David Samworth's team, and in 2009 the Nottingham University Samworth Academy opened on the old William Sharp site. The university provides far more than the governors and governance: its lecturers, students and support staff are part of the life of the school. All new pupils go on a 'transition day' at the university. The academy has a sixth form, and Nottingham's students act as mentors and tutors ('the conversations don't always stay on topic,' as one student puts it). The university also supports the academy through apprenticeships and work placements. More than twenty academy staff are undertaking masters and doctoral degrees at the university. A team from the university was recently at the school, with two playwrights and a group of local residents, making a series of plays about Bilborough past, present and future.

'For us, this project is about being the University *of Nottingham*, not just a university,' as Di Birch puts it. 'We set out to create a sense that a university is a very normal thing, not a world apart. It's an amazing opportunity for our students too.'

So 'university academies' are university-school institutions in a far broader sense simply than governance. The university relationship extends to the whole life and ethos of the academy. The universities pioneering academies view their work not only as the creation of outstanding schools in their own communities, but also a means to improve their understanding of how to promote university progression from schools with poor university traditions.

University sponsors of academies embrace the spectrum of higher education, including post-1992 universities which, as former polytechnics or local colleges of higher education, have historically had stronger links with their local state schools. The first university academy was sponsored by the University of the West of England, in partnership with Bristol entrepreneur and former chairman of Bristol City FC, John Laycock. It is in Easton, one of Bristol's toughest districts. 'The link with the university has helped hugely in raising aspirations among staff and students,' says John Laycock. Staying-on rates after GCSE have increased dramatically compared to the predecessor failing comprehensive, and the number of students going on to university has trebled since the start of the academy.

University College London, one of Britain's top research universities, is establishing an academy in its home London borough of Camden, thanks to the leadership of the Provost, Professor Malcolm Grant, and Vice-Provost Professor Michael Worton.

'UCL was the first university to admit students of any race, class or religion, and the first to welcome women on equal terms with men,' the UCL Academy prospectus announces proudly. It promises 'masterclasses, seminars and summer schools for academy students, given by UCL staff and making use of UCL's laboratory, library and other teaching facilities'. There will be a curriculum 'developed in exciting ways informed by the latest research', and university mentors 'to provide role models, classroom assistants, and sources of informal advice and guidance to students'. The sixth form will major in maths and science.

UCL is providing for its academy what Eton, Westminster and every leading public school takes for granted in terms of university connections. Indeed, this is back to the future. Historically, many of the older universities – and Oxbridge colleges – were part of foundations which also included schools. Our ancestors did not make a rigid distinction between places of learning called 'universities' and places called 'schools': there was constant overlap between them in teachers, students, governors and mission. Thus Eton is part of the same Henry VI foundation as King's College, Cambridge; Winchester part of the same William of Wykeham foundation as New College, Oxford; Magdalen College School part of the same William Waynflete foundation as Magdalen College, Oxford, and they are still located side by side. These links extended far beyond governance: until a generation ago, there were many 'closed scholarships' endowed specifically for students from named public schools to attend specific Oxbridge colleges. Only over the past century have such links finally been severed, partly because it was thought inappropriate for universities to be sustaining special relationships with exclusive fee-paying schools.

Such was the case with UCL. The university founded its own school, University College School (UCS), in 1830 because it was dissatisfied with the quality of school education of many of its applicants. UCS was one of the first schools in England to teach modern languages and sciences, and there was no religious instruction. The school was located on Gower Street, next to UCL, until in 1907 it moved out to Hampstead and became a free-standing private school. Precisely a century later, in 2007, UCL decided once again to set up its own school – an academy in its London borough of Camden – once again with the purpose of improving local school education and progression to top universities, including UCL.

'A modern university should not be divorced from secondary education in its own locality,' says Malcolm Grant. 'That's why we are setting up the UCL Academy.'

It is time for universities at large to follow the lead of UCL, Nottingham and other university pioneers. There would then be a hundred or more new university academies. The mutual benefit to both universities and state schools would be immense.

UNIVERSITY TECHNICAL COLLEGES

A variant on the university-sponsored academy is the 'University Technical College' (UTC), which is an academy for 14–19-year-olds with a focus on an area of technical education, sponsored by a business or businesses together with a university.

For the university, the sponsorship role is similar to that for a conventional academy in governance and leadership. But the technical character of the UTC gives a specific focus to its work and to the engagement of the relevant department of the university. Most of the early UTCs have an engineering focus, driven by the shortage of engineering skills in the workforce and the lack of qualified students for engineering degrees courses and apprenticeships.

JCB, the diggers and engineering equipment company, established the first UTC on its headquarters site in Rocester near Derby in 2010. It is in a converted eighteenth-century Arkwright mill, one of England's first manufacturing plants. 'Recruitment of trainees at JCB had hit an all-time low and we reluctantly considered leaving the UK to manufacture elsewhere,' says Sir Anthony Bamford, JCB's chairman. 'There were plenty of applicants but they were mostly applying because their results in English, maths and science weren't adequate for higher education.'

JCB Academy anticipates the world of work in its entire operation. The academy day and year are longer than in conventional schools, with lessons from 8.30 a.m. until 4 p.m. and then sport and other extension activities until 5 p.m. and a teaching year of forty weeks plus a week of work experience for all students. This compares to 9 a.m. to 3.30 p.m., thirty-eight weeks a year, in conventional schools and academies. Taken together, over a three-year period, this provides the equivalent of a whole extra year of schooling (not including the week of work experience), or more than two years over a typical secondary education. These are startling statistics which raises the wider issue of the length of the school day and year in England's schools at large. Why do we continue with a school day and year inherited from the Victorians?

The JCB curriculum is engineering focused yet broad. In addition to engineering, all 14–16-year-olds study maths, English, science, German, ICT, citizenship, RE and PE. Sixth-form students study for advanced diplomas – equivalent to A-levels – in engineering or business.

A second UTC opened in Walsall – The Black Country UTC – in 2011, specialising in engineering and applied science, sponsored by the University of Wolverhampton and Siemens. Siemens provides work placements, specialist equipment and uniforms, and its engineers train UTC staff. Forty other, mostly local, companies are assisting, and apprentices from local companies use workshops in the UTC.

A third UTC opened in 2012 in Birmingham, also with an engineering specialism, sponsored by the University of Aston and industrial partners, including National Grid, the RAF and E.On. Every student at the Aston UTC will have a student from Aston University as mentor.

More than thirty more UTCs are in development, stimulated by the Baker Dearing Educational Trust, a technical education charity led by Kenneth Baker.

UTCs are not restricted to engineering and classic technical disciplines. They embrace the creative and media industries, major employers of British talent and huge exporters in their own right. The BRIT School in Croydon, south London, one of the original City Technology Colleges, which majors on the performing and creative arts and their technologies, is a powerhouse for the creative industries. Its alumni include Amy Winehouse, Adele, Jessie J and Leona Lewis. BRIT recruits students at the ages of fourteen and sixteen from across London and beyond, selecting on the basis of talent for the curriculum.

A second performing arts and media technology academy – the Birmingham Ormiston Academy – opened in 2012 in Birmingham and more are planned within the UTC programme. The Lowry, the theatre and gallery next to the new BBC complex at Salford Quays, is developing one for the north-west in MediaCity in partnership with Manchester universities and Sir Rod Aldridge's education trust, and a similarly innovative partnership, led by the academy sponsor David Meller, is developing a creative arts UTC next to Elstree Studios in Borehamwood, Hertfordshire.

Every region of England needs at least one BRIT School equivalent, given the importance of the creative industries to our national life and prosperity. This ought to be an explicit goal of the UTC programme.

The age range of UTCs is one of their defining and pioneering characteristics. They recruit at age fourteen and sixteen from secondary schools across a whole region, rather than at age eleven from a narrower catchment area, as with other secondary schools. Because of their technical curriculum, UTCs recruit teenagers when their aptitudes and interests are more fully formed and apparent, hence the age range.

Kenneth Baker would like to see the age of transfer from primary to secondary schools raised to fourteen nationwide over time, alongside the wider development of more specialist UTC-style academies for 14–18-year-olds. UTCs will inform the debate on the wider case for 14–18, rather than 11–18, schools. But a hundred or so UTCs – which is the medium-term prospect – do not prejudge the issue. They will have little difficulty co-existing with the generality of secondary schools recruiting at the age of eleven. Just as students often change institution at the age of sixteen for their sixth form studies, UTCs will make it possible for a smaller number to change at the age of fourteen where their talents are better served by a specialised technical academy.

TEACH FIRST AND UNIVERSITIES

Teach First should be seized upon by top universities as a battering ram to widen access.

A few statistics say why. Of the 5,323 applicants to Teach First in 2011 (770 of them successful), 2,810 were from Russell Group universities (540 successful) and 530 of them from Oxbridge (150 successful). To put this in perspective, in 2011, the total number of Oxbridge graduate applications for conventional secondary

PGCE teacher training – which provides the overwhelming majority of teacher supply – was a mere 650 out of 25,000. Teach First
almost doubled that number. Furthermore, all Teach First teachers
are placed in challenging (ie bottom third by deprivation of their
intake) schools and academies, whereas PGCE graduates are spread
across all schools and most of those with the best degrees rapidly
end up in private schools or the top end of the state sector.

As for impact, in July 2011, Ofsted awarded Teach First its highest grade of 'outstanding' in all forty-four areas evaluated across
all the regions where it is established. Describing its participants
as 'exceptional' and recruitment as 'extremely rigorous', Ofsted
particularly praised 'their personal commitment, self-motivation,
critical reflection, and their commitment to raising the aspirations
and achievements of the students in their schools and addressing
educational disadvantage ... Even in their first year of training they
are well on their way to becoming inspirational teachers, and some
already are.'

It is time for universities, particularly the selective universities, to
get behind Teach First and help expand its numbers and reach. Every
successful Teach First teacher is not only an asset to their school, but
they are also an ambassador for their university – or Oxbridge college
– and for selective universities at large, raising the grades and the
sights of their students, encouraging them to aim as high as they are
capable in their university applications, and helping them through
the daunting UCAS application and selection processes.

As Mark Smith, a Teach First alumnus who has developed
successful mentoring schemes for students aiming for top universities, puts it:

> If selective universities concentrated more on harnessing the
> growing social conscience and entrepreneurial enthusiasm of their
> largest and most important asset, their students, rather than inef-
> ficiently allocating funds to small and isolated 'widening partici-
> pation' departments, their impact on schools and access would be
> far greater. Teach First is the way to do this.

In US Ivy League universities, where Teach For America – the forerunner of Teach First – has been recruiting for twice as long as Teach First, there are two or three times more applicants as a proportion of the graduating cohorts than apply to Teach First from top universities in England. In 2011, nearly 20 per cent of Harvard's graduating cohort applied to Teach For America. At Princeton it was 16 per cent, and 10 per cent at Yale. With a will, there is no reason why Oxford, Cambridge and all England's selective universities could not be in the same league, creating a kind of elite national service in one of the greatest causes of the age: giving children in deprived communities a good education and a far better chance of getting to university – including the top universities – than today.

To get behind Teach First, universities should support and boost its recruitment activities. Using part of their extra income from higher tuition fees intended for outreach activities, they could easily set up and staff Teach First offices within their careers services, promoting Teach First to their students, organising vacation and taster courses, and creating and supporting alumni networks.

Teach First has a key role to play in transforming both the education of children in disadvantaged communities, and the outlook and character of the next generation of England's leading graduates. It is one of the most powerful engines of social mobility in modern England.

Bexley Business Academy – the first academy to open, on the *Clockwork Orange* Thamesmead estate described earlier – has a large number of Teach First teachers. 'When I arrived, I remember thinking about Christians being fed to lions and wondering how they were coping,' says Guy Nichols, the headteacher, of his Teach Firsters. He found they were mostly coping fine. But some of the children were astonished that they were there at all. Harriet Watkins, a Teach Firster who within four years had been appointed head of English, relates: 'Students say to me "What GCSEs did you get? So why are you a teacher Miss? Why are you here? You could be an entrepreneur!" I say I want to see you get A*s like I did. It doesn't matter where you come from or that you're in Thamesmead.'

If only it didn't matter. Alas, it still does, deeply. And it will continue to do so until universities start sponsoring academies and Teach First systematically.

TOWARDS AN ACADEMY SYSTEM

English education is in transition from a low-achieving comprehensive system to a high-achieving academy system. It is a revolution which cannot proceed fast enough.

R. A. Butler said of his 1944 Education Act: 'The effect as I see it will
be as much social as educational. I think it will have the effect of weld-
ing us into one nation when it's got thoroughly worked out, instead
of two nations as Disraeli talked about.' But this did not happen. It
did not even come close to happening. Instead, the second half of the
twentieth century was numerically dominated by disgracefully bad
secondary modern schools then by scarcely better comprehensives.
Disraeli's two nations remained as segregated as ever.

Now, if we get it right, the academy system could at last weld us
into one nation.

The last three chapters start to describe this academy system.
They explain why academies work, including the fundamental
importance – for schools replacing failing comprehensives – of
governance by independent trusts and organisations with a
passion for educational transformation and the means to bring
it about. They show how academies are reinventing the comprehensive school by transforming governance, mission, leadership
and teaching together. They explain how universities and private
schools have a central role to play in sponsoring academies, bridging the historic chasms between state and private education and
between the top half of the university system and the bottom half
of the state school system.

I now describe the academy system more fully: how it has
evolved so far and how I believe it needs to develop to create 'one
nation' schools nationwide.

The starting point is that every underperforming comprehensive school should be replaced by an academy.

FAILING COMPREHENSIVES, AGAIN

I keep coming back to failing comprehensives because eradicating them remains the single greatest imperative of national education policy. Academies, and their culture of aspiration, leadership and high-quality teaching and learning, are the way to do it.

My ambition from the moment academies started to prove themselves successful after 2005 was to replace the entire bottom half of the comprehensive system with academies. I didn't put it quite like that at the time, not wanting to be burned in effigy by my admirers in the Anti-Academies Alliance even more frequently, but my direction of travel wasn't much of a secret then and I state it explicitly now.

By academies, I mean here 'sponsored academies': new schools with strong, independent governing sponsors which completely replace the predecessor comprehensives. This is the surest way to bring about educational transformation untainted by the '3 Fs' of the past: failure, fatalism and fear of change.

The replacement of failing comprehensives – rather than greater autonomy for successful secondary schools – was the main objective of Labour's academies policy before 2010 not because of any objection on my part to more successful schools becoming independent state schools but because failing comprehensives were the key national priority to be tackled. They remain so, and it is vital to maintain focus. The number of sponsored academies replacing underperforming comprehensives increased by only seventy to 337 between September 2010 and March 2012, when it ought by now to be far higher.

Transforming underperforming schools, and promoting excellent new academies in areas of historic educational failure, must be the central priority of the Education Department and its ministers, whatever their wider policy for school autonomy and reform. This is a matter of fundamental duty: if the state cannot ensure a decent basic standard of education for its people, it is failing in its most basic task and the most basic service for which citizens pay taxes. Perhaps defence and policing remain equally basic, but, in the twenty-first century, an educated population is surely what they ought to be protecting.

In 2011, the Coalition raised the floor of minimum tolerable secondary school performance – in terms of the proportion of pupils in a school gaining five or more good GCSEs including English and maths – from 35 to 40 per cent, with a view to raising it to 50 per cent in 2015. Michael Gove was right to say, when doing so, that 'there is no reason, if we work together, that by the end of this parliament [in 2015] every young person in the country can't be educated in a school where at least half the students reach this basic academic standard'. He needs now to act decisively on his own rhetoric. As of 2012, nearly 650 comprehensives are below this 50 per cent level. They should all be candidates for replacement by sponsored academies.

So the best academy chains need to become larger and more numerous, and many more outstanding academy sponsors are needed.

Consider Birmingham, England's second largest city. Birmingham used to be the 'city of a thousand trades', a global manufacturing powerhouse. Now it languishes with unemployment twice the national average despite a population 100,000 lower than fifty years ago. Under the leadership of Joseph Chamberlain in the late nineteenth century, Birmingham has a fair claim to have invented modern state education, yet its skill levels are now among the lowest in the country. The city has fifteen comprehensives still not securing five or more good GCSEs including English and maths for more than half of their pupils. Birmingham boasts some of the best private and state schools in the country, yet it has a deplorably long tail of underperforming comprehensives.

Unsurprisingly, as of 2012, Birmingham has only seven sponsored academies. It needs at least to treble this number fast.

It is a similar story in most major cities outside London, where sponsored academies continue to be thin on the ground and large numbers of comprehensives are underperforming. As of summer 2012, Bradford has seventeen comprehensives below the 50 per cent GCSE mark but only five sponsored academies; Leeds has twelve comprehensives below 50 per cent but only five academies, Sheffield nine comprehensives below 50 per cent but only three academies. Hull, Leicester, Liverpool, Newcastle, Nottingham, Stoke, Wigan and Wolverhampton between them have sixty comprehensives below the 50 per cent mark, but only twenty-two sponsored academies between them. The town of Barnsley is up there too, with nine comprehensives below the 50 per cent mark but only one sponsored academy.

Yet Birmingham also demonstrates the resources available to sponsor academies. The city has three universities, four including nearby Warwick. Only one of them sponsors an academy. None of Birmingham's major companies yet sponsors an academy.

Birmingham also has one of the most powerful school organisations in the country in the historic King Edward VI Foundation, which runs most of the city's state grammar schools as well as the King Edward's private school and its girls' counterpart. A chain of King Edward VI academies, expanding out from the foundation's seven grammar and private schools, could lead the way in transforming Birmingham's secondary education. It could dramatically bridge the division between the state and private sectors, and within the state sector between grammar and comprehensive schools. These divisions – Disraeli's two nations at local level – have balkanised Birmingham education for decades. Behind them lie the segregation of Birmingham's rich and poor, skilled and unskilled, employed and unemployed, middle class and working class, which continue to undermine the city's prosperity and cohesion. This cannot be allowed to continue into the mid-twenty-first century.

City by city there is a huge task of political and educational leadership required to replace the bottom half of comprehensives. So far, city leaders have mostly neglected this task, as Birmingham demonstrates. The reason there are still only seven sponsored academies in

Birmingham – despite my agitation when Minister, continued by my successors – is because of weak leadership by Birmingham City Council. In this case, it was – until May 2012 – a Tory–Lib Dem council seriously at odds on academies with a Tory–Lib Dem government, demonstrating my earlier point that, in tackling public service failure, political party labels matter less than whether council leaders belong to the 'do something' or 'do nothing' party.

Weak political leadership in turn makes it hard to persuade potential academy sponsors in the city that they should rise to the challenge.

This is starkly true of Birmingham's King Edward VI Foundation. From the outset of academies, the Foundation has been riven by internal disagreement as to whether it should sponsor academies. It is a classic battle of social conservatives versus social reformers, the conservatives seeking to maintain an exclusive status quo – particularly in respect of the Foundation's private schools, which fear a loss of its 'charitable' resources – while the reformers rightly want to seize the opportunity of academies to create new all-ability schools across the city in the image and ethos of the King Edward schools. So twelve years after the start of academies, there is still only one King Edward VI academy in Birmingham when there should be many more.

For Birmingham read also – in their own contexts – most of the cities mentioned above, with their large numbers of underperforming comprehensives. They need not just a few more academies but an academy system mobilising the plentiful sponsorship resources of their universities, successful state and private schools, businesses, philanthropists and foundations. London boroughs which have been slower than Hackney and Southwark to embrace academies need to do the same.

FREE SCHOOL ACADEMIES

Conceptually and legally, 'free schools' – independent state schools which do not replace an existing state school or schools – are academies and an integral part of the academy system.

Free schools are not free in the sense of there being a free right to establish them. As with other academies, the bona fides of prospective sponsors, and likely parental demand, are assessed case by case by the Education Department in deciding whether they merit state funding. And successful promoters manage their schools through a formal academy governance structure. Their funding, their freedoms, their obligations to all-ability admissions, and their accountability, including inspection by Ofsted and the publication of results, are the same as for other academies.

Free schools aren't cuckoos in the academy nest. They play a valuable role in meeting parental demand for good new schools and extra school places within the academy system, promoting innovation, diversity and choice in their approaches to teaching and learning. The academies I helped establish included more than twenty such free schools, although they were not then called such. Mossbourne Academy was one of the first. It was set up for the same reason as most free schools: to meet parental demand for good school places in a locality short of them.

The early rhetoric of free schools claimed that they would be 'parent led'. In reality, very few parents want to take on the job of setting up a new school and governing it. What virtually all parents want is a good school run by professionals in whom they have confidence. Inevitably, therefore, only a handful of free schools are being set up by parent groups. But parent groups can be highly effective sponsors, as is proving the case with the West London Free School established by Toby Young and fellow parents in Hammersmith. Several of the parents are also teachers. The West London Free School, together with the new Hammersmith Academy, a 'free school' academy established under Labour and sponsored by the Mercers livery company (sponsor of Thomas Telford School), are community academies helping to redress the large outflow of Hammersmith children to private schools and to state schools outside the borough. It is bizarre that the West London Free School has been criticised for teaching Latin. Why should children have to go to private schools, like next-door Latymer Upper School with its fees of £15,000 a year, to learn Latin?

Most free schools are being established by educational enterprises, including existing academy sponsors. Some free schools are existing private schools which have moved into the state-funded sector and ceased charging fees, as was the case with a number of Labour's academies. More than half of Labour's 'free school' academies were in London, where the shortage of good-quality school places was acute. Nearly half of the coalition government's first twenty-four free schools – which opened in September 2011 – are located in the capital for the same reason.

Many free schools are located in areas of very high deprivation with a relentless focus on overcoming disadvantage, like most of Labour's academies. Peter Hyman's School21 ('for success in the twenty-first century') in Newham, Ed Vainker's Reach Academy in Feltham, and the Greenwich Free School are all pioneered by individuals and teams passionate in their social mission. Tellingly, Ed Vainker and some of the Greenwich Free School team are Teach First alumni, while Peter Hyman is an alumni of Future Leaders, an impressive charity with a mission 'to develop the next generation of leaders for challenging schools', which talent spots the most able up-and-coming teachers in these schools and prepares them intensively for headship within four years.

Peter Hyman wants his free school to break away from 'the tired old model of one teacher and thirty children sitting in rows waiting for the next pearl of wisdom'. He explains his vision thus:

> We can't go on educating children for the middle of the twentieth century. We've got to prepare them properly for the twenty-first century and a world that requires high-quality communication skills, creativity, flexibility, resilience and collaboration. It is why we put English Language at the heart of everything we do, ensuring all children leave our school avid readers, fluent writers and confident speakers.

It is why we need to match the learning environment to what we want students to learn – small mastery classes to acquire the basics, project-based learning rooms to develop high-quality science, technology and maths teaching, Harkness tables [large oval conference-room tables] for twelve students to develop high-level thinking and debating skills, new technology to enhance learning and put power in the hands of students. In the last decade, through developments in neuroscience, psychology and studies of pedagogy, we know more than ever before about how children learn and what motivates them. It is time to develop a school system that makes this a reality.

Equally innovative is Durand Academy, an outstanding primary school in a highly deprived part of Lambeth in south London, which as a free school academy is extending its age range to eighteen and – wait for it – building a boarding school in west Sussex to which its pupils above the age of thirteen will proceed. More than nine in ten of its current eleven-year-olds are signed up to become the first boarders in 2014. They will leave for Sussex every Sunday evening and return on Friday afternoon, taking advantage of the longer school day and wider range of activities made possible in a boarding school. There will be no charge to parents, the boarding being paid entirely by the academy's trust, which generates a huge annual income through charitable endeavour and the profits of a leisure club developed by the school's remarkable headteacher Greg Martin.[†]

---

† Greg Martin has been headteacher of Durand Academy for 24 years. Durand is one of the most impressive primary schools I have visited, on a par with Thomas Telford School and Mossbourne Academy in its ethos, standards and innovation. My experience of the school is the same as that of *Times* journalist Helen Rumbelow who recounts her visit thus:

As Martin starts his tour, I notice that he repeats a single word nearly every other breath: 'structure'.
'Structure and routine,' he says, as he gestures at a class of

Such innovation is a prime purpose of free school academies, and has been since the launch of the academies programme in 2000. Many of the early academies are boldly innovative:

- Thirty academies educate nursery, primary- and secondary-age pupils from the age of three to eighteen. Before academies, there were virtually no such 'all-through' state schools. Indeed, state schools at large were banned from extending into different age ranges – another case of stifling over-regulation – despite evidence that a break of school at age eleven can harm a child's education. The early experience of these all-through academies is broadly positive. Several free schools, like Peter Hyman's and Toby Young's, are

---

immaculately uniformed children lining up for class, 'routine, structure, routine, structure,' he chants as we witness room after room of kids, heads bowed intently as they write in neatly drilled cursive. 'You say structure a lot,' I say.

'I do. A big problem in a child's life is uncertainty. What makes people feel secure is structure. That's what parents want. Those people shouting "don't put them in a sausage factory" are the very ones who can pay for their children to have structure at home. They make them do ballet, they have to do the violin whether they like it or not. And then they go private at secondary because they do want a sausage factory really.'

Now I've visited other urban academies where discipline has driven up results. It's not what's radical about Durand. Once Martin got the structure right in the classroom, he started work on the physical structure. He sold off playgrounds.

'We still have playgrounds. But yeah, I built flats on some of them. And a swimming pool. And a floodlit pitch.'

This is how he has built his dream. To be a developer of minds he has become a developer of property. He started, on school land, a thriving accommodation business and a swanky gym that is shared between students and the fee-paying public. This is what has paid for two beautiful swimming pools (all children from age four upwards get an hour's instruction a week); the loveliest, most well-appointed classrooms; and extra teachers to halve class sizes in lower streams.'

all-through, and many secondary-age academies are seeking either to integrate, or federate, with one or more of their feeder primary schools. They view this as a way of inculcating high standards and expectations in children and their families from the early years.

- Conversely, the JCB Academy, an entirely new school in Staffordshire, is only for 14–19-year-olds. Providing an engineering-focused curriculum for pupils who by the mid-secondary years want to follow this route, it is the prototype for the University Technical Colleges described in Chapter 9, whose mission is to transform the teaching of technical disciplines and skills in the state system.

- The Birmingham Ormiston Academy offers a performing arts and digital skills curriculum for 14–19-year-olds, modelled on the hugely successful BRIT School in Croydon, south London, also described in Chapter 9. Bristol Cathedral School, the first cathedral choir school to join the state system as an academy, maintains its choirs and choral excellence within a secondary school which also offers a non-specialist curriculum. These academies build on the outstanding work of 'pre-academy academies' such as the Yehudi Menuhin School, the Royal Ballet School, the Purcell School and Chetham's School of Music in Manchester, all of which are privately managed charities which take state-funded students and give them the best education in music and dance in the world. England, one of the most creative nations on earth, needs many more such academies.

- The Steiner Academy in Hereford, the first state-funded Steiner school in the UK, is an all-through academy for 3–16-year-olds following the internationally recognised Steiner Waldorf approach to teaching, with its emphasis on the practical and the artistic in learning.

- Boarding houses have opened at three academies: Wellington Academy in Wiltshire, Priory Academy in Lincoln and Harefield Academy in Hillingdon. These are partly to meet general parental demand for boarding and partly for children with vulnerable home lives who are suited to boarding, including children in care. Wellington and Priory Academies partly serve military bases and their boarding is partly geared to the needs of military parents who, unless they are officers whose private boarding school fees are paid by the Ministry of Defence, have long been short-changed by the education system.

- 'Studio schools' are small secondary academies of no more than 300 pupils. Barnfield Studio School in Luton, one of the first, opened in 2010 with a mission to promote practical skills and good qualifications among teenagers who could easily fail in a classic secondary school. It is pioneering what it calls 'a hands-on approach to skills' with project work and part of the week spent supervised in local businesses. Its sponsor, Barnfield Further Education College and its entrepreneurial principal Pete Birkett, already sponsor two academies in Luton which replaced failing comprehensives. Barnfield also intends to open its Studio School at the weekends and evenings. The Studio Schools Trust, a joint venture between Edge, the technical education charity, and the Young Foundation, a social enterprise charity, has pioneered the studio schools programme within the academy movement. Six studio schools are open and many more are planned.

- Five long-established successful private schools – including Bristol Cathedral School – joined the state system in the first wave of academies. This has become a template for successful private schools to become academies, becoming state-funded and abolishing fees without compromising their independent governance and character or their high standards, as described in Chapter 8.

Innovation and diversity have thus been at the heart of the academy system since its inception. Post-2010 free school academies build on these foundations, and combine many of these innovative strands, in immensely exciting ways. They are full of promise for the flowering of a genuinely comprehensive state education system, able to meet the needs of children in all their diversity.

Crucially, Michael Gove has not used free schools to create more grammar schools open only to children of high academic ability, as many in his party wanted. It is a testament to the success of the academy system that good state schools, even on the Right, are no longer synonymous with grammar schools.

Free schools, like other academies, are autonomous in their management. But there is no free right to taxpayer funding. In practice, the government gives clear indications as to the varieties of innovation it wants to encourage, and it makes choices about projects to fund and encourage on behalf of the public. A key part of the academy system is therefore an innovative mindset on the part of ministers, and among local authority leaders in each locality.

Promoting innovation was central to my work on academies. I actively solicited and helped to craft the all-through academies, studio schools, boarding academies, specialist academies and private school academies just described. I was struck by how little local authorities engaged in such innovation, despite their commissioning and funding powers. Their bureaucratic and producer-interest mindset tended to stifle innovation rather than encourage it, and this mentality is changing far too slowly.

So what varieties of innovation ought now to be encouraged by free school academies? As well as more academies of the kind just described, there are five innovative types of school I would especially encourage in the immediate future.

First, we need academies which provide far better for the 6,500 children a year who are permanently excluded from mainstream schools and academies. Many of these are sent to local authority 'pupil referral units' (PRUs), which are patchy at best. Far too many teenagers go straight from PRUs to the dole and the criminal justice system. There are plenty of voluntary organisations like Barnardo's with expertise and passion to make a difference in this area. They should be encouraged systematically to replace PRUs with something much better. Meadows School in Tunbridge Wells is a model: a successful state-funded school for seriously disaffected children run by Barnardo's like an academy, including boarding provision and highly trained youth workers who work one-on-one with the students. 'I would probably be locked up by now if I hadn't come here,' one of its teenagers told an Ofsted inspector who rated the school as outstanding in 2011.

Second, we need more academics promoting excellence in maths and science, subjects where England is especially weak in comparison to the best education systems overseas, particularly in Asia. The Coalition is encouraging some sixth form free schools, in effect new sixth form colleges, with a maths specialism. The London Academy of Excellence in Newham, the first free school sixth form college, sponsored by leading private schools, recruits sixteen-year-olds who have got five or more GCSE grades at B and above including in maths and English, preparing them for top universities. Free schools on this model could make a positive contribution, but equally valuable would be all-ability academies with a curriculum specialising rigorously in maths and science from a much earlier age.

In this context, it was a serious mistake of the Coalition to abolish the specialist school programme under which, for the previous twenty years, comprehensive schools and academies had been encouraged to develop centres of curriculum excellence. The specialist school policy was successful: it should have been intensified not abandoned, and maths and science ought to have been particularly encouraged as specialisms. The specialist school programme should be revived immediately as a key part of the academy system, for all secondary schools and academies. It should be extended to primary schools too, encouraging individual primary schools to develop special strengths in curriculum areas from maths and science to modern languages and sport.

Third, I would encourage the setting up of bilingual academies to provide centres of excellence in teaching the language and culture of our principal trading partners. There are hardly any bilingual schools in England's state system. Wix primary school in Battersea (bilingual French–English) and Hockerill Anglo-European College in Bishop's Stortford (offering bilingual classes in French and German) are among the few. There are no bilingual

English–Chinese state schools. I would make it a particular priority to establish a few English–Chinese bilingual academies. A deep understanding of China, and a capacity to interact with the Chinese in their own language, are critical priorities as economic power shifts East. Chinese 'immersion schools' are part of the charter school movement in the United States, including Yinghua Academy in Minneapolis and Princeton International Academy Charter School in South Brunswick, New Jersey. They have a role to play in England too. As Martin Jacques puts it in his arresting book on the rise of China: 'As China grows increasingly powerful – while remaining determinedly different – the West will be forced, however reluctantly, to confront the nature and meaning of that difference. Understanding China will be one of the great challenges of the twenty-first century.'

The pre-2010 specialist school programme led several hundred comprehensive schools and academies to develop a particular strength in the teaching of modern languages. This could and should be revived, including the development of bilingual streams in mainstream academies reviving or taking on a languages specialism.

I would also – fourthly – promote more academies to foster outstanding excellence in sport. While a number of state-funded schools and academies provide for the most talented children in music and the performing arts, as described above, there are few – beyond football youth academies – similarly focused on sport, which is equally important to our national life and culture. Where are the tennis academies, the cricket academies, the swimming academies, the athletics academies, the gymnastics academies? Organisations such as the Lawn Tennis Association and the MCC should be encouraged to sponsor highly specialised academies, either singly or in combination, to supplement their pretty fitful and unsuccessful 'outreach' activities in state schools at present.

England has nothing to match the Singapore Sports School, opened in 2004 and including two Olympic-size swimming pools, let alone, taking just tennis, the Sanchez-Casal Tennis Academy in Barcelona or the Weil Tennis Academy in California.

Mark Weil, director of the Weil Academy, describes his mission thus on the front page of his website:

> Growing up as a young tennis player, I was inspired by a well known professional football coach of the time, Vince Lombardi. Coach Lombardi told his players on their first day of training: 'Gentleman, we are going to relentlessly chase perfection, knowing full well we will not catch it, because nothing is perfect. But we are going to relentlessly chase it because in the process of chasing perfection, we will catch Excellence!'
>
> Here at Weil, we expect our players to catch excellence every day. It is ... what makes our program and our environment so special for our young players – your extraordinary children. Our players spend the time laying a stronger foundation to their games and learning to use better tactics and techniques. Then we challenge them to compete at their highest level every week. We witness an incredible transformation with 100 per cent of our players. Come train at Weil and make all your biggest dreams come true!

This is as inspirational a vision for education as any I have come across.

Fifth, we need academies with far stronger international links, not just in language teaching but also in the recruitment of secondary-age students from abroad to study at them. Incredibly, it is still the case in 2012 that state schools and academies are banned by law from recruiting overseas students. This is the kind of outdated thinking which academies exist to overcome. It is as outdated as the rigid state regulation of overseas student numbers and fees which applied to England's universities until they were liberated in the 1980s. Academies, including the new bilingual academies suggested earlier, should be encouraged to become genuinely international in their recruitment.

This is a huge agenda of innovation for the academy system over the next decade.

CONVERTER ACADEMIES

In June 2011, Holland Park School, the iconic 1960s comprehensive in the London borough of Kensington and Chelsea, voted to convert to an academy. It was a defining moment in the evolution of an academy system which will fairly soon embrace most state secondary schools.

'We believe in the spirit of comprehensive education and becoming an academy will not alter that in any way,' says Colin Hall, the school's headteacher for the past ten years, who has overseen a transformation of standards at the school. 'The reality is that academy status is looking like a successful platform; it's a template for how schools might be,' he adds. As for the school's past: 'I'm a pragmatist. Times change, contexts change, and we are not living in the 1970s any more.'

Bethnal Green Academy, a converter academy on the other side of London, has followed a similar path. The school's results have shot up from 27 per cent to 79 per cent in just four years, on the five GCSEs including English and maths yardstick. But Mark Keary, the headteacher, aims far higher and is an enthusiast for academies. 'It provides local accountability to challenge the cycle of educational underperformance,' he says, and he counters local authority objections that he is going his own way by stressing that 'the one-size-fits-all approach was never there in the first place'.

According to an interviewer, 'Keary talks of every child learning two languages and of opening an overseas branch, before admitting with a chuckle, that this is blue-sky thinking.' It would be a pity for such great ambitions to be consigned to the blue sky. They are exhilarating and precisely the international vision which academy leaders ought to have for their students and their communities, here and now. Nowhere needs it more than Bethnal Green.

Holland Park and Bethnal Green Academies aspire to achieve far more for their socially diverse communities, and their headteachers and governors view academy status as the way forward. Why? Because they want to take full responsibility for their governance and leadership, without education bureaucracies second guessing them and limiting their capacity to develop a distinctive ethos and character.

If all a successful school needed to do was to stand still, academies would not be relevant. But for today's school leaders, standing still is not only – as for the cyclist on a busy road – unwise, it is potentially fatal. With youth unemployment at a million and international competition for skilled jobs ferocious, continuous improvement is essential. Virtually all 'successful' state schools in England have a distance to go to become even among the best in class nationally, let alone world class. In the next chapter, I set out a vision for England as an education nation, including a basic standard of at least nine in ten sixteen-year-olds achieving five or more good GCSE passes including English and maths, a standard now achieved by less than six in ten. It is no good headteachers and governors saying that twenty years ago the average was three in ten and they have done well to nearly double it. They have indeed done well, but being world class, and building an open and prosperous society, requires far more. Out of more than 3,000 non-selective state schools nationwide, only twenty-eight currently achieve the basic GCSE standard for nine in ten of their students. Only 151 do so for eight in ten. Holland Park and Bethnal Green are approaching eight in ten, so they too have further to go, while they also reach for the blue sky.

Successful school leaders and governors are restlessly ambitious for change and improvement. But they need the tools for the job. This means not only the freedom, but also the unambiguous responsibility to seize their destiny. Hence academies.

What of local authorities? Some councils help their more successful schools to become better and leverage their success; some are a hindrance. Some provide cost-effective support services; others don't. Some promote positive collaboration; all too many, alas, promote the lowest common denominator. In none of these respects – school improvement, support services and collaboration – does academy status write local authorities out of the script. Rather, it enables schools to forge co-operative rather than dependent relationships with their councils. And local councils continue to have a role in regard to academies, championing the interests of parents, ensuring sufficient school places, and organising provision for children outside of mainstream education. They also play a key role in commissioning new academies and free schools.

The very fact that councils are no longer the managing agent, as in the old local authority comprehensive system, frees them to speak up for parents uninhibited. They are no longer the 'producer interest', defensively stifling criticism. I have seen this first hand in my neighbourhood in Islington. It took years to persuade the council to agree to the replacement of Islington Green, one of the borough's worst failing comprehensives, with an academy. Now the academy is established, the leader of Islington council is rightly dissatisfied at its slow pace of improvement and has said so loudly in the local media and to the sponsor. Rapid action is being taken.

The academy system puts successful schools and independent sponsors, rather than education bureaucracies, at the heart of leadership and decision-making.

Consider two issues of burning importance to many successful secondary schools: their right to expand, and their right to open sixth forms. Many schools are held back by historic patterns of local school organisation, in the case of post-16 provision often dating back to the 1970s and 1980s when staying-on rates beyond the minimum school leaving age were pitifully low. As part of comprehensivisation, even the minority of secondary schools with sixth forms often had them removed in order to create sixth form or further education colleges drawing from large numbers of comprehensives. Some of these colleges are successful, some less so. Either way, the number of post-GCSE students staying on in full-time education has increased significantly in recent years, providing more than enough students for successful schools as well as colleges, and for them to collaborate and compete in offering the best courses. Yet local authorities and state regulatory agencies consistently stand in the way of schools wishing to open sixth forms. Nearly half of comprehensives still do not have sixth forms.

I spent months personally intervening, when Minister, to enable Arden School, a highly successful comprehensive in Solihull, to open a sixth form, with passionate support from students and parents but against the opposition of Solihull Sixth Form College, the local authority and the Education Department's own post-16 funding quango. The sixth form finally opened in 2006. Five years later, Arden has an annual sixth form intake of 180 students. Virtually all its sixth-formers go on to university, and it is one of those twenty-eight all-ability schools nationwide to have got more than nine in ten of its pupils above the five GCSE level including English and maths. Unsurprisingly, Arden was the first comprehensive in the West Midlands to convert to an academy in 2010. Had it been an academy five years earlier, it would have been better placed to secure its sixth form without a protracted struggle.

Tellingly, the first step Bethnal Green Academy is taking as an academy is to establish a sixth form. Mark Keary expects to be educating 180 sixth-formers within two years. His plan is to provide intensive additional support in English language skills to make up for the fact that most of the academy's East End students have English as a second language. 'There won't be free periods or casual dress,' he says. 'It will be full-time and professional, which is what the students want.'

Converter academies should have an absolute right to expand and to open sixth forms – areas still hedged around with bureaucracy – provided they possess or can supply the necessary accommodation. This will liberate them to serve their communities better. Academies are about independence for a purpose. There is no higher purpose than meeting parental demand for good school places and promoting better post-GCSE education – both A-levels and technical courses – for the coming generation of 16–18-year-olds, in the face of mass youth unemployment and underemployment.

Academy status also gives schools an opportunity to reconstitute their governing bodies. For a start, where necessary they can make them smaller and more professional, as described in Chapter 7. It is also open to converter academies to partner with academy chains and other sponsoring organisations, not necessarily to take over the governance as in a sponsored academy but to enrich the school's networks and improve its support systems. A quarter of converter academies have joined chains for this reason.

Innovation, better governance, and ambition for improvement are compelling reasons for successful schools to convert to academy status. The worst reason, however, is simply to pocket the £25,000 the government gives to converter academies. Converting to academy status, but with nothing changing to improve the school or enlarge its mission, is simply a gimmick.

ACADEMIES SPONSORING ACADEMIES

Converter academies are expected to assist an underperforming school or schools. In my experience, 'advice and assistance' arrangements generally amount to little unless there is hard leadership and governance involved. The most successful converter academies should become academy sponsors in their own right.

The City Technology Colleges are trailblazers in this regard. Ten of the sponsors of the CTCs – and there were only fifteen in total – are now sponsors of academies also. Often the headteacher of the 'parent' CTC has, in effect if not in name, become chief executive of the emerging academy chain. Between them, these ten CTCs are sponsoring more than thirty new academies, virtually all of them a by-word for quality. The Harris, Thomas Telford and Haberdashers academy chains – under the continuing or initial leadership of Dr Dan Moynihan, Sir Kevin Satchwell and Dr Liz Sidwell respectively – have already been mentioned. Impressive academy chains have also grown out of John Cabot CTC in Bristol, under the leadership of its headteacher David Carter, and out of Brooke Weston CTC in Corby, under its headteacher Sir Peter Simpson.

To expand this model, in the early days of the academy programme I encouraged a number of successful comprehensives with outstanding headteachers to convert to become academies in order to sponsor new academies within a single governing trust. Garforth Academy in East Leeds and Outwood Grange Academy near Wakefield are trailblazers under the inspirational leadership of Sir Paul Edwards and Michael Wilkins respectively. Garforth's 'School Partnership Trust', led by Sir Paul, now sponsors three secondary-age academies which replaced seriously underperforming schools, one in highly deprived South Leeds and two in equally challenging communities in Doncaster, plus a primary-age academy in Leeds. A large number of converter academies are also joining the trust. Outwood Academies, the trust growing out of Outwood Grange, now sponsors five academies.

Still more ambitious is the Academies Enterprise Trust (AET), founded and led by David Triggs, the extraordinarily entrepreneurial headteacher of Greensward Academy in Hockley, Essex. AET now sponsors eighteen academies, both primary and secondary age, from nearby Clacton and Ashingdon in Essex to Ryde in Kent and Richmond in London.

If this is what three outstanding former comprehensive schools have already done as academies, the potential is immense for educational transformation led by the best of the thousand or more converter academies. Historically, virtually no attempt was made to 'clone' or leverage successful state schools to provide new or replacement schools. This was left to local council bureaucracies, which by and large did it badly because they lacked expertise, commitment and passion. Now, in the academy system, the most successful schools have the opportunity and responsibility to lead school reform. Academies, private schools, sixth form colleges: all have a part to play. Their governors, management teams, teachers, ethos, support services and curriculum programmes are hugely valuable resources which ought to be deployed for wider benefit.

What of 'middling' schools? I support the decision by Sir Michael Wilshaw, the Chief Inspector of Schools, to eliminate 'satisfactory' as an inspection grade so that all schools which are not rated excellent or good are designated as 'requiring improvement', where they are not failing. By this token, all failing comprehensives, and those without a credible improvement plan, should in principle be candidates for replacement by sponsored academies.

Basically, schools – like all organisations – are either succeeding or failing, in that they are clearly (or relatively) on the way up or the way down. Where they are on the way down, they should become academies under the governance of other schools or organisations with the capacity and mission to inspire them anew.

GRAMMAR SCHOOLS

Just as decades of isolation in respect of private schools, vis-a-vis the state schools, did deep damage to the education system and society at large, so have decades of isolation in respect of the 164 state grammar schools, which are a powerful and underexploited national resource.

With much of the Left trying but failing to abolish them, and much of the Right trying but failing to replicate them, the state grammar schools which survived comprehensivisation have mostly spent the last thirty years churning out great results for their students but keeping their heads down for fear of provoking attack.

However, if history explains the isolation and timidity of the grammar schools, it should not be allowed to perpetuate it. By converting to become academies, grammar schools have the opportunity to sponsor all-ability academies to replace secondary modern schools in their localities, leveraging their ethos of excellence and outstanding teaching. In Kent, across the Medway towns and the declining coastal towns, grammar schools exist in some of England's poorest and most socially divided communities. Grammar school-led academies could bring about fundamental improvement. Given the strength of their A-level provision, they could start by pioneering joint sixth forms offering both academic and technical courses across selective and non-selective schools in their areas. Most secondary modern schools still have no sixth forms. Grammar schools could lead the way in transforming post-16 education in their localities.

A few grammar schools have taken a lead. Skinners', the City livery company which sponsors one of the most prestigious grammar schools in Tunbridge Wells, now also sponsors Skinners' Kent Academy, which in 2008 replaced a neighbouring secondary modern school. The academy has a sixth form and a strong partnership with Skinners' Grammar School, including a group of Skinners' students who spend their gap year between A-levels and university as teaching assistants at the academy. The old secondary modern ethos has been entirely eradicated. In the three years since its opening, the academy's GCSE scores have doubled and are now above the national average. Invicta Grammar School in Maidstone, which became an academy in 2006 in order to federate with neighbouring Valley Park secondary modern, has brought about a similar transformation. Both schools are now governed by the Valley Invicta Trust, with a single chief executive.

Other grammar schools nationwide should follow suit.

WHAT HAPPENS WHEN ACADEMIES FAIL?

Academies do not always succeed. There needs to be an effective process for dealing with failure.

Proposals for local or regional 'educational commissioners' are being bandied about in pursuit of a supposed need to fill a 'middle tier' between Whitehall and academies. This is a solution in search of a problem.

Local authorities are alive and well in respect of many of the functions which would be performed by any new 'middle tier'. They remain responsible for ensuring there are sufficient school places in each locality, for special educational needs, for excluded children and other children out of school, and for school transport, among other system-wide services. Local authorities are also, vitally, a commissioner of new schools, including free schools, alongside the Education Department. This commissioning role flows not only from their education powers: as public landowners they are crucial in facilitating the establishment of new schools, whose biggest set-up challenge is often finding suitable land and premises. Furthermore, most primary schools are unlikely to go down the academy route any time soon, so, even if most secondary schools become academies, local authorities will continue to play a direct supervisory role over a large proportion of schools in each locality.

It is essential that local authorities embrace these important continuing roles positively, rather than behaving as if they are on the way out. For there is no gain in replacing them with new quangos which would comprise largely the same local education officials wearing new hats, let alone in setting up new bureaucracies alongside them.

School inspection is another vital 'middle tier' function, undertaken by the school inspectorate Ofsted. Ofsted is fully competent to identify school failure and there is no need for a new bureaucracy to be doing this either.

There is, however, one important missing link in the developing academy system: namely, what should happen when Ofsted identifies an academy as failing? At present, no one has the job of 'managing' failing academies, and it is undesirable that this role should be taken on by the Department for Education, either in its bureaucratic or its political guise.

To supply this missing link, I suggest a simple reform. Where a 'sponsored' academy is found to be failing, Ofsted should conduct an audit of the academy's governance to answer one critical question: are the sponsors and their governors up to the job of improving the academy radically? Where they are, they should be given appropriate time to set improvement in train before re-inspection. Where they are not, Ofsted should replace the sponsor (using the Secretary of State's existing powers in this regard), conducting an open competition for a successor sponsor and brokering the transfer of sponsorship. In the case of a failing 'converter' academy, the competition should be for a sponsor to replace the existing governing body, turning the converter academy into a sponsored academy. In both cases, the choice of new sponsor ought to be made in collaboration with the relevant local authority so that a judgement on the purely educational bona fides of potential sponsors is tempered by local democratic judgements on, for example, the desirability or not of particular faith or business sponsors.

PRIMARY SCHOOLS

Many primary schools, successful and unsuccessful, are becoming academies, some on their own, some in federations with other primary schools and/or with secondary-age academies. Many free schools are primary or all-through and I would also expect soon to see the rise of chains like the existing chains of secondary-age academies.

The typical secondary school has about 1,000 pupils and an annual budget of £6 million, whereas the typical primary school has about 400 pupils with an annual budget of £2.3 million. In itself, size is a determinant neither of the suitability nor the likely success of an academy, but it is undoubtedly the case that many primary headteachers and governing bodies find management more daunting than their secondary counterparts, and they are more reliant on their local authorities. Academy status is therefore likely to spread more slowly across the primary than the secondary sector.

However, many of the arguments for academies apply equally to primary as to secondary schools. A minority are seriously underperforming. In 2011, 1,310 primary schools were failing to achieve basic literacy and numeracy standards for more than four in ten of their eleven-year-olds, as well as being below average in the academic progress made by their children between the ages of five and eleven. Unless these schools are rapidly improving, they should be replaced by sponsored academies. Meanwhile, successful primary schools need to become steadily more so and play a wider leadership role, which they can do by becoming academies – including by taking responsibility, as sponsors, for struggling primary schools. By raising the scale of ambition and capacity, academies can bring new entrepreneurial zeal to primary education: in overcoming disadvantage, in building community missions, in the teaching of literacy and numeracy, and in the systematic introduction of the subject-specialist teaching which is so sorely lacking in most state primary schools, although it is general practice in private prep schools.

The lack of specialist teaching in primary schools flows from the outdated model of the generalist primary school teacher, without a subject honours degree, which is ripe for challenge by academy pioneers. It also needs to be changed by means of national reform to teacher recruitment and training, as suggested in the next chapter.

CHAIN REACTIONS

Academy chains are one of the most innovative aspects of the academy system, vital to its future. The secret of their growth and success is simple. In Aristotle's words: 'We are what we repeatedly do. Excellence, therefore, is not an act but a habit.'

As of March 2012, there are nearly fifty organisations or individuals sponsoring more than one academy. All these are 'chains' or 'federations' but they come in very different shapes and sizes. Most of them are small, embracing no more than a handful of schools, typically in a single locality or region. There are only seven sponsors of more than ten academies and the largest of them, ULT, sponsors only twenty-one. However, in addition to sponsored academies, 'converter' academies are joining chains, in effect creating a two-tier membership with sponsored academies being directly governed by chains while converter academies join as (in effect) associate members without the hard governance dimension. About a quarter of the first 1,775 schools converting to academy status have joined, or founded, chains in this way and, as of March 2012, one in ten of all secondary schools is sponsored by, or belongs to, a chain.

The growth in chains and schools joining chains looks set to be driven mostly by a steady increase in the number of chains, and by smaller chains becoming medium-sized, not by the larger chains becoming huge.

The largest chains do not conform to a single model. ULT, E-ACT. Oasis and the Ormiston Trust are national in their coverage. AET is a national chain but with a strong focus on Essex growing out of its founding academy, Greensward. ARK is largely London-based but is building a second academy hub in Birmingham. Successful regional chains include the Harris Federation in (mainly south) London, Thomas Telford in the West Midlands, the Cabot federation in and around Bristol, and the Outwood Grange and Garforth 'School Partnership Trust' Academies in Yorkshire.

Some chains are faith-related, like Oasis Education (fourteen academies, growing out of a Christian education charity serving disadvantaged children). The largest single sponsor of academies is the Church of England, with forty academies, although these are sponsored by individual dioceses and, beyond the C of E label, do not constitute a meaningful chain, which also explains their highly variable quality.

The University Technical Colleges described in Chapter 9 are becoming a 'curriculum' academy chain. Although each UTC has different lead sponsors, drawn from higher education and businesses, they share a common focus on technical education, together with a common 14–19 age range, a common sponsorship model and a common partnership with the Baker Dearing Educational Trust, the technical education charity promoting the UTCs.

Chains spanning the private and state sectors, described in Chapter 8, are also integral to the academy movement.

Some chains also have a particular view of school organisation, such as Harris with its 'houses', breaking down academies into smaller vertical units providing pastoral support and as a basis for competitive sport and other activities. Chains often have common policies, procedures and curriculum approaches. The best chains grow their own leaders and deploy them across their academies. Thomas Telford has exported eight headteachers in the last ten years, including to its new academies, while nine of the Harris Federation's headteachers are home grown.

The sponsor-managers of the larger chains invariably possess substantial school management or other business experience. Mostly, they are outstanding ex-headteachers, but not invariably so. Lucy Heller, managing director of ARK, is a former media company director, while Steve Chalke, founder and director of Oasis, one of the largest chains, is a charismatic and entrepreneurial Baptist minister-cum-community organiser.

How large could or should chains become?

I would not set arbitrary limits to their growth for so long as standards remain high and an individual chain is not becoming unduly dominant within a particular conurbation or large area, which is not yet the case anywhere. Quality, parental demand and diversity should be the guiding lights in the growth of chains.

What of the relationship between chains and their individual academies? Only rarely has this become problematic, since most 'sponsored' academies are bound to their sponsor by foundation, while 'converter' academies which have joined chains can leave them pretty well at will since there is rarely an integral governance dimension.

However, chain–academy relations could – and in some cases already have – become unsustainable in one or both of two circumstances. First, when schools are transferred between sponsors. The controversial transfer, at the behest of the sponsors alone, of the Emmanuel Schools Foundation (ESF) and its four academies from Sir Peter Vardy's sponsorship to that of the ULT in 2010 was resented by the highly successful ESF schools, which are now seeking to break away, with the agreement of ULT.

The second scenario is where there is discontent about the services and/or leadership being provided by the parent chain. The charges levied by some of the larger chains are likely to become a factor here. The larger chains typically top-slice between 4 and 6 per cent of the budgets of their constituent schools in order to provide central services. One academy chain has (in 2012) a central budget of £4 million and forty staff. The quality of central services and support needs to be very high to justify such charges or they will soon become a source of contention, in the same way that local authority top-slicing of budgets has been in the past.

The solution is simple. Successful academies – that is, those rated as outstanding by Ofsted – should have a straightforward right to leave a chain, and either to become a free-standing academy subject to its own governance or to join another. It would be quite wrong for academy chains to become resented local education authorities in new guise.

‡

The growing number, range and size of academy sponsors is injecting dynamic energy into the education system and systematically enlarging the network of social enterprises committed to the success of state education. This will intensify as academy sponsors become steadily more numerous and powerful, beyond the 150 already engaged.

As the dozens of universities and state and private schools sponsoring academies become hundreds doing so; as the few dozen major businesses sponsoring academies and University Technical Colleges become hundreds doing so; as the dozens of free school academies pioneering innovation and combating disadvantage become hundreds doing so; and as the seven larger chains of academies sponsoring more than ten academies apiece become dozens of chains embracing dozens of academies each, the academy system will broaden and deepen as a movement for educational transformation nationwide. This cannot happen too soon.

EDUCATION, EDUCATION, EDUCATION

ruth, Knowledge, Vision. Three words, emblazoned over the entrance to the American Museum of Natural History facing Central Park in New York, conveying the purpose of education as surely as the injunction of President Theodore Roosevelt, one of the museum's patrons, which adorns its rotunda: 'Character, in the long run, is the decisive factor in the life of an individual and of nations alike.'

When I visited the museum, the facade, undergoing restoration, was masked by hoardings advertising two exhibitions: 'The World's Largest Dinosaurs' and 'Journey to the Stars', narrated by Whoopi Goldberg.

Truth, knowledge, vision, character, deep curiosity about the cosmos, the story of evolution and the human race. All of these have been woven into the fabric of liberal and humane education for more than a century since education took its rightful place alongside liberty and democracy as the bedrock of civilised society. Together with inculcating skills for life – literacy, numeracy, technical and social skills – they are the mission of modern schools. What changes is not their relevance or salience but how they are imparted and made of deep and lasting value to the largest number of young people.

The 'fierce urgency of now' – Martin Luther King's injunction to make a difference while we can and refuse to be imprisoned by the past – is to expand education. To expand, dramatically, the number of young people being well educated. To expand the content and means of education to make it more urgent, more exciting, more empowering, more character building. And to expand education to encompass the full limits of individual potential.

To achieve this, England needs world-class schools in every community nationwide. The reform challenge ahead is summed up in three number sets:

- **60 to 90.** The imperative to increase radically the proportion of school leavers reaching a basic modern education standard to at least 90 per cent, from 60 per cent today.
- **90+.** The imperative to expand the scope and impact of education far beyond exam-based school qualifications.
- **50:50.** The imperative, beyond the age of eighteen, to increase the proportion of young people gaining higher-level academic and technical qualifications to at least half, and to provide good-quality apprenticeships and training to those going straight into work.

60 TO 90

In the past twenty-five years, England has advanced from a '30 per cent' to a '60 per cent' education system. We cannot now move too rapidly from 60 per cent to 90 per cent and beyond.

The figures 30, 60, 90 signify the proportion of school leavers reaching at least the basic standard of five GCSE passes at grade C or above including English and maths.

Most education systems have such a benchmark. The French have their baccalaureate; the Americans their high school diplomas; the Germans and the Finns their Abitur. The closest overseas benchmark to England's is the basic Singaporean standard of five O ('ordinary') levels above grade C. O-levels are the exam sat by sixteen-year-olds in England before the introduction of GCSEs in the late 1980s. Singapore's are still set and marked by the Cambridge exam board.

A generation ago, in most industrial nations, such qualifications were achieved by a minority, and were only intended to be so. Now they are achieved by the majority, and the imperative is to extend them to the overwhelming majority as soon as possible.

In 2011, the proportion of England's sixteen-year-olds achieving the basic GCSE basic standard reached 59 per cent, a record

level. However, in the quarter century during which this proportion nearly doubled from 30 per cent, the proportion of French
schoolchildren gaining the baccalaureate also nearly doubled to
66 per cent in 2010, the proportion gaining the highly demanding
Abitur and its technical counterpart in Germany doubled to 50 per
cent and the proportion gaining five or more O-levels in Singapore
also nearly doubled to 82 per cent. It is a similar picture across the
developed world.

The United States stands partially apart from this trend. The US
high school graduation rate has fluctuated around 70 per cent for
decades. For all the debate about the crisis in American education,
and high schools as 'dropout factories', the striking thing about
US high school graduation is how democratic and egalitarian a
concept it was in a twentieth century when most industrial nations,
England included, designed their schools so that most teenagers
dropped out of full-time education with inferior qualifications
well before the age of eighteen. The high school graduation rate
peaked at 80 per cent in the late 1960s and stood at 70 per cent back
in the mid-1950s when most Europeans and Asians weren't even at
school at the age that most young Americans were gaining their
high school diplomas.

In his 2012 State of the Union Address, Barack Obama hailed
the post-war generation which 'built the strongest economy and
middle class the world has ever known'. It did so on the foundation of America's schools, and President Obama's injunction for
America once again to become 'a country that leads the world in
educating its people' harks back to Thomas Jefferson's observation
at the founding of the United States that 'if a nation expects to be
ignorant and free, in a state of civilisation, it expects what never
was and never will be'.

In England, by contrast, even a decade or two ago slogans like
'more means worse' held sway. Every increase in the number of young
people gaining qualifications was allegedly the result of 'dumbing
down'. Indeed, the exam board rules had only recently been changed
to allow an increase in the proportion of students allowed to pass

public examinations, and gain higher grades, as standards rose, rather than abiding by fixed quotas year after year.

'Dumbing down' has been a source of vexation to those possessing qualifications since time immemorial. But more deeply, 'more means worse' reflected a conservative social reflex that GCSEs, A-levels, the baccalaureate, the Abitur and so on should only be attained by an elite. Such views are now rightly prehistoric. Now, political leaders worldwide play variations on Obama's 'race to the top', George W. Bush's 'no child left behind', and Tony Blair's 'education, education, education'.

Today's debate on school reform is about how, and how soon, the best can become the norm.

David Hopkins writes in his inspirational book *Every School a Great School*:

> It is salutary to recognise that whether the goal of 'every school a great school' is achieved or not, its realisation is more about professional and political will rather than strategic knowledge. It is now twenty-five years since Ron Edmonds asked his felicitous question: 'How many effective schools would you have to see to be persuaded of the educability of all children?'

This is a question which politicians and educators barely need to ask, for virtually all their children achieve well above the basic GCSE standard. This is true whether they want to become doctors or dancers, engineers or electricians, and almost whatever is happening in their home life. And most go on to university as a matter of course. So how can it be acceptable that still only one in four white boys from the poorest families (those eligible for free school meals) in England achieve the basic GCSE standard? Bridge this class divide and 60 quickly becomes 90.

The target for every all-ability secondary school in England should be to reach the 90 per cent basic GCSE standard soon, and by 2020 at the latest. The rest of the world is not waiting for England to get there, least of all China, now producing seven million graduates a year, one for each school-age child in England. More than 90,000 Chinese students are studying in the UK alone.

In international surveys of school standards, England's teenagers do OK but not brilliantly. The OECD's latest (2009) standardised international assessments of attainment by fifteen-year-olds in numeracy, literacy and science rank the UK 25th for reading, 28th for maths and 16th for science out of sixty-five countries. The previous assessment, in 2006, placed the UK similarly. Another reputable international assessment, of attainment in maths and science among 9–10-year-olds and 13–14-year-olds in 2007, placed England higher, at 5th in science and 7th in maths out of forty-nine countries among fourteen-year-olds. But looking at the raw scores in these assessments, as well as the rankings, it is striking how far behind the East Asian leaders (Singapore, Taiwan, South Korea, Japan, and Hong Kong and Shanghai in China) we are in maths in particular.[†]

Let's look further at Singapore, with its multi-racial population of five million, two-thirds the size of London. Singapore ranked within the international top four in maths and science in both these international assessments, and ranked 5th in reading in the OECD assessment. This should be no surprise given its O-level success rate: 82 per cent of sixteen-year-olds gaining five or more O-levels at grade C or higher, almost all of them including English and maths, compared to 59 per cent of their English counterparts at broadly equivalent GCSE level. So about 40 per cent more Singaporeans are reaching the basic GCSE standard. One hesitates to specify this difference as the scale of the performance gap between schools in England and Singapore but it is clearly large, particularly given that most Singaporeans are taking O-levels in their second language,

---

[†]   The OECD's 2009 'PISA' study does not assess China as a country but only Shanghai, Hong Kong and Macao. But given the very high rankings of Shanghai in particular – which ranks not only far above Britain but also above Singapore, Finland and Korea in all three of science, reading and maths – the Chinese challenge of the future is glaringly obvious.

English. The performance gap appears to be greater still at A-level. A remarkable 80 per cent of all subject A-levels in Singapore are sat in maths and the sciences, compared to fewer than 30 per cent in England.

It is therefore no surprise that the National University of Singapore ranks 23rd in *The Times*'s 2012 global ranking of universities, above almost all Britain's universities, despite the country's size and the fact that so many of the brightest Singaporeans study abroad. Singapore also has five polytechnics offering highly rated three-year 'diplomas' – good honours degrees, by English standards – in technical and vocational disciplines. Fifty per cent more Singaporeans go on to higher education than a decade ago and 44 per cent of Singaporeans between the age of twenty-five and thirty-nine now have higher education. The controversy in England about a '50 per cent target' for higher education misses the point that virtually all the world's most advanced countries now have more than half of their young adults embarked on academic or technical courses akin to English honours degrees. The issue isn't whether a majority should be going on to higher education, but the nature of the higher education institutions they should be attending (how meaningful is it to call them all 'universities' as we have in England since 1992?) and the types of courses they should be pursuing in these institutions.

Further education, another of England's perennial weaknesses, has been similarly transformed in Singapore. Twenty years ago, the initials of Singapore's Institute of Technical Education – ITE – were commonly dubbed: 'It's The End'. Now the ITE resembles a multi-campus university, and standards and applications are high.

Study visits to schools in Singapore, Finland, Germany, Taiwan, Hong Kong and Japan have transformed my thinking on the scale of the task we face in England. All these countries are improving their schools fast – all their schools, not just their elite schools. And not just the East Asians, whose educators nowadays spend almost as much time discussing 'creativity' as maths, but also Finland, where the school graduation rate is now well above 90 per cent, and

Germany, which has extended the school day for all schools as well as phasing out its bottom tier of 'hauptschulen', so that virtually all teenagers progress to higher-level academic or technical courses. None of these countries has a performance gap of our size between top and bottom, within or between schools.

Getting to 90 is the 'fierce urgency of now', not just for our schools but for our whole society.

In this international 'race to the top', England's schools have done well to get from 30 to 60, and to narrow the gap between top and bottom. An analysis by Chris Cook of the *Financial Times* of GCSE results in maths, English, science, history and geography (the subjects of the Coalition's EBacc) between 2006 and 2010 finds 'sustained improvement in the results achieved by children from the poorest neighbourhoods ... the gap closed by one-sixth of a grade in every one of these GCSE subjects'.

This may indicate a turning of the tide, at last, on social mobility. But it is only a start, and accelerating the trend is only partly about tackling failing schools. Another study by Chris Cook, of GCSE grades achieved by pupils from the poorest families compared to their wealthier counterparts in all schools, shows that, while the poorest do worst in the worst schools, they tend to achieve far less than their wealthier counterparts in almost all schools. And the wealthier their family, the better children do in almost all schools. He argues: 'The killer problem for social mobility is not that there are a few schools which have all the poor children in them (though that is a factor), it is that poorer children tend to do badly even when they go to good schools.'

It is because of this underachievement by children from poor families, even in most higher-achieving schools, that in 2011 only twenty-eight non-selective schools in England, of 3,170 nation-wide, reached the 90 per cent GCSE level. But these twenty-eight, and the further 123 which were above 80 per cent in 2011, show it is not impossible to close the gap. Crucially, in these 151 schools achieving 80 per cent plus, pupils from the poorest families achieve almost as highly as the average for all pupils in the school. There are also 446 secondary schools, one in seven, where pupils from the poorest families achieve above the national average GCSE score for all pupils.

'I'm on the side of the optimists,' says Kevan Collins, the former education director of Tower Hamlets, one of London's poorest boroughs, who identified these 446 schools. 'We know that teachers and schools can make a difference.'

And this is what the optimists would say: for a typical secondary school in size and attainment, getting from 60 to 90 by 2020 means an extra six students each year reaching the basic GCSE standard. Any good teacher in the school could probably name these six students long before they reach GCSE and say what would get them there.

Great schools nationwide are what will get England from 60 to 90. Schools with strong, positive governance and leadership, driven by powerful vision, ethos and innovation. These are the outstanding academies, and other schools like them in their ethos and leadership, described in earlier chapters.

However, while ethos and leadership are essential, they are not sufficient to generate a surge in the number of great schools. Great schools also need a supply of outstanding teachers. They need a modern, inspirational curriculum. They need to build on excellent nursery and under-fives education, and support for parents in the earliest years of bringing up children. They need state and society to value and promote community service and civic engagement by teenagers and young people. They need robust 'supply chains' to higher education and to apprenticeships and jobs.

Well-led schools make a big difference in all these areas. They are proactive in recruiting and developing teachers and leaders, in improving their curriculum, in deploying technology, in networking, in engaging their communities. Sport, the arts and clubs flourish and students do community service. University, college and apprenticeship places are secured year by year like a military campaign. And because they are well run and inspirational, great schools squeeze more out of their state budgets and attract other funding on top.

But even great schools can't do all this on their own. They need the state to do a far better job of supporting them and their work. This needs to start with teacher recruitment and training.

A NEW DEAL FOR TEACHERS

The quality of a school rarely exceeds the quality of its teachers for the obvious reason that teachers cannot teach what they do not know. Children of course teach themselves and each other to a large extent, and parents are their first teachers. But in these respects too, culture and practice are critically affected by schools and their teachers.

It is a sobering thought that children typically spend only about 12 per cent of their childhood at school. But half of the rest is spent asleep. As for the other half, parents and relations are obviously critical, but a good deal of it is spent hanging out with school friends. Here again, schools and teachers really matter.

We know this from our own childhoods: the teachers who inspired and changed our lives; the ones who didn't, and also changed our lives. It is almost superfluous to read studies like those in Tennessee and Dallas which show that, if you take pupils of average ability and giving them teachers deemed in the top fifth of the profession, they end up in the top 10 per cent of student performers, but give them teachers from the bottom fifth and they end up at the bottom.

The imperative is therefore simple: to recruit the nation's teachers from its most able students. Yet in England this is not happening. It is not even close to happening.

The state is the prime marketer, regulator and funder of teacher recruitment and training. It will remain so, however many academies and free schools there are, so the state clearly needs to raise its game fundamentally.

From its analysis of education in more than fifty countries, the consultancy McKinsey says it 'has never seen an education system achieve or sustain world class status without top talent in its teaching profession'. The best education systems regard great teachers as their 'north star' and have 'systematic approaches to attract, develop, retain and ensure the efficacy of the best educators'.

We therefore need to learn from Singapore, Finland and South Korea, the three nations with arguably the three most successful school systems in the world, and three of the most successful economies, which recruit virtually all their teachers from the top third of their graduates. South Korea's come mostly from the top 5 per cent. England, by contrast, recruits mostly from the bottom half. Well under half of maths teachers recruited in recent years, and barely half of science teachers, come with first or upper second class degrees. As for their universities, out of 53,745 applications for postgraduate teacher training in England in 2011, a mere fifty-five (0.1 per cent) were from the London School of Economics, and scarcely more (100) were from Imperial College London, England's premier science and engineering university (0.2 per cent). Oxford and Cambridge between them supplied only 650 (0.6 per cent each). Include the 255 from University College London (0.5 per cent), and England's five top universities between them supplied a mere 2 per cent of graduate teacher training applicants.

As for primary school teachers, the first B. Ed course for primary teaching I found on Google – at the University of Wolverhampton – requires only two Cs and a D at A-level or vocational equivalent for admission, not including either maths or English, and it is top rated by Ofsted.

Drop-out figures tell a similar story. About 20 per cent of England's teacher trainees drop out within two years and nearly half drop out within five years, compared to less than 3 per cent a year in the world's best education systems.

In Singapore, Finland and South Korea, there are ten or more applicants for each teacher training place. By contrast our Education Department regards it as a triumph that, unlike in the 1980s and 1990s, there are now enough applicants to fill the advertised training places. Even so, state school teaching in England is only just a selective profession, with barely 1.5 applicants for training places to teach crucial secondary-level subjects including maths, physics, chemistry, modern languages and IT. Even for primary school training, the most competitive part of the profession, there are just over two applicants per place. And there are still not nearly enough specialist teachers. One in six maths classes in state secondary schools are taught by non-specialists and only one in three science teachers has a degree in either physics or chemistry. This is why so many secondary schools do not teach the three sciences to GCSE but only 'general science'. They simply don't have the specialists.

'Don't even step on the shadow of a teacher' is a Korean proverb. If that sounds a bit authoritarian, I like the idea that 'people know that if you've been trained as a teacher you must really be something special', as Pasi Sahlberg describes social attitudes in Finland. Among Finnish men, teaching is the most desirable profession in a spouse, according to social surveys, while Finnish women rank male teachers as only less desirable than doctors and vets. Among Finnish students, teaching is the most esteemed career, outpolling the law and medicine.

Finnish teacher training is concentrated in eight of Finland's top universities, and universities can only select candidates who have passed a national screening process. (In England, teacher training takes place in more than eighty universities and colleges, and there is no national screening.) Furthermore, all Finnish teachers either have a masters degree or are working towards one, often including a thesis on an issue of practical relevance. On a visit I paid to a primary school in Helsinki, the teacher showing me around had just completed her masters thesis on the best ways to organise home to school transport for children with disabilities, a critical issue for schools. The headteacher of the school startled me when I asked what was her biggest staffing problem. 'My best teachers going to do PhDs,' she replied. No headteacher in England has ever said that to me. Even the national drive for the best teachers to take masters degrees has been abandoned by the Cameron government, which withdrew the funding. I hope that headteachers are nonetheless supporting their best teachers to study for higher degrees.

Equally concerning is the lack of support for basic teacher training in England, again in contrast to the best systems abroad. Teachers in England are expected to train at their own expense, getting even further into debt over and above their now onerous fees and loans for first degrees. Some bursaries are available and the Cameron Coalition has rightly reformed them so that larger bursaries are payable to graduates with better degrees in maths, physics, chemistry and modern languages. But even for graduates with a 2:1 in these disciplines, the larger bursary of £15,000 does not even cover fees and living costs for the teacher training year. Teaching also needs to be made far more attractive to suitable mid-career-switchers, who bring vital experiences as well as technical skills to teaching.

Then there is the problem of poor teaching. Effective school leaders motivate their teachers and get the best out of them, often transforming the performance of previously poor or mediocre teachers. They are also skilled at moving on those who continue to let down their pupils. However, it is true to say that, because of the hassle of competency proceedings, poor performers too often reappear in other schools rather than leaving the profession. If, as someone said, autobiographies are a branch of fiction, so are all too many job references.

What is to be done? Radical reform, not further incrementalism, is required to make teaching a career of choice for the best graduates. I suggest an eight-point reform plan: a new deal for teachers.

Reform one: Teach First, the highly successful charity which recruits, trains and places high-achieving graduates into challenging schools, as described in Chapter 3, should be expanded to make it one of the main routes into secondary school teaching.

With its seven applicants per place, mostly drawn from top universities and the top quarter of graduates, Teach First should be expanded as fast as consistent with maintaining quality. Teach First will recruit 1,000 graduates in 2012. If this were increased by 500 a year, to reach 5,000 by 2020, concentrated on secondary school posts in harder-to-recruit subjects including maths, science and IT, Teach First would by then be supplying one in four new secondary school teachers and larger proportions in subjects with the biggest recruitment challenges at present. This alone would be transformational.

For this to happen, Teach First needs to change its existing model in one significant respect. At present, it gives schools no choice of teacher, but simply agrees to supply a certain number of teachers. As a result, it is often the supplier of last resort, even for schools which take Teach First teachers each year, because head-teachers understandably want to test the market before deciding which vacancies to fill unseen by Teach Firsters. For Teach First to become a large supplier of first resort, a simple but essential reform would be to give schools a choice of Teach First teachers.

Reform two: learning from Singapore, Finland, South Korea, Teach First and Teach For America, mainstream teacher recruitment and placement beyond Teach First should be professionally managed on a national basis, and training should be entrusted to the best universities and schools.

Instead of the complex and uneven regime which now applies, where students apply for teacher training places to a large number of individual universities, each with their own admissions criteria and procedures, there should be a national recruitment process, adopting high admissions standards and best international practice in selection and assessment techniques. It should focus with equal passion on recruiting teachers from all ethnic and social backgrounds, and on recruiting far more men to a profession which has become seriously unbalanced so that teachers better match the children they teach and the communities they serve.

I would set up an independent trust akin to the BBC to take on this vital job, with a board comprising educational, business and social leaders. It is essential that teacher recruitment is seen as a national, not a government endeavour, and that it is not politicised. The training of teachers recruited by this National Teaching Trust should be commissioned from a small number of the best universities and schools. At present, for essentially historical reasons, teacher education takes place in more than eighty universities and colleges, which place their trainees in large numbers of schools in their area chosen only partly, if at all, for their excellence. Instead, training should take place in at most a few dozen universities of high standing, and trainees should be placed only in schools ranked outstanding by Ofsted. The National Teaching Trust should promote rigorous standards and quality control, and support teachers directly throughout their training and their early years in teaching.

Reform three: schools rated outstanding by Ofsted should be allowed to recruit trainees directly, outside this national process and Teach First, provided they are prepared to pay them and train them properly, with or without a university partner. This option might prove particularly attractive to the best academy chains and federations.

Reform four: teacher trainees should be paid a salary from the outset. This effectively happens in Teach First and is a significant part of its appeal. In return, again learning from the practice of Teach First, graduates should be employed by a school, and they should work a standard 48-week year for their initial two training years. They should teach or assist at their school during the whole of the thirty-eight-week term time, with out-of-school university courses taking place in the other ten weeks, starting with a summer training programme in the six weeks before their first autumn term.

Reform five: there should be a much higher starting salary for target groups of teachers, and if this helps transform intake it should be extended more widely.

Pay is of course only one factor in attracting the brightest and best into teaching and in motivating them thereafter. Finland, for example, pays its teachers at about the OECD average. By contrast, Singapore and South Korea have the best-paid teachers in the world, relative to average earnings in their countries, and most of the better education systems pay above average. In the case of South Korea, this is made more affordable by a high student : teacher ratio of 30:1, against the OECD average of about 17:1.

McKinsey's analysis of international evidence on teachers' pay and performance, with particular reference to the United States, emphasises two points which very likely apply in England too. First, finalists and graduates tend to focus on starting salaries more than salary progression when choosing careers. Second, students and graduates generally underestimate how much teachers are actually paid. This is itself a function of the low status of the profession, but it is exacerbated by the complexity of teachers' pay scales, where the numbers are never round and the scales resemble the departure board at Waterloo station. An additional factor in England is the high cost of postgraduate training, which is a big disincentive even to getting past 'go'.

McKinsey's research suggests that it is attractive and simple starting salaries and top salaries – that is, salaries for new teachers and salaries for new headteachers – which make a big difference in attracting far more high-performing graduates to teaching, rather than salary progression. Since the critical policy objective is to attract excellent graduates into teaching in the first place, front-loading the salary and making it as attractive as possible makes obvious sense. An excellent teacher aged twenty-three is worth far more than a mediocre one aged forty or fifty, and many of those twenty-three-year-olds will still be teaching or leading schools at forty or fifty. Tellingly, far more than half of Teach First teachers have stayed in the profession beyond the two years for which they signed up at the outset. Once recruited to teaching, even the best graduates tend to stay.

It is not just the twenty-one- and twenty-three-year-olds that these reforms would be intended to attract. They would also improve the appeal of teaching to career-switchers, who will become all the more important to the age and experience profile of new teachers as Teach First becomes a principal route into the profession. Schools need a good balance of younger and older teachers, and teachers with all kinds of backgrounds: academic, practical and pastoral. But the forty-, fifty- and sixty-year-olds in the classroom – or in the detention room or on the football pitch or leading the school visit to Beijing – need to be as enthusiastic and committed as the twenty-one-year-olds starting out with their sense of mission and adventure.

A career-switchers scheme (the 'Graduate Teacher Programme') has increased the number of career-switchers in recent years. But again, the application process is an obstacle course with weak national branding and quality control. And career-switchers start on a salary below the bottom of the standard teachers' pay scale. This could hardly be less attractive or fair to mid-career or late-career entrants on reasonable salaries and with family commitments whose contribution to a school – if they are any good, and only the good should be recruited – will be akin to that of their fellow teachers within days of their arrival. It was a policy breakthrough that career-switchers were allowed to be paid a salary at all during their school-based training year, which further demonstrates the need to break free from incremental change and reinvent teacher training and employment in fundamentally new ways.

From its market research in the US, looking also at alternative uses of additional education spending, McKinsey concludes that the best value for money – if the money is available – comes from offering a starting salary of $65,000 and a maximum salary of $150,000, which its projections suggest would be likely to yield a more than one-third increase in the number of 'top third' graduates becoming teachers.

Like the McKinsey analysts, I am unpersuaded that alternative uses of extra education investment – apart from an increase in Sure Start provision for under-fives from poorer families, and their parents – would raise standards as much as incentives to recruit substantially more of the brightest and best into teaching. I am especially unpersuaded, from the evidence, that further reductions in class sizes, by expanding the total number of teachers and assistants beyond the big increases which have already taken place in recent years, would be remotely as productive.

So reform five, in conjunction with rigorous quality control, would be to raise the starting salary for target groups of teachers significantly, perhaps to £30,000 out of London and £35,000 in the capital in one go for new secondary school teachers of maths, physics, chemistry, IT and computing. These are crucial secondary subjects where the challenge to recruit the most able graduates is greatest. (The average graduate starting salary in 2010 was £23,000 and teacher starting salaries ranged between £21,600 and £27,000.) If this proves a game changer, then the reform could be extended more widely as resources allow.

I would do the same for headteacher starting salaries – perhaps £70,000 for heads of larger primary schools and £100,000 for heads of secondary schools as basic starting salaries, and higher in London.

Targeted in this way, the costs would be manageable. Together, these reforms would add less than 2 per cent to the total teacher pay bill, and far less should they succeed in cutting drop-out rates, as is likely. But to make these high starting salaries fully worthwhile and cost-effective, they ought to be introduced alongside reforms six and seven, which they make possible.

Reform six would be an end to nationally determined increments beyond these higher starting salaries, leaving pay progression at the discretion of the school.

Reform seven would be a longer probationary period within which ineffective teachers and headteachers could be removed without claims for unfair dismissal. I would extend the probationary period to three or four years for both new teachers and headteachers, during and at the end of which employment could be ended for less than good performance without recourse to claims of unfair dismissal. This would be in place of the current system where 'qualified teacher status' is gained (or not) after just a year in the classroom on the basis of 'satisfactory' performance. There is generally no probationary period whatever for heads. An important corollary would be an expectation of training and professional support throughout these longer probationary periods, which would further raise standards and address poor performance.

Reform eight would be to phase out the B. Ed (and equivalents) in primary education and replace them with largely subject-based degrees.

Excellent teachers and teaching are just as important in primary as in secondary schools. Yet, while secondary teachers have for several decades been expected to have subject honours degrees and deep subject knowledge as well as pedagogic skills and training, primary school teachers mostly come from general education courses – B. Eds and equivalents – in university departments which are often the old teacher training colleges amalgamated or renamed. We need to do better than this, both for primary-level teachers themselves and for primary school children who have few – if any – teachers with specialisms in most areas of the curriculum, and few even with graduate-level knowledge in English and maths. In stark contrast to private junior schools, most state primary schools do not systematically employ historians, musicians, geographers, science graduates, drama and PE specialists, and so on. It is time they did so, which requires radical reform to teacher recruitment and training.

In place of the B. Ed, primary school teachers should in future either be recruited with honours degrees in specific subjects and then undertake postgraduate training – as at present for secondary school teachers and a small proportion of primary teachers – or they should study for combined 'academic subject plus pedagogy' degrees, with a large proportion of these joint honours degrees majoring in literacy and numeracy. Then every primary teacher would have deep subject knowledge and the primary curriculum could be broadened and deepened significantly.

A start could be made on all eight reforms immediately. Taken together, I believe they have the potential to improve significantly the calibre of teachers and teaching.

At this point, I could wax lyrical, as do many of those envisioning the future of schools, on the potential of this or that technology, this or that teaching or learning technique, this or that social or networking trend, to change education as we know it.

There is a lot that is new and different in education which impresses and inspires me.

There is education in wellbeing – relationships, health and happiness – which is vital to personal resilience and which barely featured in the classroom when I was at school.

There is the use of wireless and digital technology to 'flip the classroom', in the brilliant vision of Salman Khan and his online Khan Academy, with instruction at home and outside the classroom through excellent video lectures and digital materials while classroom time is used more productively for individualised support, discussion and feedback on tasks and exercises. The number of unique visitors to Khan Academy – with its 'free world class education' offered online via short ten- to fifteen-minute videos – grew from one million to four million a month during 2010 and 2011. The not-for-profit academy, founded only in 2006, now offers a collection of more than 3,000 micro lectures via YouTube.

There is the teaching of presentational and debating skills to all teenagers, not just to debating teams in private schools. The UK charity Debate Mate, run by current and former university debaters, runs programmes for more than 150 secondary schools, including the entire ARK and Haberdashers' chains of academies. It is having a remarkable impact in helping teenagers express their ideas clearly, confidently and reasonably, skills which ought to be at the heart of modern education.

There are supplementary schools using school premises in the evenings and at weekends to provide extra education for specific language and cultural communities. In London there are steadily more and larger supplementary schools serving most of the capital's language, faith and ethnic communities, led by teachers, parents and community leaders, often in close association with mainstream schools.

There is the use of the 'Harkness table', pioneered in Phillips Exeter Academy, a leading private school in the US. Classes become seminars with students and teachers sitting and interacting around a large oval table instead of in rows of desks with the teacher looming at the front.

There are 'extended schools', open twelve hours or more a day and at weekends and in the school holidays as a social, cultural, sporting, artistic, community learning hub, all the more valuable now that so many schools have new or refurbished facilities.

I could go on. But it is not from top-down prescription, let alone tips from politicians like me, that the best innovation, the best technology, the best teaching and learning and the best national and international practice will sweep through our schools. The wind of change takes the form of outstanding teachers and school leaders, dedicated to doing the best professional job within their power.

We need far more brilliant teachers, brilliantly led. That is the essence of education, education, education.

In terms of state reform, we also need better under-fives services, a better curriculum, the transformation of schools into community hubs, and far better promotion of citizenship and democracy among young people.

SURE START

As the Scandinavians realised long ago, unless children gain social skills, and start learning, from their earliest days, and unless parents get the support they need to help them – including the childcare and nursery provision needed for them to work and earn – society is impoverished, education undermined and the poor lose out most.

As with the impact of good and bad teachers, academic studies are almost superfluous in the light of our personal experience. But the Millennium Cohort Study – tracking 19,000 children born between 2000 and 2002 – is there, demonstrating that, even by the age of five, children from disadvantaged families lagged nearly a year behind their middle-class contemporaries in social and educational development.

The last fifteen years have seen a transformation of under-fives nursery provision for three- and four-year-olds, alongside the establishment of Sure Start providing childcare, health, early education and parenting support for more vulnerable parents from before the birth of their children. Both nursery and Sure Start provision need to expand. While four-year-olds can generally secure full-time places in primary schools in 'reception' classes, there is only an entitlement to three hours a day of nursery provision for three-year-olds and this needs to be increased substantially as an entitlement for all parents. Sure Start, and its 3,600 children's centres nationwide, then needs to focus not only on providing additional childcare and parental support for parents of the most disadvantaged children, but also on ensuring that they are ready to learn when they start school.

TIME FOR AN A-LEVEL BACCALAUREATE (A-BACC)...

As well as good qualifications, every young person needs life skills, resilience, broad horizons, and a strong sense of duty and citizenship. Schools need to do a steadily better job of helping young people acquire all these.

It is often asserted that the 'basics' of literacy and numeracy and an 'exam culture' are driving creativity and other worthwhile activities out of schools. This claim does not stand up to serious scrutiny. Nationally and internationally, schools which excel in the arts and sports, and in virtually every other aspect of a wider curriculum, are almost invariably those which also do best at literacy and numeracy and equipping their students with good qualifications. Apart from some brilliant schools for pupils with certain disabilities, I have yet to discover the school which excels in creativity and sport which can't also point to good test and exam results. Schools which fail in the basics rarely achieve anything much else.

What mainly holds schools back from broadening their curriculum is not the exam system or the national curriculum but inadequate and unimaginative teaching and leadership. Great teachers, well led, teach a great curriculum and constantly push at its boundaries, inside and outside the classroom. Here again, attracting more of the brightest and best into teaching is the essential policy. For the best schools, there is little benefit from the national curriculum when set against its rigidity and bureaucracy, and I would remove the requirement to follow the national curriculum for all schools rated outstanding by Ofsted.

On exams, there is no virtue in pulling up the existing GCSE and A-level system by its roots without consensus about a better system to replace it, or worse still with a vague sentiment that fewer or less demanding exams would be a good thing. GCSEs, A-levels and the International Baccalaureate are the currency of universities and, adding in B Techs and reputable technical qualifications, of employers too. If the state waters them down, the better-off in their private schools will continue to trade in reputable qualifications ruthlessly, however much they complain about the stress over their dinner parties.

However, there is a broad consensus as to certain weaknesses in the national exam and assessment system in respect of 16–18-year-olds. The current A-level system, of typically three or four closely related subjects with no requirement to study English, maths, science or a modern language, is narrower than the pre-university courses in virtually every other country, while the landscape of post-16 technical and vocational courses is hard to navigate and the qualifications themselves are often of low status. The time is ripe for two significant 'next steps' reforms to help put this right.

Reform one: A-levels should be reformed to give them more of the subject and skills breadth of the International Baccalaureate (IB).

The IB is a far broader programme than A-levels, with very strong international credentials built up over the more than forty years since the Geneva-based independent IB Foundation established the IB diploma. The IB is now studied in more than 2,300 schools across 140 countries worldwide. The largest concentration of IB schools – 750 – is in the US, with large numbers also in Canada, Australia, Mexico, India, China, Spain and Germany.

The IB requires study of six subjects, including English, maths, a second language, and a subject each within broad groupings of mainly humanities and the sciences. There is also a 4,000-word extended essay, an interdisciplinary 'theory of knowledge' course, and a requirement to demonstrate involvement in 'creativity, action, service', both as an individual and as part of a team. This is an excellent post-GCSE course for academically inclined students.

Tellingly, Singapore – rarely behind the curve in promoting excellence in its education system – adopted key features of the IB in its 2006 reform of A-levels. Singaporean students are now required to take at least one 'contrasting subject' within, typically, a four-subject programme, three at equivalent of A-level and one at AS. Students majoring in the humanities and arts have to take a maths or science course and vice versa. Compulsory 'knowledge skills' have also been introduced alongside A-levels, including project work akin to the extended essay in the IB, plus a requirement to demonstrate 'life skills' through participation in a Community Involvement Programme and other 'co-curricular activities'. This is in effect the IB but allowing for more specialisation, which is the strength of A-level. The introduction of AS in England more than a decade ago was a mouse of a reform by comparison, simply encouraging Year 12 students to study one more subject, typically the 'next door' subject to their other two or three.

More than 220 schools and colleges in the UK now offer the IB. The private sector led the way, but two-thirds of IB providers are now in the state sector. The Blair government's policy was for each local authority area to have at least one state sector IB provider, to give more sixth-formers a choice between A-levels and the IB. This has now largely been achieved. With this prevailing wind, I hoped that A-levels could be reformed consensually on the Singaporean model, or possibly that over time England would simply replace A-levels with the IB.

However, the growth of the IB has not been obstacle free. There are training and transitional costs, which the Blair government subsidised for new providers. There is also the greater ongoing cost of the IB, which requires teaching time equivalent to five A-levels. And the IB has not always been welcomed by universities, whose tutors sometimes cavil at the lesser degree of subject specialisation of the IB (i.e. lesser specialisation in *their* subjects) compared to A-levels and unfairly make tougher offers to IB students than to A-level students. Top universities often make IB offers of forty-two to forty-five points (the maximum possible is forty-five). This is notably tougher than three A grades at A-level.

The IB has nonetheless been gaining ground for the good reason that it is broader, more engaging and more international than A-level in both subjects and skills. Expansion of the IB should be encouraged by covering the additional costs to schools of offering it. The government should also broker agreement between school and university leaders on fair comparability between IB and A-level offers.

Going further, I believe the time is ripe to follow Singapore and carry through an IB-style reform to A-levels to create an A-level Baccalaureate (A-Bacc). This should include a 'contrasting subject' requirement, a project-based extended essay and an interdisciplinary theory of knowledge course as a standard part of A-level, and a requirement to demonstrate community service. Students would receive an overall A-Bacc mark, as in the IB. Reform on these lines would notably improve the post-GCSE curriculum for the half or more of teenagers on track for higher education or higher-level technical qualifications.

... AND FOR A TECHNICAL BACCALAUREATE (TECH BACC)

For the equally important half of sixteen-year-olds not on track for higher education, the requirement is for qualifications which lead reliably to apprenticeships and jobs, and these presently are too scarce. As Alison Wolf puts it in her 2011 report on vocational education: 'The staple offer for between a quarter and a third of the post-16 cohort is a diet of low-level vocational qualifications, most of which have little to no labour market value.'

The stark, deplorable fact highlighted in the Wolf report is that only 4 per cent of sixteen-year-olds who have failed GCSE English and maths go on to pass them by the age of nineteen. The vocational qualifications – if any – that they acquire are not only generally low level; they mostly do not even include GCSE-grade

competence in the core skills of literacy and numeracy, which
goes part way to explaining the youth unemployment rate of
22 per cent in 2012. 'Every other country in the developed world
concentrates on improving the language and maths skills of its
post-16 vocational students, and so, belatedly, should England,'
concludes Wolf.

England's fastest-growing major occupational groups since
2000 are nursery and educational assistants, and care assistants
and home carers, of whom there are now more than 1.2 million
combined. The caring professions will be major sources of new jobs
in the future, alongside, one hopes, employment in new industries
and services. What most of these jobs have in common is that,
while they do not require higher-education-level academic or technical skills, they do require literacy, numeracy, reliability, social
skills and a capacity to understand, implement and operate instruc-
tional and IT systems.

It is vital that young people are equipped with these skills,
and that they acquire them in tandem with occupation-specific
qualifications. Where possible, they should lead directly into – or
be acquired alongside – apprenticeships, so that they lead directly
to jobs, with employers playing a bigger role both in providing apprenticeships and work experience at earlier stages, and
also in supporting the training system within their occupational
area in the way, for example, that German employers have done
for generations.

The good news, thanks to strong state support over the past
decade, is that apprenticeships are back, and their number and
range is growing steadily. The bad news is that many apprenticeships are short and unstructured – one in five lasting less than six
months – providing neither skills nor secure pathways into stable
and well-paid jobs.

Part of the answer, I suggest, is to implement the Wolf
recommendations in the form of a new 'Tech Bacc' (Technical
Baccalaureate) for post-sixteen-year-olds not studying the A-Bacc,
to comprise three simple elements: English and maths GCSE, a

reputable qualification in an occupational area or areas, and work experience including a formal reference from the employer for future use. For those who have reached the basic GCSE level including English and maths, but wish to acquire further technical qualifications, there should be a higher-level Tech Bacc comprising higher literacy, numeracy, problem-solving and project-working skills, together with a reputable technical qualification, either to be taken alongside an apprenticeship or, if beforehand (as will be the case for most students under the age of eighteen), including substantially more work experience and a formal report on performance during it.

The Tech Bacc, with more and better apprenticeships and work experience, will help make a reality of the 50:50 education system, investing more in young people not proceeding to higher education. However, the numbers going on to higher education should continue to rise. This serves the national social and economic interest for a steadily larger skilled workforce, quite apart from the personal fulfilment involved, provided it includes a significant proportion of young people gaining technical diplomas or degrees akin to those conferred by Germany's Fachschulen and Singapore's polytechnics. With market-based higher education fees covering much or most of the cost, individuals should be left to decide for themselves whether they wish to proceed to higher education and not be held back by the knee-jerk conservatism of those who think that too many go to 'university'. Fifty years ago, social conservatives thought too many went to secondary school, and 150 years ago they doubted the value even of primary education beyond a year or two of the '3Rs' and instruction in the Bible.

A striking finding of the Millennium Cohort Study is that, among the mothers of children born in the UK in 2000, 98 per cent wanted their children to go to university. Applying R. H. Tawney's excellent principle that what the good parent wants for their child, the state should want for all children, we should encourage young people to realise their ambitions and make the best of their lives, university included.

DEMOCRACY AND SCHOOLS

'There are no GCSEs in values or league tables for citizenship,' Estelle Morris remarks. Yet values and citizenship ought to be integral to 21st-century education and the state has an important role to play in making them so.

England is altogether too timid and half-hearted about the role of schools in building citizens and citizenship.

We complain that teenagers show too little responsibility, yet we give them too little responsibility.

We complain there is too little volunteering and social commitment among the young, yet this is mostly done outside school, not as part of a modern education.

We complain that young people are uninterested in politics and do not vote – only 44 per cent of 18–29-year-olds voted in the 2010 general election – yet most of them do not get to cast their first general election vote until they are aged twenty or older. Furthermore, the act of voting is totally unrelated to citizenship education in schools and virtually no attempt is made to engage teenagers and young adults in local government.

Democracy and social responsibility need to be taught and learned in schools. We can't carry on, as with sex education a generation ago, expecting them to be learned spontaneously or informally, and then complain when this doesn't happen.

Part of the benefit of secondary schools having sixth forms is that sixth-formers are great role models for younger teenagers. Sixth-formers are also well able to take on significant responsibility within schools, not only individually as prefects but in organising and leading activities outside the classroom, and also in decision-making. Sixth-formers, in particular, are good judges of the bona fides of teachers and headteachers, and they can play a valuable role in selecting teachers and school leaders.

School councils have an important role. Virtually all secondary schools now have an elected school council, and increasingly they are given real tasks and real budgets. I am a convert to elected school councils also in primary schools, since I visited Millfields primary school in a highly deprived part of Hackney, under the leadership of Dame Anna Hassan, and watched the school council – including children as young as six and seven – discuss bullying, school food and the state of the school toilets.

It is essential to relate the teaching and learning of citizenship in schools to important practical objectives. That is part of the argument for reforming A-levels to include the 'community, action, service' element of the IB, as suggested earlier. Good schools foster and reward these activities anyway, but giving them formal recognition in the assessment system, including in UCAS forms and exam certificates, would help further. This ought to happen at GCSE level too.

Voting is a critical responsibility of citizenship, and the political debate and campaigns which precede voting are the most intense exercise of democracy in our national life. I favour giving young people the vote at sixteen, so that political debate and democracy fully include young people and so that young people start to consider and discuss how to use their vote while they are still at school. Sixteen is the age of responsibility in most other spheres. It is hard to make an argument of principle against giving the vote to sixteen-year-olds as already happens in Austria, Brazil and the Isle of Man. Like votes for women, and lowering the voting age to eighteen, I expect that votes at sixteen will become the international norm, and England could and should lead the way.

Alongside extending the vote to sixteen- and seventeen-year-olds, there should be a polling station in every secondary school in local and national elections, turning on its head the perversity of some schools being closed on polling day so that the 'adults' can get on with democracy. Just as in schools mock exams lead to real public exams for the older students, so mock elections should lead to real elections for the older students. This would give the teaching of citizenship a practical objective. And politicians and candidates would treat teenagers with a wholly new seriousness if they knew their electoral prospects depended upon it.

For the same reason, it should be possible to become a local councillor at the age of sixteen and parties should actively promote younger candidates – including school sixth-formers – to stand for council elections, in the way they have started seriously to promote women and ethnic minority candidates in recent years. Most local councils have hardly any young councillors, even in their twenties, yet education and services for children and young people are among their main responsibilities. The city of Leeds, I discovered on a recent visit, has more councillors over the age of seventy-five than under the age of thirty-five. No wonder local government is so remote from young people. And no wonder civic engagement by young people is so negligible, when it ought to be a hallmark of modern society.

SCHOOLS AS COMMUNITY HUBS
Schools should become community hubs, not remain isolated buildings just for teaching school-age children.

For education to be a central community activity, schools need to be central community institutions. It is also wasteful to invest in state-of-the-art school facilities and facilities, including sports facilities, cafes, restaurants and theatres, and for them to be closed or barely used for a quarter of the year, and at weekends and half the working day even when schools are in session. This becomes all the more urgent as other community services – including health centres, post offices, libraries and community centres – are closing or under threat in the face of public spending cuts, when imaginative solutions for the co-location of services on school sites should be explored. The co-location of public libraries with schools is the most obvious synergy, but, with innovation and imagination across the public services, far more ambitious projects would be possible.

A good example of such innovation is the St Paul's Way Transformation Project in London's East End. A £36 million regeneration scheme is rebuilding St Paul's Way secondary school as an integrated project including wider community facilities including a health centre, an internet cafe and careers service. This needs to be the first of many such ambitious projects nationwide.

THOMAS TELFORD

I started this book at Mossbourne Academy, an exemplary academy in so many ways, including the four in five of sixteen-year-olds achieving the basic GCSE standard in one of the most deprived communities in the country. I finish it at Thomas Telford School, one of the original all-ability City Technology Colleges, in Telford new town between Birmingham and Shrewsbury, which was a prime inspiration for today's academy movement.

At Thomas Telford, 160 out of 2011's 163 GCSE students achieved five or more higher-grade passes including English and maths. Nine in ten of the sixth form leavers go on to university each year.

The school's entire curriculum is accessible to students and parents on the internet. There is a report to parents on their child's progress every four weeks, using GCSE grades from the age of eleven: that is nine reports a year or sixty-three reports during a school career.

Along with its formidable academic provision and achievements, the school matches the best private schools in the arts, clubs and sports. Sports take place in what is called 'session three' of the longer school day, between 4 p.m. and 5.40 p.m, which gives students the equivalent of an extra day's schooling each week beyond the standard school day. Thomas Telford students in the past year include the captain of the England U16 girls basketball team, the girls 100m backstroke national champion, the U15 girls English biathlon gold medallist, a national finalist for the 100m schools hurdles, and members of the Great Britain junior cadet and senior judo squads. Most students pursue the Duke of Edinburgh award, many of them gaining gold or silver.

All Thomas Telford's GCSE-year students get the chance to go on a university summer school taster course at Aston University. They also do two weeks work experience in Year 11 after their GCSEs, and all sixth-formers also have the opportunity to do another two weeks work experience. On one visit to the school I was surprised – and impressed – to find that the careers adviser, based in a 'hub' near the school's dining area, was a retired senior executive at Tarmac, one of the school's founding sponsors. 'They think I know a thing or two about jobs,' he said drily.

In its first twenty years, Thomas Telford generated a £16 million profit, although a state school, from selling leading-edge IT courses to more than 1,000 schools nationally as a spin-off from its innovative IT curriculum and systems. It used much of this income to endow the three academies – all Thomas Telford look-alikes in their curriculum, leadership, ethos and standards – it has established across the West Midlands since 2001 in partnership with its own original sponsor, the Mercers livery company.

Thomas Telford is an exemplary employer. In return for the longer school day, all staff have a lesson-free day each week for planning and preparation. There is an on-site subsidised nursery, including baby unit places, for all employees' children.

All of this has taken place under the inspirational leadership of Sir Kevin Satchwell, the school's headteacher since its founding twenty-one years ago. The headteachers of all the new Thomas Telford academies were not only trained at the school, they were also personally mentored by Sir Kevin for their first three years.

Sir Kevin has a new vision: to make Thomas Telford the premier school in the country for training new teachers. His Thomas Telford-led training programme will this year (2012) take 150 trainees. His plan is to increase this to 500 over the next five years with successful trainees not only meeting the national requirements for 'qualified teacher status' but also studying for masters degree programmes. The reinvention of teacher recruitment and education nationwide, essential for England's schools to become world class, could begin at Thomas Telford.

Thomas Telford sets out its mission in ten simple objectives:

To admit students of all abilities.

To develop qualities of enterprise, self-reliance and responsibility.

To involve, as fully as possible, the wider community, including industry, business, commerce and parents in the education and training of the students.

To operate a longer school day.

To share research with the neighbouring schools and the educational community and where possible support collaborative developments locally.

To remove the artificial barrier that exists between vocational and academic courses.

To improve post-16 staying-on rates to that comparable with France, Germany, USA and Japan.

To deliver the national curriculum with extra science, mathematics, technology and business education.

To ensure that all students obtain their educational entitlement, irrespective of gender, religion, ethnicity or special need.

To provide a safe and secure environment for students, staff and visitors.

This is education, education, education for the twenty-first century.

HOW TO BE A REFORMER

This is a book about education. It is also a book, by a professional optimist, about how it is possible for government to bring about radical change for the better. Boiling down my views and experience, I offer twelve general reflections.

1. Address the big problems
Power is finite and evaporates much faster than you expect. It is vital to expend it on large not small objects. And to be moral, these objects should never be sectional but for the general good.

This is a counsel of conscience. For the democratic politician it is also a counsel of self-interest, for, as Tony Blair used to say, 'the best policy is the best politics'. There is no better – meaning purer or more effective – way of securing and holding power than to appeal beyond sectional interests to a credible and honestly felt conception of the national interest, which is rarely the same thing as repeating worn-out party claptrap.

In the case of education, England's single biggest problem in the mid-1990s was the chronic underperformance of the bottom half of its comprehensive schools. Fundamental change was obviously required; in its absence, millions of children, and the country at large, were suffering. Yet the Labour party was largely in denial, campaigning for more investment without the radical reform needed alongside it, while the Conservatives were largely in escapism, offering opt-outs to benefit small numbers of children while under-investing in mainstream state education and ignoring the mass of failing schools. An education policy which did not offer a fundamental solution to the biggest problem of the day – that half of comprehensives were basically failing – was a national betrayal not worthy of government. It was vital to see it in these terms.

There are still far too many underperforming comprehensives and their replacement remains a national imperative. The same imperative for radical change extends, in 2012, to youth unemployment; to the council estates and substandard housing in which so many people still lead a miserable existence; to the north–south divide and the state of so many of England's provincial cities, which are generating neither the jobs nor the businesses and amenities needed for the future; to the national infrastructure; and to strategies for growth and systematic business creation in the face of a sustained economic downturn. England needs big transformational policies not more of the failed policy of the past with a few tweaks.

As a political historian, I am struck by how few ministers leave much of a mark, despite the supposed power of their offices. Prime ministers, dealing with great crises, can hardly fail to make an impact, positive or negative. But few even of them make much impact as reformers as opposed to crisis managers.

My role model for the bold reformer, addressing the big issues with courage and conscience, is Roy Jenkins as Home Secretary in the first Wilson government in the mid-1960s. Astonishingly, Jenkins was Home Secretary for only twenty-three months, yet in that short time he carried, or paved the way for, the legalisation of abortion and homosexuality, the introduction of no-fault divorce and majority verdicts in criminal trials, the abolition of theatre censorship and flogging in prisons, and the most radical reform of policing since the war. He changed the face of society for the better, exploiting the full resources of politics and government with bold daring.

Crucial to Jenkins's ability to accomplish all this was that he came to office with a fully and carefully worked-out plan, which he had spent the best part of a decade forging. He also saw conventional party politics as something to be overcome and reshaped, while being an effective party politician himself.

For the same reasons, I have long admired the unlikely duo of Ken Livingstone and Michael Heseltine. Neither of them ever fitted comfortably into their parties and both are political loners who went through periods of intense media vilification for straying from the conventional wisdom of Left and Right. Yet both have constantly focused on big problems and successfully carried radical and controversial reforms which tackled them successfully.

Council house sales, Docklands, the Thames Gateway, High Speed One, the Jubilee Line and Docklands Light Railway, the O2 Arena. All were carried through by Heseltine. Even where he failed – failing to persuade Thatcher to follow an active industrial and regional policy in the 1980s; failing to persuade Major to introduce elected mayors to provide real leadership for England's cities – he was on the right lines and many of his policies are coming to fruition a generation later.

As for Livingstone, there is the London congestion charge, Crossrail, Oystercard, the reinvention of London's buses, a bold approach to tall buildings in the City making possible the Gherkin, the Shard and Heron Tower, and championing the rights of gay people and ethnic minorities long before this was politically mainstream. In his memoirs, Ken records that as Mayor of London he was the only member of his own team who supported the introduction of the congestion charge in 2003. 'We went round the table as each of them urged me to put it off until my second term because they feared it might cost me the 2004 election ... my head of media remarked: "It's lonely at the top."'

2. Seek the truth and fail to succeed

Outside the natural sciences, there are few undisputed truths. Reasonable people differ, and progress generally follows a painful iterative process not a blinding flash of revelation. But that is no excuse for not rigorously seeking the truth by seeking out and weighing honestly the relevant data, research and experience. 'Without data, you are just another person with an opinion,' in the words of Andreas Schleicher, the OECD's education director, who has pioneered comparative international data on education systems.

In the case of England's secondary schools, by the late 1990s, there was plenty of data, from independent test results and studies, Ofsted inspections, and the OECD, of the crisis of standards in English state education and the vital importance of strong, independent leadership and governance to successful school reform. It was from this evidence, and visits to dozens of failing comprehensives and successful schools including the fifteen outstanding City Technology Colleges, that the academies policy grew.

However, academies didn't come in a blinding inspirational flash. Just as truth is contested, reforms are not obvious – or rather, the obvious ones have already been done. Reform requires trial and error, learning from failure and adapting anew. Tim Harford has written a stimulating book on this theme – *Adapt: Why Success Always Starts With Failure*. It is the story of the evolution of both Teach First and academies, as told in Chapter 3. These were two of the most successful and groundbreaking reforms of the Blair years. Both followed failed initial attempts at dealing with the same problems, and painful adaptation from this failure. However, there would have been no attempt at reform in the first place but for the decision to confront an unpopular truth: that the status quo, in terms of failing schools, was far worse than generally believed within my own party, and incremental change was never going to be enough to put it right.

3. Keep it simple

In my experience, almost all the solutions to big problems are simple. Complexity comes in trying to avoid or qualify the simple solution because it is unpalatable. Of course, you need to be simple and right, not simple and wrong; and a good deal of research and experience – and, where appropriate, piloting of policy – needs to go into getting to the right simple solution. Simple doesn't mean simplistic. Nor does simple mean easy. It means getting to the heart of the problem and making the fundamental change which makes the fundamental difference.

In the case of academies, the concept is simple: not-for-profit independent state schools with dynamic sponsor-managers committed to educational transformation. This goes to the heart of the fundamental problem with failing comprehensives, which is their generally low-grade governance and leadership, and their dependence on generally low-grade local council bureaucracies. This radical simplicity is also what made – and still makes – academies controversial. There was constant pressure to compromise the simplicity: to put academies back under new forms of local authority supervision, to subject them to the regulation applying to comprehensives, and to undermine their independent sponsorship. Keeping it simple, and not compromising the simplicity, was my constant preoccupation throughout the hurly burly of design and implementation.

4. Be bold, but go with the grain as far as possible

The English, with their long unbroken history and sceptical cast of mind, breed experts whose deep knowledge of the status quo tends to fatalism and inaction. This is certainly true of education, where those who have best understood the roots of present discontents – whether it be the problems of teacher recruitment, or the history of the private schools and the comprehensives – have generally been those most resigned to the status quo.

It takes a crisis and a leader – or rather, a leader who can paint the status quo as a crisis – to break this mentality. But this still being England, the trick, for the leader, is to harness expertise and precedent to the cause of fundamental change. And to do so in the way that Roy Jenkins, my mentor, used to say was the hallmark of the successful political adviser, by arguing to solutions not conclusions. Radicalism about goals but pragmatism about means, with a pragmatism born of deep knowledge and familiarity, is key to effective reform.

This is the approach I sought to apply to academies, which drew substantially on the City Technology Colleges set up by Kenneth Baker in the late 1980s, and on the status of church schools within the state-funded sector going back to the Butler Act of 1944, although they are distinctly different to both. This minimised legal and procedural innovation, maximised the precedents and, crucially, avoided the need for controversial new legislation.

It is particularly important not to confuse worthwhile reform with legislation or with the creation of new bureaucratic structures. Ministers and senior civil servants love rearranging quangos, government departments and local government. Because it is easily within their power to do, they do it all the time to make it appear that they are acting on this or that issue. But mostly this is a time-consuming and expensive distraction from what matters. Sometimes it is fatal. It is the same with legislation, where ministers and departments compete fiercely for precious parliamentary time to introduce Bills, yet little of the voluminous legislation on education, health, criminal justice or local government – four of the areas subject to most Acts of Parliament over the last thirty years – has had a positive effect. A good deal of it has made things worse.

5. Lead and explain, lead and explain

As a reforming minister, you need every day to lead and explain, lead and explain. The civil service and your party look to you for leadership and a 'narrative', and so do the allies of reform outside. If you don't lead and explain, the Whitehall machine stops, your party becomes restless, and opponents seize the momentum. You have to be a message machine on constant 'replay'. And you need to be passionate and persuasive in what you believe, and convey this every day.

For me, this was the most difficult and stressful part of the job, being fairly shy and uncombative, and with only limited broadcasting experience before becoming a minister. The thought of being interviewed by John Humphrys and Jeremy Paxman made me physically sick, but they are only the tip of the iceberg. Equally important are the local and regional media, the influential columnists, and the growing online world. And you need to try to do the same job with civil servants, business leaders, professional groups, think tanks, parliamentarians, councillors, trade unions, academics, students, the lot. Barely a day passed without my setting out the case for radical school reform and academies before some audience or meeting or media outlet. Every time it was important to start from scratch – why it was unacceptable for there to be so many failing comprehensives, how it could be so different, what academies were, and how they could bring about radical transformation. Rebuttal of misunderstandings, errors and downright lies in the media is also a constant preoccupation.

6. Build a team

Sir Frank Lowe, one of the first academy sponsors and a marketing genius, used to urge me on with G. K. Chesterton's line: 'I've searched all the parks in all the cities and found no statues of committees.' There can be no leadership without leaders, and government is no exception. Equally, leaders achieve almost nothing alone. If you don't build a team, you build nothing.

However, that is not the same as taking the team which you are given. As a minister, you have only limited capacity to determine which individuals occupy which posts, because ministers do not make civil service appointments, at least not directly. But even where you are unable to make appointments, you can spot the capable can-do individuals, irrespective of grade, and work with them directly. This capitalises on one feature of being the leader: you are one of the few people in the organisation not constrained by hierarchy, unless you constrain yourself. I always affected not to understand civil service grades and reporting lines, and dealt with officials largely on the basis of their expertise and dynamism. Also, as leader, you are almost the only person in an organisation able to meet and deal freely with outsiders, and this too is vital to being effective.

7. Build coalitions not tabernacles

To carry major reforms, you cannot have too many friends and you should seek to make them at every turn.

A key element in the success of academies was the support they attracted from school and education leaders across the state and private sectors, and politically from the left of the Labour party through to the right of the Conservative party. Diane Abbott, Bob Marshall-Andrews, Simon Hughes, Nick Gibb, Michael Howard all became strong supporters, initially because they were persuaded that academies could make a real difference to specific schools and localities in their own constituencies. Local authorities controlled by all three parties became strongly committed after intense wooing of their leaders and chief executives.

I spent little time discussing ideology about school organisation with MPs or council leaders, just the state of their schools and what we could do, together, to replace them with something better. What I learned from the experience was to be relentlessly practical; to talk about people and their welfare, not about ideas; to keep party politics out of it as far as possible; to be prepared to meet almost anyone any time; to be as flexible as possible; not to make capital over opponents coming to agree with you, particularly within your own party; not to create unnecessary political dividing lines (there are quite enough of them already without new ones which only undermine your capacity to carry through major reforms); and always, where goals or policies do not conflict and are equally valuable, to replace 'or' with 'and'.

Academies combine the best of comprehensive schools *and* grammar schools *and* private schools. They are state-funded *and* independently managed. They are intended to educate rich *and* poor *and* middling. They are commissioned by central government *and* local government. They aim, unashamedly, to get their brightest pupils into Oxbridge *and* to develop the talents of all other pupils to the full, including children with learning difficulties. It is possible to do all these things together *and* it has to be done if England is to have a decent education system.

8. Champion consumers not producers

As a reformer, you need constantly to put yourself in the position of the citizen and consumer, and seek to judge things from their viewpoint.

My rule of thumb as Schools Minister was not to agree to anything, nor tolerate anything, that wouldn't be acceptable if applied to my own children. My test of whether a school was good enough was simple: would I be prepared to send my own children to it? If this answer was no, then I thought it was straightforwardly immoral to stand by and let it continue. My regret is that I didn't enforce this rule strongly enough, in the face of political or bureaucratic pressure or from sheer exhaustion.

When I went on to Transport, I spent a week travelling by train around Britain unaccompanied, which gave me a mass of horror stories as well as a lot of favourable impressions. I also spent a day driving around the M25, stopping at every service station and talking to drivers and staff about their experiences. All this was invaluable in guiding my decision-making as Minister.

Douglas Hurd once said that the politicians who do best are often those who seem least like a politician. The same, in my experience, is true of ministers, and indeed leaders at large.

9. On important issues, micro-manage constantly

Micro-management by leaders is supposed to be bad and 'being strategic' good. But in my experience, micro-management is essential around decisions and projects which determine the success or failure of a policy. And strategy is too often an excuse for higher waffle.

Barely a day passed in my years pioneering academies without my spending at least an hour on academy business, usually pushing forward or facilitating individual projects. I dealt personally with sponsors and local authorities in putting together virtually all the early academy projects and many of the later ones.

It is also essential to be clear about fundamental elements of a policy which should not be traded except presentationally, where facility in drafting is a useful skill, and secondary areas where compromise buys goodwill and might in any case be right. For example, when deciding on particular academy sponsors for particular projects, I would usually go with the judgement of the local authority or local MP, even where I disagreed with it.

They knew the local context better than me, and they were the ones who had to 'sell' the decision locally.

It is vital not to separate policy from implementation. Whitehall tends to compartmentalise the two, but they go together. To succeed, policy needs constantly to be adapted and modified in the light of experience in implementation. For example, the process of procuring academy buildings was radically changed in the light of early cost over-runs and poor cost control. It also proved untenable to require all sponsors to put up £2 million apiece to sponsor an academy; this was first reduced, then selectively waived, then abandoned entirely.

10. Keep calm and carry on

Virtually every week of my government life yielded a panic or crisis of some sort, and the pressure was often intense.

Most of these alarums and excursions were in areas other than academies, so the challenge was to manage them while keeping academies moving forward. But some of them went to the heart of the academy programme itself. For example, I was constantly in the courts as opponents of academies challenged fundamental aspects of the policy. Had any of these cases succeeded – and the government's ever-cautious lawyers said that several of them might do so; they even suggested I suspend the whole programme at one point because of a challenge under EU procurement law which they said was almost certain to succeed (it didn't) – then the whole programme would have shuddered to a halt. I soon learned that the greater the crisis, the more important it is to project calm and confidence, even if you don't feel it. And always blame yourself in public for mistakes, never blame subordinates. And always try to learn and improve.

11. Reform is a marathon not a sprint

Luke Johnson writes of the entrepreneur:

> My experience is that new companies generally take from five to ten years to break through. Those enterprises that are doomed will

fall by the wayside in this period; only the viable ones remain. These
are the enduring undertakings that are self-sustaining and have
potential. They are led by determined founders who are persistent
and who have invariably matured over the life of their creation.

I concur entirely. It took four years of hard pounding before academies moved from being a small experiment to a national policy,
with the decision to set a target for the creation of 200 academies
at a point when there were still only twelve open. Even then, it took
another year – until the aftermath of the 2005 election – for the
programme to gain decisive momentum, and a further two years to
achieve consensus behind the policy within the governing Labour
party and with the opposition Conservatives.

Only eight years into the academies programme did I feel
confident that my personal leadership was no longer essential
to its survival and development. Probably this was ridiculous
self-importance, but that is how it seemed to me at the time and
it is certainly true that I was the only point of continuity in the
programme across these eight years.

12. *Always have a plan for the future*
This is Bill Clinton's maxim. You constantly need a plan for the
future, and you constantly need to be adjusting it – like the satnav
which resets after each new turning – in the light of events.

My reason for writing this book is that I have an education
reform plan for the future and I want to share it. Academies have
now passed the thousand mark, but academies and other successful reforms of recent decades are only the beginning of the transformation of the English school system required for England to be an
open, classless and prosperous society in the twenty-first century.

MANIFESTO FOR CHANGE

1. Basic education standards

It should be a national objective for at least nine in ten of sixteen-year-olds to achieve the basic GCSE standard of at least five GCSEs at grade A* to C including English and maths as soon as possible and by 2020 at the latest. This should be the objective for each individual school too.

2. A new deal for teachers

No school can be better than its teachers. The best education systems in the world recruit their teachers from their top third of graduates. Transforming teacher recruitment is the most urgent priority for England to build a world-class education system. This requires a new deal for teachers – radical reform, not incremental change. The New Deal involves eight reforms:

Reform one: Teach First, the highly successful charity which recruits, trains and places top graduates into schools with more deprived intakes, should be expanded to make it one of the main routes into secondary school teaching. Teach First should increase its recruitment by 500 a year to reach 5,000 a year by 2020, by when it would be supplying one in four new secondary school teachers and perhaps half in more challenging schools and academies. Universities should systematically support Teach First to achieve this recruitment target.

Reform two: mainstream teacher recruitment and placement beyond Teach First should be professionally managed on a national basis, with training entrusted to the best universities and schools. Instead of the existing system, where more than eighty universities recruit trainees and provide teacher education, in partnership with many thousands of schools, training should be concentrated in a far smaller number of the best universities and schools. There should be a national recruitment process, adopting higher entry standards and best international practice in selection and assessment techniques, managed by an independent trust akin to the BBC with a board comprising educational, business and social leaders. This National Teaching Trust would commission the best universities and schools to undertake training, and support teachers directly throughout their training and their early years in teaching.

Reform three: schools rated outstanding by Ofsted should be allowed to recruit trainees directly, apart from the national recruitment routes, provided they are prepared to pay them and train them properly. This option would be particularly attractive to the best academy chains and federations.

Reform four: teacher trainees should be paid a salary. Learning from Teach First, graduates should be employed by a school, and work a standard forty-eight-week year for two initial training years. They should teach or assist at their school during the whole thirty-eight weeks of term time, with out-of-school university courses taking place in the other ten weeks, starting with a summer training programme in the six weeks before their first autumn term.

Reform five: on the evidence that starting and top salaries matter most to recruiting good teachers, there should be a much higher starting salary for target groups of teachers. For new maths, physics, chemistry and IT teachers, the salary should be in the region of £30,000 outside London and £35,000 in London, and for new headteachers I suggest a starting salary of £70,000 for larger primary schools (£80,000 in London) and £100,000 for secondary schools (£115,000 in London). These higher starting salaries would be contingent on reforms six and seven below, and, if they help transform recruitment, they should be extended more widely.

Reform six: for teachers and headteachers on these higher starting salaries, there should be an end to nationally determined increments. Pay progression should be at the discretion of the individual school.

Reform seven: teachers and headteachers on these higher start-ing salaries should be subject to a longer probationary period of three or four years, during and at the end of which employment could be ended without recourse to claims of unfair dismissal.

Reform eight: the generalist B. Ed degree (and its equivalents) in primary education should be phased out and replaced with subject-based degrees. In place of the B. Ed, primary school teachers should in future either be recruited with honours degrees in specific subjects and then undertake postgraduate training – as at present for second-ary school teachers and a small proportion of primary teachers – or they should study for combined 'academic subject plus pedagogy' degrees, with a large proportion of these joint honours degrees majoring in literacy and numeracy. Then every primary teacher would have deep subject knowledge and the primary curriculum could be broadened and deepened significantly.

3. Academies

To move from 'academies' to an 'academy system' driving national educational transformation six reforms are required:

Reform one: every underperforming secondary and primary school should be replaced by a sponsored academy. As of 2012, nearly 650 comprehensives are failing to achieve the basic GCSE standard for half or more of their students. These, and the 1,100 most seriously underperforming primary schools, should be the priority for the next wave of academies.

To provide for this, high-achieving academy chains need to become larger and more numerous, and many more outstand-ing academy sponsors are needed, including universities, and successful state and private schools. Every university and Oxbridge college should sponsor at least one academy replacing an under-performing comprehensive or providing new school places in areas of low standards. So should every highly successful state school or academy, and every successful private school and private school foundation. The most successful state primary schools should also become academy sponsors, setting up academies to replace low-performing primary schools, with the best of these developing chains.

Reform two: successful schools converting to become academies should use their new status to help underperforming schools systematically, and the best of them should become academy sponsors themselves.

Reform three: all secondary-age academies should include sixth forms.

Reform four: all academies should consider operating a longer school day, from 8.30 a.m. to 5 p.m., and possibly increase the length of the school year from thirty-eight weeks to forty or forty-one, including work experience for Year 11, 12 and 13 students. A longer school day on these lines, equivalent to an extra two years of education for every secondary school pupil, provides for a broader and deeper curriculum, including far more opportunities for clubs, sports and the arts.

Reform five: where an academy is found to be failing, Ofsted should conduct an audit of the academy's governance to answer one critical question: are the sponsors and/or governors up to the job of improving the academy radically? Where they are not, Ofsted should replace the sponsor, conducting an open competition for a successor sponsor and brokering the transfer of sponsorship. In the case of a failing converter academy, the competition should be for a sponsor to replace the existing governing body, turning the converter academy into a sponsored academy.

Reform six: academies rated outstanding by Ofsted within a chain should have the right to vote to withdraw from the chain. Academy chains should not be allowed to become resented local education authorities in new guise.

4. Free schools

Free schools – being academies without a predecessor state school – have been a central part of the academies policy since its launch in 2000. Where properly led and focused, they play an important role in overcoming deprivation and promoting choice and innovation.

Successful 'free school academy' innovation since 2000 includes entirely new academies in disadvantaged areas, 'all-through' academies educating children from the age of three or four through to eighteen, academies with boarding facilities, and academies – including University Technical Colleges – with specialist curriculums in fields such as engineering and the performing arts. These four types of free school academy should all be expanded in line with parental and employer demand. The government should also encourage five other innovative types of 'free school academies' in the immediate future.

First, academies which provide far better for the 6,500 children a year who are permanently excluded from mainstream schools and academies.

Second, academies promoting excellence in maths and science, subjects where England is especially weak in comparison to the best education systems overseas, particularly in Asia.

Third, bilingual academies to provide centres of outstanding excellence in teaching the language and cultures of our principal trading partners including China.

Fourth, academies to foster outstanding excellence in sport, including tennis, cricket, swimming, athletics and gymnastics.

Fifth, academies with far stronger international links, not just in language teaching but also in the recruitment of secondary-age students from abroad to study at them.

5. Specialist schools

It was a serious mistake of the Cameron government to abolish the specialist school programme under which, for the previous twenty years, comprehensive schools and academies had been encouraged to develop centres of curriculum excellence. The specialist school policy was successful; it should have been intensified not abandoned, and maths and science ought to have been particularly encouraged as specialisms.

The specialist school programme should be revived immediately for secondary schools and academies. It should be extended to primary schools too, encouraging individual primary schools to develop special strengths in curriculum areas from maths and science to modern languages and sport.

6. Overcoming the private–state school divide

Every successful private school, and private school foundation, should sponsor at least one academy, true to its charitable mission and leveraging its success and its networks within the state-funded as well as fee-paying sectors.

Successful private day schools should be enabled and encouraged to join the state sector as academies, on the model of the first wave of 'direct grant' academies since 2000. On this model, the private school becomes an academy, retaining its independent management and character but without fees. It exchanges academically selective admissions for all-ability admissions, but with a large catchment area and 'banded' admissions to ensure a fully comprehensive ability range. It also continues with a large sixth form, underpinning continued very strong academic performance.

7. An A-level Baccalaureate

The IB has been gaining ground in recent years for the good reason that it is broader, deeper, more engaging and more international than A-level in both subjects and skills. Expansion of the IB should be encouraged by covering the additional costs to schools of offering it.

Going further, England should follow Singapore and carry through an IB-style reform to A-levels to create an A-level Baccalaureate (A-Bacc). This should include four key new components: (1) a 'contrasting subject' requirement, so that students majoring in the humanities, arts and languages take maths or a science and vice versa. (2) A project-based extended essay. (3) An interdisciplinary theory of knowledge course as a standard part of A-level. And (4) a requirement to demonstrate community service. Students would receive an overall A-Bacc mark, as in the IB.

8. A Technical Baccalaureate

There should be a new 'Tech Bacc' (Technical Baccalaureate) for post-sixteen-year-olds not studying the A-Bacc, to comprise three elements: (1) English and maths GCSE, (2) a reputable qualification in an occupational area or areas, and (3) work experience including a formal report back from the employer.

For those who have reached the basic GCSE level including English and maths, but wish to acquire further technical qualifications, there should be a higher-level Tech Bacc comprising higher literacy, numeracy, problem-solving and project-working skills, together with a reputable technical qualification, either to be taken alongside an apprenticeship or, if beforehand (as will be the case for most students under the age of eighteen), including substantially more work experience, also with formal evaluation.

9. Sure Start and under-fives provision

Both nursery and Sure Start provision need to expand. The existing entitlement to only three hours a day of nursery provision for three-year-olds should be doubled for all parents. Sure Start, and its 3,600 children's centres nationwide, should provide additional childcare and parental support for parents of the most disadvantaged children, ensuring that they are ready to learn when they start school.

10. Democracy, community and schools

Part of the benefit of secondary schools having sixth forms is that sixth-formers are great role models for younger teenagers. They are also well able to take on significant responsibility within schools, not only individually as prefects but in organising and leading activities outside the classroom, and also in decision-making. School councils have long featured in secondary schools. They should be established in all primary schools too.

Young people should be given the vote at sixteen. This would boost citizenship education, and ensure that political debate and democracy fully include young people. Alongside extending the vote to sixteen- and seventeen-year-olds, there should be a polling station in every secondary school in local and national elections. Just as in schools mock exams lead to real public exams for the older students, so mock elections should lead to real elections for the older students, in which they take a real part. This would give the teaching of citizenship a practical objective.

For the same reason, it should be possible to become a local councillor at the age of sixteen and parties should actively promote younger candidates – including school sixth-formers – to stand for council elections, in the way they have started seriously to promote women and ethnic minority candidates in recent years.

11. School governing bodies

Learning from the success of academies, all state schools should consider reducing the size of their governing bodies to fifteen or fewer, while ensuring that the membership comprises more governors with high levels of commitment and professional experience.

It is especially important that governing bodies are effectively chaired. Three reforms would promote this: (1) The appointment of the chair of the governing body should be separate from the appointment of its members. (2) The chair should be appointed by the governing body through open competition. (3) Governing bodies should be allowed to pay their chairs.

12. Schools as community hubs

Schools should become community hubs. This becomes all the more urgent as other community services – including health centres, post offices, libraries and community centres – are closing or under threat in the face of public spending cuts, when imaginative solutions for the co-location of services on school sites should be explored. The co-location of public libraries with schools is the most obvious synergy, but, with innovation and imagination across the public services, far more ambitious projects would be possible.

REFERENCES

FOREWORD

- Ben Okri, 'Lines in Potentis'.

CHAPTER 1

- Hackney Downs: draws on Michael Barber, *The Learning Game: Arguments For An Education Revolution* (Victor Gollancz, 1996), pp.113–119.
- Mossbourne: draws on personal information and interviews with the author and also: Sir Michael Wilshaw interviews in *The Times*, 16 July 2011 and 15 September 2011; Christopher Middleton, 'The school that beat the rioters', *Daily Telegraph*, 16 August 2011; *The Economist*, 22 July 2011.

CHAPTER 2

- Failure of the secondary moderns and statistics on pre-comprehensive system: *The Crowther Report – Fifteen to Eighteen*, Central Advisory Council for Education (England), Ministry of Education, 1959.
- David Hargreaves: *Social Relations in a Secondary School* (Routledge and Kegan Paul, 1967), pp.86, 87.
- Tony Crosland: Susan Crosland, *Tony Crosland* (Coronet, 1983), p.148.
- Bruce Liddington quotes here and in following chapters: interview with author.

CHAPTER 3

- GCSE and other statistics for 1997: *Promoting excellence for all – School Improvement Strategy: raising standards, supporting schools*, Department for Children, Schools and Families (2008).

- Adonis and Pollard: *A Class Act: The Myth of England's Classless Society* (Penguin, 1998), p.61.
- Melissa Benn: *School Wars: the Battle for Britain's Education* (Verso, 2011), pp.xi, xii.
- Charter schools: I was particularly influenced by Chester E. Finn, Bruno V. Manno and Gregg Vanourek, *Charter Schools in Action: Renewing Public Education* (Princeton University Press, 2000), because of its combination of passion for transformation yet detailed, methodical description of the nuts and bolts of establishing good schools to overcome social disadvantage and the need in particular for strong governance, leadership and accountability.
- Reaction to launch of academies: http://news.bbc.co.uk/1/hi/education/677996.stm and *Times Educational Supplement*, 'Academies' Kiss of Life', 2 June 2000.

CHAPTER 4

- St Mary Magdalene High Court ruling: *The Guardian*, 26 July 2006.
- Evelyn Grace Academy: Rowan Moore, 'Evelyn Grace Academy, Brixton', *The Observer*, 17 October 2010.
- 'It was the most striking school building I had ever seen': Ian Gilbert, foreword to Gill Kelly, *Where Will I do My Pineapples? The little book of building a whole new school* (Crown House Publishing, 2011).

CHAPTER 5

- *Guardian* reaction to Education Five-Year Plan: Rebecca Smithers, 'Comprehensive change drives Labour's agenda', *The Guardian*, 9 July 2004.

CHAPTER 6

- David Bell: 'Schools inspector backs academy programme', *The Guardian*, 4 August 2005, and interview with the author.
- My memo advising Tony Blair not to announce his departure date: Tony Blair, *A Journey* (Hutchinson, 2010), pp.163–165.
- Willetts speech on academies and grammar schools: 'Tories abandon grammar schools', *The Guardian*, 16 May 2007.

CHAPTER 7

- Independent studies of academies: Stephen Machin and James Vernoit, *Changing School Autonomy: Academy Schools and their Introduction to England's Education*, Centre for the Economics of Education, LSE, 2011; the same authors, 'Academy schools: who benefits', *CentrePiece*, Autumn 2010; National Audit Office, *The Academies Programme*, two separate reports, 2007 and 2010. For persuasive recent analysis of the positive impact of school autonomy within state education systems in developed countries, see Eric A. Hanushek, Susanne Link and Ludgar Woessmann, 'Does school autonomy make sense everywhere? Panel estimates from PISA', *National Bureau of Economic Research* (2011), working paper number 17591.

- Pupil absence and truancy data: 'Pupil Absence in schools in England: Autumn Term 2010 and Spring Term 2011', DfE, 19 October 2011; and DfE Press Notice, 12 July 2011.

- Views of parents, pupils and teachers: *Academies Evaluation: Fifth Annual Report*, PWC, 2008.

- 'It's really down to the sponsor': Elizabeth Leo, David Galloway and Phil Hearne, *Academies and Educational Reform: Governance, Leadership and Strategy* (Multilingual Matters, 2010), p.63. This is the best study of academies to date, by three authors with in-depth experience of school leadership and policy.

- David Ross, Lord Harris and Paul Marshall: interviews with the author.

- 'You are left with, on the one hand, a kind of widespread anarchy ...': Melissa Benn, *School Wars: the Battle for Britain's Education* (Verso, 2011), p.112.

- Lynn Gadd and Dan Moynihan: interviews with the author.

- UK corporate boards data: Viral Acharya, Conor Kehoe and Michael Reyner, *Private Equity vs. PLC Boards in the UK: A Comparison of Practices and Effectiveness* (European Corporate Governance Institute, 2008).

- Study of 16 academies: Philip O'Hear and Eric Blaire, *Early Academies: Making a Difference* (Specialist Schools and Academies Trust, 2011).

- Michael Marland obituary: *The Guardian*, 4 July 2008.

CHAPTER 8

- Sutton Trust reports on educational background of leading social groups: *The educational backgrounds of leading scientists and scholars* (2009), *Responding to the new landscape for university access* (2010), *The educational backgrounds of the UK's top solicitors, barristers and judges* (2005).
- 60 per cent of chart acts educated at private schools: 'Music and Meritocracy', *New Statesman Blog*, 6 December 2010.
- Michael McIntyre: *Life and Laughing: My Story* (Michael Joseph, 2010), pp.84, 112, 148.
- Stats on private/state school teachers: Francis Green, Stephen Machin, Richard Murphy and Yu Zhu, *Competition for Private and State School Teachers*, Centre for the Economics of Education (2010).
- 1944 report on private schools: Fleming Report.
- Roy Jenkins: *A Life at the Centre* (Macmillan, 1991), p.170, and interview with the author.
- Anthony Seldon, Graham Able and Lord Turnbull: interviews with the author.
- For excellent studies of private/state collaboration through academies, see *Working Together: Academies and Private Schools*, edited by Bill Watkin (The Schools Network, 2012).

CHAPTER 9

- Private/state school stats on progression to higher education: *Degrees of Success – University Chances by Individual School*, (Sutton Trust, 2011).
- Di Birch, John Laycock and Malcolm Grant: interviews with the author.
- JCB Academy: drawn in part from Jane Ware, *The JCB Academy: Year One* (Baker Dearing Educational Trust, 2011).
- Teach First Ofsted inspection: report, July 2011.
- Mark Smith quote: interview with the author.
- Guy Nichols and Harriet Watkins quotes: from Teach First case study of Bexley Business Academy.

CHAPTER 10

- Peter Hyman: interview with the author.
- Helen Rumbelow on Durand Academy: *The Times*, 27 October 2011.
- Meadows School: from Ofsted inspection report, 2011, p.5.
- Martin Jacques: *When China Rules The World* (Penguin Books, 2012), p.564.
- Weil Academy: http://www.weiltennis.com/
- Colin Hall: Joanna Moorhead, 'Holland Park comprehensive to become an academy', *The Guardian*, 27 July 2011.
- Mark Keary: interview with the author and Josh Neicho, 'Bethnal Green Academy is top of the class', *Evening Standard*, 27 January 2012.

CHAPTER 11

- David Hopkins: *Every School a Great School: Realising the potential of system leadership* (Open University Press, 2007).
- OECD and international maths and science assessments: from the OECD's Programme for International Student Assessment (PISA studies) and the Trends in International Mathematics and Science Studies (TIMSS).
- Chris Cook data: Chris Cook, 'Poorer children close education gap', *Financial Times*, 30 September 2011; and Chris Cook, FT blog, 'The social mobility challenge for school reformers', 22 February 2012. http://blogs.ft.com/ftdata/2012/02/22/social-mobility-and-schools/#axzz1wofhNZq1
- 'I'm on the side of the optimists': Kevan Collins, *Times Educational Supplement*, 4 May 2012.
- McKinsey reports on teachers: *Closing the talent gap: Attracting and retaining top-third graduates to careers in teaching* (McKinsey, 2010), and *How the world's best-performing schools come out on top* (McKinsey, 2007).
- Stats on PGCE applications from top universities: *House of Lords Hansard*, 27 February 2012, col 15283.
- Teacher salary and drop-out figures: House of Commons education select committee, 9th report (2012), pp.20, 21, 31.

- Pasi Sahlberg: *Finnish Lessons: What can the world learn from educational change in Finland?* (Teachers College Press, 2011), Chapter 3.
- Data on early-years development of children: from Elizabeth Washbrook and Jane Waldfogel, *Cognitive Gaps in the Early Years* (Sutton Trust, 2010).
- Alison Wolf quotes: from her *Review of Vocational Education* (Department for Education, 2012).

CHAPTER 12

- On Roy Jenkins as transformational Home Secretary: see my 2011 lecture on Roy Jenkins in Mr Speaker's series on great twentieth-century parliamentarians, available on andrewadonis.com.
- Ken Livingstone quotes: from *You Can't Say That* (Faber & Faber, 2011).
- Luke Johnson quote: from *Financial Times*, 27 July 2011.

THANKS AND ACKNOWLEDGEMENTS

This book would not exist without Roy Jenkins and Tony Blair, who inspired my politics, and Ed Victor, who stimulated me to get writing.

The academy movement is the work of thousands of individuals, and I have personal debts to many of them. However, to name simply those who generously assisted with, and commented on, some or all of this text, I am hugely grateful to Michael Barber, David Bell, Di Birch, Malcolm Grant, Mark Greatrex, Ewan Harper, Philip Harris, Lucy Heller, Peter Hyman, David Leam, Bruce Liddington, Alasdair Morgan, Sally Morgan, Dan Moynihan, Philip O'Hear, Nick Pearce, Conor Ryan, Kevin Satchwell, Anthony Seldon, David Shepherd, Mark Smith, Michael Wilshaw, Brett Wigdorz, Alison Wolf and Michael Worton. A number of civil servants prefer to remain anonymous but they know how grateful I am to them too.

The Biteback team – Iain Dale, Sam Carter, Suzanne Sangster, James Stephens, Namkwan Cho – are brilliant, and fully deserve their reputation as one of the most exciting things in British publishing.

Kathryn, Alice and Edmund were wonderful throughout.

INDEX